That's Enough in Anyone's Life

The Autobiography of

Clare R Grant

First published in 2010 by:

ISBN: 978-0-956-678-904

Printed and bound in Great Britain by:
BookPrintingUK, Remus House, Coltsfoot Drive,
Woodston, Peterborough, PE2 9JX

ACKNOWLEDGEMENTS

My everlasting thanks to Sally – Sarah Pakes-Newton A.I.S.T., B.H.S.A.I – who willingly offered to take on the laborious task of typing this account. She has done a marvellous job having had to juggle her life between being a farmer's wife, a mother and find the time to plough through endless pages of scribble.
In the early stages of setting up I asked Sally to give her constructive criticism and comments. One particular chapter I had started various paragraphs with the same word. In the margin she wrote, Oh! No, not again!
Sally not only has a sense of humour, but has been a pleasure to work with and has become a treasured friend.

Indebted gratitude to Rob Braddick for his time and patience. He willingly gave invaluable assistance when I needed a second opinion, and spent many hours proof-reading this autobiography.

I wish to thank Patricia Spink B.A who works as an artist and was assigned to clean and photograph the portrait for the cover. It was drawn in pastels by Gasgoigne Thompson in 1953 when I was 11 years of age.

Finally, my thanks to Susan Titcombe for her time and support, in encouraging me to go ahead and publish my autobiography!

To Paloma, Carlos and Sir Snorkles.

And to all those wonderful people who will never be forgotten. In my darkest hours of desperation they were there to help me.

Chapter 1

My first experience of terror came shortly after my birth. The year was 1942, and around the age of six months, a bomb hit our home. Mother heard the air raid siren but instinctively knew we were going to be hit. Lifting me out of the bath, dripping wet and still clutching a sponge, she ran out of the house. Mother never remembers her feet touching the stairs at all. We were both in a state of shock as we hid under the stairway amongst the rubble until help came. I dug my little nails into her skin and clung to her absolutely petrified. It seemed an eternity, as mother crouched in the dark, before help arrived. Hot drinks and blankets brought comfort and we were taken off to stay at someone else's house.

It was at this point that father, on surveying the damage to the family home in broad daylight, decided that mother and I were to be evacuated to Cornwall where he considered we would be much safer. Due to a spinal injury during childhood, father was unable to join the forces, so during the war years he dedicated his time to helping those in need. Father obtained his certificate of Anti-Gas Training in 1939 and became an A.R.P. Warden working day or night shifts; many times around the clock. He would bicycle about with a tin helmet on, organising rescue parties for those that were bombed. He had the most amazing ability to comfort the injured and the bereaved.

Meanwhile, a tiny cottage had been rented cheaply so that mother and I could move in. It was extremely basic with water having to be pumped from a well in the garden. The walls had thick layers of wallpaper, all serving as insulation. One evening, having been put in my cot to go to sleep, I became fascinated with a tiny bit of paper which was hanging from the wall. Through the bars of my cot I managed to get a grip with my sturdy little fingers and pull. To my utter delight I discovered that layer after layer of wallpaper had different colours and patterns. Eventually tired with all my exertions, I fell asleep. Mother found the hole in the wall later that night and nearly had a fit. She was expecting a visit from the landlady and quickly had to find someone in the village to put things right. From then on mother made quite sure that my cot was kept well away from any wall! On another occasion when mother came to check on me, she entered the room to find a mouse sitting on my forehead busily washing itself whilst I slept quite peacefully, unaware as to what was going on.

Eventually we moved to a house in Kingston near Lewes, surrounded by the beautiful Sussex Downs. It was at this house that we had an assortment of animals. A mongrel dog called Pickles who couldn't have been more appropriately named. He was always in a pickle, devouring carpets or clothing and running off with anything that took his fancy with mother chasing after him and shouting, 'Grr.... you naughty dog!'

It all became too much for mother and in the end Pickles was considered too difficult to cope with and causing too much havoc. Sadly he had to be given away.

We had a beautiful black and white cat and she produced a

large litter of kittens—all black with white patches, except one. He had a wonderful grey coat with a white bib and four white socks. This cat was to become my childhood companion and was named Silver. Being an only child, I was left alone quite often and it was a question of amusing myself. I had a large doll's pram and Silver spent hours in it. He would lie there quite happily and I would have long conversations while wheeling him around in the garden. I don't think there ever could be another cat like Silver. I used to dress him up in doll's clothes with a bonnet on his head and tuck him underneath the blankets just like a baby. He didn't mind at all and would lie there for hours on end; in fact I think he must have loved all the attention. Father, having had a chicken farm in his younger days whilst studying agriculture at Cambridge University, insisted on keeping chickens at the bottom of the garden. It was while living at Kingston mother managed to get milk, butter and a few extras from a local farmer. This meant that from a very early age I had to learn to use my little legs and walk long distances with her.

My first visit to the seaside was almost my last! Mother had taken a rug for us to sit on. I was supposed to be playing with a bucket and spade but soon got bored and ambled off to the shore's edge where I proceeded to lie on my back and slowly drift out to sea. Meanwhile, mother had been engrossed in a complicated knitting pattern and was counting the stitches on a jersey she was making. Suddenly, she realised that I wasn't there and saw this little body floating away. I always remember my mother telling me that as she waded into the sea, fully dressed, a man

stood nearby and never even attempted to help her. When she rescued me I was apparently having a wonderful time gurgling and laughing to myself, thoroughly enjoying this new experience of being carried away by ripples of water.
The war having ended, it was at this point that a Swedish governess appeared in my life. She was called Heidi and turned out to be simply delightful. A wooden cabin had been erected in the garden and there Heidi would spend many hours teaching me. She not only made my lessons interesting but was great fun as a companion.
Around this time, I also remember a blue-coloured Ford car with a canvas roof appearing on the scene. We would all clamber into the car while father turned the starting handle and cranked up the engine. On one of these occasions we had set off for an afternoon drive and suddenly smoke started to pour out of the engine. Father opened the bonnet to find a rag on fire which some mechanic had inadvertently left behind. That little car on its narrow wheels did a very good service for many years.

Chapter 2

Father had had one younger brother who died tragically, at the age of fourteen, from pneumonia. While still a young man, he had also lost his mother, so when his father died, he inherited everything. It came as a tremendous shock to discover that, although his family had lived well, his father had made a fortune on stocks and shares. He had been an extremely astute business man. This was the turning point which changed my parents' lives and mine. The love of money is the root of all evil! Too much money can destroy people's lives and in many cases doesn't bring happiness, because happiness cannot be bought.

Unfortunately, and very sadly, father didn't have the ability to sort out his financial affairs and this, in later years, was to be the downfall of us all. Added to this was the fact that, on hearing how much had been inherited, mother immediately made plans for the future. So, before my sixth birthday, we moved to a large three-storey house with six bedrooms on Blatchington Hill in Seaford. It was surrounded by a tall flint-stone wall and in the grounds there was a cottage with two garages alongside it. Through an iron gate was an entrance into an enormous vegetable garden with extensive fruit canes. Father's chickens were installed in a huge chicken hut and pen for them to scratch about in. Next to this fifteen rabbits were kept as well. Silver came with us, much to his annoyance—firstly, at being uprooted to another home and, secondly, due to a young black poodle called Rufus appearing on the scene. My parents obviously felt that they had to bring me up

with animals as playmates. Next on the scene appeared a chinchilla rabbit called Poppet, who was mated and produced a whole lot of little poppets.
A pond in the garden was filled with goldfish and two pet lizards. The tortoise had a hole drilled in his shell and was attached to a long string and had the run of one of the lawns, but preferred to bury himself in the flower beds.
Unfortunately, money had gone to mother's head and she soon realised that the house was ridiculously large and she would have to have help. Apart from the gardener and his wife who lived in the cottage, a French cook came in daily and Mrs. Marr always came on a Thursday to do the ironing and polish the silver.
One morning father and I were getting breakfast as usual and I dropped a piece of toast underneath the cooker. As I bent down to pick it up I saw something curled up. Immediately, I had visions of a snake, but father put my mind at ease and went off to get a broom handle. Prodding at whatever it was, eventually, after considerable hassle, a hedgehog appeared. It was bitterly cold and frosty and he had come through the dog's trap door, walked across the scullery to the kitchen where there was an Aga. We named him James Esq. and he became so tame that when he heard us banging a spoon on the back of a plate, he would trundle up the garden path to the back door for his food.
Next door to us was a school for partially blind boys and we could hear them playing their recorders. Adjoining the school was a small church and father eventually settled in as Church Warden. He really enjoyed going to the service

on Sundays and talking to all the boys.
My parents took Heidi and I on a holiday to Switzerland during the summer. It was all very exciting and we stayed in an hotel overlooking Lake Lucerne. It was here that Heidi took me out on her back to an island in the middle of the lake and taught me to swim. Shortly after this trip, sadly Heidi had to return to Sweden, but to this day we have always kept in touch.
The dust having settled from the move, mother decided it was time to do some socialising. She started to have clothes and evening dresses by top designers, making special trips to London for fittings. Her wardrobe was extensive, with a mink coat, silver fox wrap, leopard skin coat with matching hat and an endless list of jewellery, and so it went on. Father should have imposed more control over mother, but he didn't and would give in just for peacesake.
Mother did make our lives extremely unhappy, which brought about a tremendous bond between father and myself. I was his pride and joy and he was my consolation and companion. We never had a cross word and, looking back, I can remember only happy times whilst in his company. To this day I miss him and always will. Father was one in a million for he was made up of the most amazing qualities. He was gentle, kind, humble, generous, totally unselfish and a wonderful listener. He was respected and loved by all who met him. Father became very well-known all over Sussex and further afield for his tireless efforts in organising and raising money for charities. In recognition for all his work father was invited

to Buckingham Palace on 11th July 1968 to meet Her Majesty Queen Elizabeth II.
His charity work became so demanding that he was often out late at meetings or up at the top of the house in his office, tapping away on his typewriter. He was a member of the English Speaking Union, International Friendship League, Rotarians and Toc H Society, to name but a few of the organisations. In 1977 father was presented with a book from the Past Rotarians Club of Brighton, Hove and District. The inscription inside the cover was:-

Past Rotarian Dudley H. PRYOR
Founder Member
President 1962/63
Secretary for 16 years

in token of their great respect and their deep appreciation of his loyal services to the club.

We had all sorts of famous people to the house to raise money at garden fetes. It was an ideal setting because of its size with plenty of room for side stalls and teas on the lawn. Whatever father decided to do for charity he managed to achieve. He was brilliant at organising and raising large amounts of money for, literally, umpteen charities. His work didn't stop there either for a tremendous amount of effort, money and time was also spent on orphaned children who seldom went out anywhere. Father would plan a wonderful outing and go with them and love every minute of their company.
He was just as much at ease with the blind, the disabled, the homeless and the sick. In short, he dedicated his life to

others and was never happier than when he could bring a smile to someone's face or help those who truly needed him. Helping others was what motivated his every day and there were many times when the demands upon him must have been, without a doubt, very tiring.
Mother had been an S.R.N. before she married and it became very clear that she was a career woman. Her life had been nursing and that was what she really loved doing more than anything else. It was a great mistake that she ever tried to take on the role of wife and mother. Without a doubt, she would have got her gold medal had she not married, and in her earlier days had been in charge of young nurses at Guy's hospital. There was simply nothing mother didn't know about medicine or illnesses and, in that respect, I learnt a great deal from her. So it's difficult to imagine a person being such an outstanding nurse and yet so bitter, cold, hard and cruel.
I shall never forget, at the age of seven, the day that mother ordered me to lie on my bed face downwards. She pulled my knickers down, knelt on my legs and thrashed me with a large hard-backed hair brush. I couldn't breathe, as the pillow was suffocating me, and I couldn't move due to having mother's full weight on top of me. I remember thinking that I was going to die because she got so violent that she winded me. When mother eventually stood up, the expression on her face was one of panic as I fought in gasps to breathe.
Mother was incapable of giving me a hug or a kiss. She barely had time for me and told everyone I was a difficult child because she didn't know what to do with me. In

actual fact, she had thought of a way out of not enjoying a six-year-old and plans were already being made. It was so indescribably cruel that, as I write, I can still hear her words and see her expressionless face whilst pronouncing them to me.

It wasn't any different to any other evening and, at the required time, I would go down and say goodnight to my parents and then go upstairs. I walked into the sitting room and mother was reading a book on the sofa. She told me to sit down because she was going to tell me a story—something she had never done in my short life–so I found this quite extraordinary.

She started: 'There was once a little baby whose mother didn't want her, so she gave her away to another mummy and that little girl is you.' After a slight pause she said, 'And now you can go to bed.'

There was no loving cuddle or hug—nothing. Can anyone imagine how I felt trying to understand what had been said to me? This was the turning point in my life when I realised I hadn't really been wanted and wasn't loved. How right my intuition turned out to be.

I went to bed and curled right up, cuddling a beloved blue rabbit that went everywhere with me. Father came in soon after from a meeting and came to see me. He would usually stand in the half light of the doorway and play peep bo round the door, which sent me into fits of giggles. On leaving, after giving me a big kiss and a hug, he would always recite a funny rhyme.

This time I didn't laugh and I didn't cry. I was too shocked, but I remember my little arms reaching up and putting them very tightly round my father's neck, for I knew that he truly loved me. He was a real father and we never ever thought of each other as anything else.

Chapter 3

Next morning, mother informed me that we were going up to London for the day. Mother's mother lived in Highgate and I loved going to stay with granny. However, on this particular occasion we did a fleeting visit and I heard mother say, 'I'm taking Clare to Harrods to get her uniform for boarding school.'

Granny replied, 'But she's so young still, you shouldn't send her away, Irene.'

The convent did not take children until the age of seven. However, it seemed that whatever mother had told the nuns, the rule in this case had been dismissed. A school trunk appeared and everyone was frantically sewing on Cash's name tapes, whilst rushing backwards and forwards to mother's commands. Eventually, I was packed off with my school trunk, plus liberty bodice, jars of malt with cod liver oil and clutching my blue rabbit. Father drove down to Hastings and hardly uttered a word. He was horrified to think I was being sent away at six to a convent but, as always, mother got her way every time. Father couldn't bear the arguments or mother's complete lack of consideration for our feelings.

Mother was all dressed up with one of her dreadful hats, to impress Mother Superior, for she insisted on having a word about me. In actual fact, she just wanted to make sure that both Mother Superior and the other parents heard what she had to say.

In a loud voice she announced, 'Dudley and I are going abroad on a luxury cruise, so you won't be able to contact us if anything happens to Clare.'

I stood watching parents talking, nuns flapping about, girls greeting each other and giggling, car doors opening and shutting, fathers struggling with trunks, while a continual stream of cars arrived. Meanwhile, my parents, through the din, were saying goodbye and I was left alone watching the car disappear through the school gates.

Once we were settled in the dormitory and the lights were out, it was then that I vowed I would find my natural mother one day. The tears flowed for the first time until I drenched my pillow whimpering like a hurt animal. My only consolation was hugging a blue rabbit. Nobody knew that I was under shock, nobody knew what mother had said or done to me and nobody knew or cared how I felt. All that the nuns knew was that I was a terrible child who, due to being so awfully naughty, had forced her mother to go away abroad for a holiday.

We were awakened by Eleanor and Margaret. Eleanor was very large and always wore a blue overall and never smiled. Margaret was extremely thin and wore a green overall, and, of the two, Margaret was the kindest. Eleanor would pull my hair as hard as she could to get the knots out, and then pull my head backwards while plaiting. It was an agonising performance every morning for I had very thick waist-long hair. From then on nothing went right. I would stand alone in the recreation ground during the day. At night the other girls would tell the nun on duty that I was crying and that they were being kept awake. Every night the tears would flow and I would fall asleep through sheer exhaustion on a sopping wet pillow.

One afternoon, while outside, I sat on a mound of grass and the next thing I knew someone was rushing me off to the nuns. I had sat on a hornets' nest and was very severely poisoned. They say that if you get stung really badly, you never get colds. I believe there must be some truth in it, for I rarely get a cold and seem to escape most flu epidemics.

A routine was soon established whereby mother would insist on planning to travel abroad whilst it was my school holidays. Mother's question was, 'Do you want to come with us abroad or go to a riding school?'

The idea of travelling about in a car didn't appeal to me at all. Besides, I was crazy about horses and this had been very much encouraged by my parents, as I had had riding lessons from a very early age. The riding school I stayed at was great fun, and all the children there were allotted a horse to look after. There was never a dull moment, for we had to muck out, groom, ride, clean and polish tack. There were lectures in the tack room on certain days of the week and excursions out riding all day with picnics. In our spare time we would play hide and seek in the beautiful grounds surrounding the old rambling house. One of the sitting rooms, where we were allowed to sit in the evenings, was full of trophies, prizes and photographs. It was one mass of glorious merit to an outstanding horsewoman.

Mrs. Nelson was an exceptional horse rider and always rode a horse called Nelson. She had a short, cropped hairstyle, always wore trousers, striped shirt, bow tie, tweed jacket and a gentleman's grey hat. She must have been in her late sixties when I first had the privilege of meeting her and becoming one of her pupils.

In later years I appreciated how much she had taught me, for her style and knowledge was far beyond many riders. It was amazing how the moment she walked out to the yard, with crop in hand, and was assisted up onto Nelson, that somehow over twenty children would be ready and paying attention. Sometimes, instead of riding across the Downs, we would have classes on a cinder track. There was no messing about. Not only would her critical eye pick up any faults but we were also made to perform all sorts of feats on top of our horses. We had to prove that we were in full control of what we were doing and were made to ride with pennies—yes, the good old ones—between our knees. But we loved all the hard work because we all had one thing in common—our love of horses and the desire to learn.

Chapter 4

My other passion from a very early age was dancing and so I was taken along to classes. It soon became quite obvious that I had a natural talent and was far more interested in anything artistic than I ever would be sitting still in a classroom. At the age of seven and a half, the nuns started to prepare us for our first Holy Communion. Suddenly, we were the centre of attention with endless instruction in religious teaching. Rehearsals for the big day took place in the school chapel, while dressmakers made our long white dresses and veils. I was getting very excited because my parents would be coming in June for Mass and then a special breakfast afterwards.

Disaster had to strike! One of the girls in my class was jealous of all the attention we were getting and decided to pick on me. There was a rule that stealing was not only considered as damnation in hell for all eternity but that such a crime had to be punished extremely severely. This particular girl put, of all things, an expensive dental plate into the back of my locker. She then went and told the nun of our class that the box containing her plate had disappeared from her locker. This little girl had a famous father in high places, and she also managed to get away with far more than we ever could! Of course, she put on a wonderful act and said her parents would be extremely annoyed. Having managed to send all the nuns into an alarmed state of emergency, every girl in our class had to empty the entire contents of their desks and hunt high and low.

Obviously, this procedure didn't bring to light the whereabouts of the plate. So this little girl calmly suggested to the nuns that we ought to search our lockers. These consisted of large wooden cupboards, with separate pigeon holes, which had each girl's name on. Here, you were allowed to keep personal belongings and so, along with the rest of the class, I started to empty my pigeon hole. There, sitting in its box, was this girl's plate which she had hidden right at the back underneath all my possessions. I was told that I had committed a mortal sin and would be condemned to hell. I was marched off, like a criminal, to be locked in a room by myself. Nobody would listen as I pleaded innocence and the argument was that it had been found in my locker. I was told that, under these circumstances, I was not fit to make my first Holy Communion. Later, someone appeared with my night clothes, sponge bag and a tray of food. I was told that I was being isolated from everyone. I got myself in such a state I could not eat and did nothing else but cry. I was kept in isolation for three days and eventually the girl in question owned up, saying it had been a joke!
After the summer holidays, the Christmas term brought quite a few surprises. In the pitch dark we had a fire drill and all the girls were made to climb out of the dormitory windows in their night clothes. It was freezing cold and terrifying, as the height was considerable. We had to launch ourselves over the window sill hanging from a rope ladder and, as we descended, the rough wall of the building grazed our knees and caused them to bleed. Amazingly enough, while at this convent, there was a real

fire in the laundry room, which wasn't far from the dormitories. One of the staff had put some clothes near an electric fire and forgotten to switch it off. Whilst the fire engines, bells ringing, roared up the school driveway, half the girls slept right through all the action. Only in the morning, during recreation, did we all go and survey what was left of the laundry room!

The new school year moved us into another classroom where there were eight highly-polished stairs to negotiate—not a sensible idea for young children with no grip on their uniform shoes.

On one particular day, we were getting into line to leave the classroom and I was at the top of the stairs. I slipped down them and my head crashed straight into the iron corner of a desk at the bottom. Blood poured everywhere and I remember nearly passing out as the nuns held me over a bath discussing whether I should be taken to the hospital for stitches or not. Eventually, to my utter relief, they decided against it due to my blood clotting very quickly. Literally an inch higher on my temple, it would have killed me instantly and to this day I bear the scar.

I wasn't happy at boarding school, and even less in a convent. Therefore, I made little progress where lessons were concerned. Always a very energetic, active, outdoor child, I found stuffy classrooms quite unbearable. I have tremendous willpower to learn if I am interested, but otherwise it is a complete waste of time. Literature, essays and anything creative or artistic would always hold my attention. The little girl with boundless energy, happy disposition, generous and kind, started to change, hating school, hating being away from her home. Finding out how cruel other little girls could be, I became thoroughly miserable.

The turning point was when my parents came to see me during an epidemic of measles. My mother was horrified that, firstly, there was no one with nursing qualifications looking after us and, secondly, we were all sitting in our beds with the sun streaming through the tall dormitory windows. So when the summer holiday came, I was taken home and didn't return, much to my absolute relief.

During my time at school I made friends with two girls named Jennifer and Patricia. To this day Patricia and I have kept in contact and she comes into my story later on.

It was to be a glorious summer and my parents had invited Jennifer and her mother to stay with us for three weeks at a cottage they had rented in St. Ives, Cornwall. I was very fond of Jennifer and we had great fun together on several occasions. Picnics were organised, a trip out to sea, endless walking and playing on the golden sands with visits to the surrounding villages. One afternoon we had been galloping up and down, running races on the beach and playing hide and seek with Rufus in tow. It all proved too much for him and while we girls slept, worn out in bed that evening, Rufus had a heart attack. It was only due to my mother's professional nursing skills that he pulled through. She spooned whisky down his throat and massaged his chest, nursing him all night. By the morning he had pulled through and went on to live for another three years.

One morning Jennifer and I escaped on the pretence of

going to the village shop to buy some sweets. In actual fact, we had heard the villagers talking about an old lady who lived with thirty cats. We were fascinated by this information and determined to investigate further.
Her house was round with a thatched roof with one door and a tiny window. It was situated up a steep hill with steps leading to a wicket gate. By this time we were totally convinced that it was a witch's house and it took nerves of steel to pluck up the courage to eventually knock on the door. The old lady, dressed in black, opened the door, and behind her in the one dark room were thirty pairs of cats' eyes staring at us. We dashed back to the gate, out into the street and down the hill as if we were going to have a spell put on us. Before the holiday came to an end, we discovered that the old lady had once been a district nurse!
Summer holidays nearly over, it was decided by mother to have another governess. Her name was Eva and she turned out to be a lovely person. We seemed to make some progress with lessons for they were made interesting, which seems an all-important point when teaching a child. Eva stayed with us for six months and, meanwhile, mother was interviewing for a replacement.
After Eva had gone, a battle-axe appeared. Miss Connington was never referred to by her Christian name and arrived at the front door with two enormous battered suitcases. She was a large, plump woman in her late fifties, with hair that was three colours—yellow, white and grey—scraped back into a large bun. She wore wire-rimmed glasses at the end of a pointed nose and had a moustache. To my way of thinking, she was extremely

ugly. That wouldn't have mattered, had she had a sense of humour or tried to make my life enjoyable. Mother had obviously thought that life had been too easy-going for me with Eva and was determined to change all that.
Miss Connington hadn't the slightest idea of how to cope with me and she spent her time saying, 'Mrs. Pryor, I must have a word with you about Clare.' She had the most ghastly false teeth that I have ever seen. The gums were bright orange and the teeth were far too big for her mouth. On the rare occasion that she tried to give a smile, it was a terrible sight.
Of course, I had taken an instant dislike to Miss Connington. There was no way on this earth that I was going to obey her or learn anything at all. My father never understood how mother could have employed such a woman in the first place and eventually, after several months, she had to go.
By this time, mother had decided that she had had enough of governesses and didn't want me around either. This time father did manage to strongly object to having me put back into a boarding school. So I was sent to a local girls' school and was allowed to bicycle back and forth.

Chapter 5

Starting day-school meant that life suddenly got extremely hectic, due to having to fit in all the extra classes my parents insisted on me having. By this time, it was quite obvious that I would never be a budding academic and clearly was a hyperactive child. So every spare moment had a lesson fitted in somewhere, with tennis, ice-skating, maths, riding, embroidery and ballet. The latter was progressing with glowing reports and from a very early age my mind had been made up to become a ballerina.

Whilst attending school I made friends with a girl in my class called Rosalind. She lived about a quarter of a mile up the road from our house. Her parents had lived in Kenya for many years. When they returned to England they brought their man-servant, Nicholas, with them. Rosalind's mother had set up a riding school at their home. Imagine my joy when my parents announced that they were going away on one of their jaunts abroad and that I was going to stay at Rosalind's house for a month. It was one of the few times in my life that I can look back on and remember as being blissfully happy. Rosalind and I shared a bedroom and each day Nicholas would appear with a hot cup of early morning tea. After breakfast, if horses were available, we would go out riding. Sometimes Rosalind and I would ride in the afternoon together and gallop across the Downs.

There was a lovely informal atmosphere despite the hive of activity going on. Nicholas would stand in the kitchen with his white apron on, preparing the next meal, with lots of saucepans bubbling away. High tea was great fun because there was always lots of conversation, laughs and delicious food. Rosalind had two brothers and there was invariably a groom, plus a friend eating as well. Time flew by and all too soon it was time to leave.

On returning, I had to prepare for an operation which was to be performed at home. Apparently, all my milk teeth were rotten and the dentist decided that the only way to save my second lot of teeth was to remove milk teeth and molars, a total of twelve! It had been decided that gas would not give time to extract them, so an injection in the arm would be given by our family doctor. In attendance was a second doctor.

Dr. Sudbury was a fairly tall man and, while returning from our bathroom, he nearly knocked himself out in the doorway. In a state of concussion, he spent twenty minutes trying to get a needle into my vein. By this time, I was terrified and the dentist and doctors decided to clamp the gas mask over my face. Consequently, there was not enough time to perform the operation properly and I was left with bits of root imbedded in the gums.

The pain was indescribable; my face became so swollen and bruised that eating became out of the question. I remember so well that it was father who spent hours stroking my hand, just sitting quietly by me, as I lay in bed and drifted in and out of consciousness. It was a long, agonising recovery and father would read umpteen story books to alleviate the pain and boredom.

Although it seemed quite barbaric at the time, it did prove the dentist right. He did save my second teeth and, although they all have fillings, I haven't lost many. Due to the fact that my second teeth found no obstructions, they have developed abnormally large roots and extractions have to be performed in hospital.

During the holidays, I was allowed to go and stay with granny. Mother would take me up on the train and, when we arrived there, my favourite pudding would be waiting for me. I have never tasted a tapioca pudding more delicious than the one that granny used to make. She would thoroughly spoil me and we would have a lovely time. I was only allowed to stay for a few days, but granny would always have tickets for us to go to a pantomime. Every day we would call at a neighbour's flat and fetch her poodle, Scrappy. Then we would walk to Hyde park, taking a bag of bread to feed the ducks.

Granny was the most elegant lady I had ever seen. She was thin, tall, beautifully dressed and always wore lovely hats. She walked with the aid of an ebony walking stick with a silver handle. At night she would sit on my bed and tell me all sorts of interesting stories and I would ask her to show me her jewellery box. It was full of fascinating earrings, necklaces and rings. On one occasion, granny showed me the most exquisite pearl necklace with a large diamond clasp. She told me that one day it would be mine because she wanted me to have it. Unfortunately, when granny was dying and being taken away in an ambulance, she was wearing the pearl necklace. It was never seen again.

Granny had married a widower, who already had seven children from his previous marriage. She then produced a daughter and son. I mention this because mother's only brother, supposedly meant to be an uncle, decided, most of his life, to totally ignore me. I never once received a Christmas or birthday present from him. As a child, it hurt terribly and for many years I longed to be accepted by mother's brother.

I shall never forget one day, on a visit to granny, the front door bell rang and my mother went to open the door to her brother. Henry walked into the sitting room, pointed at me and said, 'Irene, get her out of here, she's not one of the family!' There was, without a doubt, a streak of terrible cruelty in both brother and sister. Amazing, when you think that both of them were in the medical profession. They never got on together and for over thirty-five years had little to do with each other.

It must have been around the age of eleven when I broached the subject of my adoption to granny. She could see I was upset and that nothing had ever been explained to me. So she decided, quite rightly, to tell me the truth. Due to the fact that mother had not got pregnant after quite a few years of marriage, she eventually decided to adopt. She had always said that a boy was what she wanted. The adopted baby was not a healthy one and was continually getting ill with one thing after another. As nothing was known about his parents or their medical background, she finally sent him back to the orphanage. Granny's doctor was a kind old man and one day, while visiting the surgery, she explained to him how her daughter desperately wanted to adopt a baby. Doctor Putt told granny that one of his lady patients had asked him for

help in getting her baby adopted when it was born. Eventually, everything was decided and mother was to have the baby, be it girl or boy.
There was just one condition that Doctor Putt insisted on and that was that the baby was to be given a good start in life by being breast fed. She was to stay with her natural mother for the first month. Then granny fetched me and brought me back to her flat where her daughter was waiting to receive the tiny bundle.
Granny finished her story by quietly saying, 'Your natural mother was a very attractive lady and life hadn't been easy for her.' I was so grateful to granny for this information and that at last I knew the truth.
Mother was incapable of giving me a kiss or putting her arms around me or really loving me, so staying with granny was extra special because she really adored me. But, little did I know, in my innocence, that I was never going to be allowed to stay with granny again.
I can't remember how the situation arose, but either I blurted something out or mother cross-examined me. Anyway, when mother found out that granny had told me about my adoption, I was immediately sent up to my bedroom. Tears poured down my face as I heard mother on the phone calling her mother 'wicked .... and how dare you do such a thing'. It went on and on. Father tried to intervene, but mother told him not to interfere, and the next thing I knew was mother calling me downstairs. In her hands she held a notepad and pen.
I was made to sit at a table with mother behind me and was told to write: 'Dear granny.' By this time, I was reeling

from shock and totally stunned by mother's reaction. 'You are not moving from this chair until you have written what I am going to tell you to write. You will never be allowed to stay with granny again.'
The details of that letter were awful and when I protested that I didn't want to write a letter like that to granny, I was slapped across the face and told, 'Write!' There was nothing I could do about it and in the end, completely and utterly against my will, I was forcibly made to write that letter. It was then promptly taken away to be posted.
The last time I saw granny was on 2nd June 1953, on the day of Queen Elizabeth II's Coronation, and that didn't turn out to be a pleasant day. It had been arranged that granny and uncle Henry would meet us at an hotel in London for lunch.
From one of the hotel balconies we watched the endless procession and, despite the heavy drizzle of rain, Queen Salote of Tonga refused to have the hood of her carriage erected, in order that the millions lining the street and watching from the windows and balconies could see her.
Lunch was a tedious affair and I wasn't hungry so mother made a fuss, whilst Henry wouldn't speak to his sister and granny and daddy told mother to leave me alone.

Chapter 6

After this incident mother became even more domineering, totally lacking in any kind of affection for either father or myself. She only needed father for his money and her one aim was to spend it. Every year on Boxing Day the house would be filled with three hundred people invited to a cocktail party. Food was sent down from London at great expense and I would spend the evening handing dishes of this, that and the other around. Mother would excel in airs and graces and constantly prod me in the back when she thought I should be circulating with some more cocktail sausages, vol-au-vents or whatever. Occasionally, mother would grab me by the arm and, in a loud voice, would say to a group of people, 'This is my daughter Clare.' She would then go on to explain where I was at boarding school, etcetera, etcetera. I would stand there amidst all the legs and agree with mother's dialogue. It was so embarrassing.

Father was the total opposite and didn't like to hold forth, but quietly made sure that his organisational skills were put to good use at birthday parties and Easter. He would spend hours preparing and planning and there would always be chocolate eggs hidden in the garden for us children to find. Clues were given on a typed piece of paper and we would spend Easter morning hunting. When not at boarding school, birthday parties with the usual party games were great events. Father being such a natural person would put all the children at ease and I don't know who enjoyed it most, us or him.

Conveniently situated within a three minute walk from our house was the local tennis club. I was lucky enough to have an elderly ex-Wimbledon gentleman to coach me. He was a perfectionist with a tremendous style. Father bought me a Slazenger racquet and had my initials put on it and I was determined to learn everything I could about tennis. I took to the game as if I had been born with a racquet in my hand and from then on I was often to be seen on a tennis court.

The loving attention I got was from father, which inwardly annoyed mother. He would find time to play tennis with me, go for walks or outings, because he knew that I spent a lot of time by myself and did get lonely. Although we lived well, I was never allowed to be spoilt and for this I am truly grateful. When life gets tough, you can only cope if you have been taught discipline. Father put a lot of emphasis on good manners, politeness and respect for other people. He not only expected it from me, but gave a shining example himself.

However, having said all this, I knew perfectly well that there were times when I could have twisted father round my little finger, but I can truthfully say that I never asked him for anything. I remember so vividly walking by a shop window and there was what I had set my heart on—a walking doll. I stood looking at her whilst holding on to my father's hand and knew I could literally melt his heart if I wanted to. We passed on and I just hoped I might get one for a birthday or Christmas, but never did. To this day I'm glad I never asked my father. Later in life, in my most horrific financial struggles, I did not feel I had the right to tell him and make him worry, so I kept it all to myself. Sometimes during the summer my parents and I would go down to a place called Birling Gap. Occasionally, I was allowed to bring a friend and, once everyone had been assigned with something to carry, we would make our way down to the beach. I always remember my parents repeating the same thing every time we went out anywhere. Should I find any object, on no account was I to touch it, but to come and tell them. There were unexploded bombs and many other things for children to pick up that the Germans had dropped during the Second World War.

Birling Gap has miles of rocks where you can spend hours with a net and bucket catching crabs, shrimps etc. I would tease the sea anemones by giving them a tiny stone which they would suck in and then spit out again. Mother would take a Primus Stove and cook the shrimps and whatever else she had brought for a meal. We would sit and watch the sun setting while we ate before going home. I used to get ravenous after filling my lungs with sea air and using up boundless energy. My idea of bliss was Marmite sandwiches, but I never understood why mother couldn't or wouldn't make enough of them.

Totally against father's wishes, mother decided, once again, that she wanted me out of the way, so plans were made to put me back into another convent in Kent. Out came the school trunk from the attic and an exhausting day followed in London, traipsing around after mother, trying on endless school uniform. Then there was an hour and a half return journey sitting in a stuffy train. I had been quite alright at the local school in the knowledge that, at the end of the day, I could pedal off home, but the idea of being put into another prison was alarming, to say the least.

The dreaded day came and I was left surrounded by high brick walls where the outside world was never seen. Nothing motivated me to study anything. I didn't want to learn and, apart from this, we had a continual disruption of new teachers practically every term. Only the brainy girls could cope with the diabolical changes we had. My mind has never been a studious one so, of course, I got lost in the first term and never caught up. Eventually my parents realised that all I was interested in were my ballet classes. I was born to dance and had a natural talent for it. I had a wonderful ex-Sadler's Wells teacher and she soon realised that I was an outstanding pupil, never happier than when dancing, tireless in my efforts for perfection and determined to show my mother that I was going to be a ballerina. This was my goal, my ultimate dream and what I worked so extremely hard at to try and achieve.

Convent life was extremely boring and tedious with nothing exciting ever going on. So I used to gaze out at the high brick walls surrounding me and wish it would all disappear. I was never happy there and I used to put up with a lot of bullying. To add to the misery, the nuns opened and read all our letters, unless they were from our parents. The way round this was to have any friends send their letters to your home address. Parents would then put them in a second envelope and send them on.

My parents had great friends in London and their son

Charles was like an uncle to me. He was a charming person and I used to enjoy his visits. Sometimes during the term-time he would ring and the nun who answered the phone would want to know who he was.
'Uncle Charles', he would reply.
During the holidays he would ring and say, 'Clare, I'm coming to see you and to take you out to dinner.'
We would go to lovely places and once he took me to his naval club in London. He had ordered the most beautiful bouquet of freesias for me and it made me feel very special. I was extremely fond of Charles. He took a job out in Canada and, although we corresponded and he sent me presents, I only saw him once again on a brief visit to Britain. Tragically, he died of cancer some years later. In loving memory, I named my son after him.
Shortly after settling in at school, when we were not considered 'new girls' any longer, the nuns started preparing us for our Confirmation. It turned out to be the most embarrassing day. Everything was prepared for the Bishop's arrival. The nuns all had spotless bibs and tuckers on and us girls wore clean veils. Parents were allocated to their pews in the chapel and then took their turn in walking up to the Bishop, kneeling on one knee to kiss his ring and walking back to their pew. My mother was down on one knee kissing the Bishop's ring and, as she rose to her feet, she heard a slight 'twang' and there on the floor, for all to see, was her petticoat! She bent down and stuffed it into her handbag and hurried back to her pew, to the sound of one-hundred-and-eighty girls twittering and giggling.

My mother had never understood me and as I went through my teens she made life for father and me quite unbearable. Neither of us could ever do anything right and, as far as she was concerned, I really wasn't good at anything and never would be. My escape came in the form of an Irish family who lived ten minutes' walk down the road. Mrs. O'Hara had eight children and no matter what was going on, or how busy she was, you were always made very welcome. 'Come in Clare, stay for lunch, stay for tea, stay for dinner.'

The house could be bursting at the seams with children, dog, nanny and visitors, but I was always included in the next meal. It was all so different from our home and I loved being at Mrs. O'Hara's house. There were lots of comings and goings with a front door that worked overtime. It was a lovely easy-going atmosphere and Mrs. O'Hara was always pleased to see me, no matter what hour of the day it was. In one word, she was an absolute sweetie and very fond of me.

Her eldest son was often around at weekends or in the evenings after work when I was playing with one of his sisters. I didn't realise it at the time, but he fell in love with me. He would write whilst I was at school and must have gone through torture for many years. I was a young teenager and he was in his thirties. Apart from the odd crush on a boy or 'puppy love', I hadn't a clue what falling in love was all about. Looking back, I realise now how much he had adored me and how I must have hurt him. His mother had always hoped that we would marry and was upset that nothing became of it. We both eventually married other people and went our different ways.

Chapter 7

School dragged on and the boredom was only made a little more bearable by my becoming tennis and netball Captain. The tennis team was of a high standard and soon we were invariably winning both the away and home—if you can call school 'home'—matches.

Just before one of the Easter holidays, I discovered that a French girl called Monique was spending the whole of the holidays with the nuns. Her mother was widowed and had made great sacrifices to educate Monique in England. This meant that financially the cost of travelling back to France at the end of each term was impossible. I asked my parents if Monique could come home with me.

We had just got through our holidays to the last week when disaster struck. Getting up one morning, father appeared, looking completely shell-shocked and drained of any colour. I immediately realised something dreadful had happened and also that mother—who always had breakfast in bed—was nowhere to be seen.

'Where's mother?' I asked.

'She's been taken ill and has been rushed into hospital,' replied my father.

Monique and I were hurried along to the dining room for breakfast by our French cook.

'You be good Miss Clare,' she said. 'Your father 'as 'ad ze most terreeble shock.'

No more explanations were given and father drove off in his car, leaving me still wondering exactly what was going on.

It was many years before I found out the real truth of that ghastly morning. Mother had taken an overdose and had been rushed to hospital in an ambulance in the early hours of the morning. We were taken to see mother the next day and took her a bunch of flowers. Father then somehow coped with us girls for the next few days and got us back to school. He was always so loyal to her and never let on what had really happened. Monique's mother, on hearing that mother had been taken ill, decided to have me for a month during the summer and I couldn't wait for the term to finish. I was so excited for we were travelling by train to Paris. We then spent a few days at her house and then on to Monique's grandparents who lived in a chateau in Normandy. Monique had a collection of cousins and we all had a marvellous time. We went on bicycle rides in the surrounding countryside and played in the vineyards, eating so many grapes until we felt quite sick. Neither Monique's grandparents nor cousins spoke any English so there was a continual buzz of French conversation around me. Monique got carried away with her cousins at meal times and I soon learnt that I would have to learn the French language pretty sharpish or get left out.
Meals were fun with so many people and, regardless of age, a glass of red wine was naturally considered part of the meal. By the time we got back to school for another term, I could speak fluent French. The rest of my class just couldn't believe what they were hearing, for I had taken not one iota of interest in French lessons and had spent my time being punished outside in the corridor. Later on, I was to return again with Monique and stay

with her other grandparents, this time in Brittany, but only for a week or so and then back to Paris. Monique and her mother took me to see Notre Dame, Champs Elysees, Arc de Triomphe and Versailles. At the Eiffel Tower we went up to the very top in the lift and watched the cars below which appeared like ants running around. Then we walked down every step to the ground.

My parents, meanwhile, had had another trip abroad and mother couldn't face the idea of Christmas at home. So they decided to go to Switzerland for the festive season. We travelled out to Zurich by night and then by train. At Wengen our luggage was piled onto a sleigh. I spent my time skiing, ice-skating or on the toboggan run where I enjoyed careering down a three-mile stretch at really dangerous speeds. Before we departed there was a skiing test and immediately mother muttered that it would be a waste of time for me to attempt such a thing. However, I did enrol that afternoon and rushed back to the hotel to proudly show my parents my bronze medal.

The atmosphere at home had been difficult for some time, but was now getting quite unbearable. Father buried himself deeper and deeper into his charity work and kept working all hours. He could not stand mother's constant nagging and her belittling remarks. He had even stopped going to his Church of England service and had been baptised a Roman Catholic to keep the peace.

For some unknown reason, mother also flatly refused to have anything to do with any of father's relatives. So father used to take me to visit a sister of his mother's who lived in Eastbourne. She had one daughter who never

married and was always known as aunt Doris. We would go for afternoon tea and I would sit and play the piano, my feet dangling from the stool. Father also had two other cousins. Alan lived in London in a large rambling house and Molli lived on the Isle of Wight. She became, in later years, a surrogate mother to me and her love, support and companionship gave me the strength to endure all that was yet to come in the future years.
Christmas had been such a success that we went back to Wengen the following year. Terrain being familiar this time round, I rushed off down to the ice rink to skate. By the afternoon I was starting to feel ill and by the evening had developed an alarmingly high temperature with bronchitis. I was so ill that the doctor wanted to put me in hospital, but mother wouldn't hear of it. I kept drifting into a delirious state and remember little of what went on. It took three weeks before I was sufficiently recovered to negotiate travelling back to England.

* * *

Eventually, after eleven long years, my last few weeks of boarding school arrived. It was time to leave and aim for an entrance to Sadler's Wells. Although mother was making father's life a misery, the devastation that was about to hit me, at the age of seventeen, never entered my head.
My parents had apparently thought about separating many years previously, but decided, for my sake, not to do anything about it. It didn't occur to either of them to

choose any other time to go ahead with final legal proceedings but the day before my final exams. I sat in an absolute stupor during the next week with my exam papers in front of me. All the girls around me had heads bent and were writing frantically. The shock was so great that I was incapable of making any sense of the questions and sat gazing down at the white blank paper or out of the window. I kept telling myself that there might be a mistake and couldn't imagine separated parents. I was told by mother over the phone that I was to take a train home and to arrange for my trunk etc. to be sent on.

When I arrived home, father wasn't there. He would suddenly appear on a visit and just as suddenly disappear again. Mother was having furniture removed, some into storage, the rest sold. She then told me that, although they had done everything possible to sell the family home and had had it on the market with several estate agencies, they hadn't managed to sell it. It was to be auctioned the following week and they had got two paid bidders to try and get the best possible price.

I cannot put into words the agony of it all, only to say my world had literally and very truly fallen apart. The shock that I felt left me numb and almost speechless. I watched in horror as bits of furniture disappeared out of the house before my very eyes. A man was going round with a clip-board tying labels which read 'for sale' onto furniture, pictures and treasured ornaments.

My mother and I sat in the auction room and the tears welled up as I fought them back, but when they started bidding for our family home, it became so painful that I just sat with tears pouring down my cheeks. Eventually, the house that we loved so dearly with all the childhood memories was sold over our heads. It never even reached a good selling price, leaving my parents with even less than they had expected. A middle-aged couple bought it and I wondered, at the time, what on earth they were going to do with such a large house and no family. The final blow came when mother turned round with no feeling whatsoever and quite coldly announced, 'Of course, you do realise that you will not be able to take up a career as a ballerina.'

Mother had arranged for us to go and stay with a friend a few streets away and, armed with umpteen suitcases and Silver in a basket, we arrived on her doorstep. Helen was very kind and had known us for years. After something to eat we retired to the bedroom which I was sharing with my mother. She showed no emotion at all; for that matter, no feeling for me either. I was now even more of a burden round her neck, so she sat bolt upright in bed and suddenly said, 'And what are you planning to do?'

I sat on the edge of my bed and thought how can this woman be so insensitive? Here I was, at seventeen, only just finished school, parents separated, family home gone and my dancing career destroyed. Everything that I had loved had gone in a matter of ten days. Mother felt nothing for me at all and hadn't even given me a kiss or a hug—and hey presto, here we were at a friend's house being given a roof over our heads! I hadn't answered the question because, as far as I was concerned, I didn't care about what was going to happen. I felt total indifference.

'Well,' said mother, 'if you are refusing to answer me, then I will arrange something.'
To be quite honest, I didn't care what she was going to do with me. I quietly crept off downstairs to sit in the kitchen where we had left Silver for the night. He, too, was upset not knowing what was going on and he rubbed his head against me as I cuddled him in my arms and cried bitterly. He was all that was left.
A few weeks later, mother announced that she had arranged for me to go to Spain to a family for a year and that I would be leaving at the end of August. That meant there was only a month before leaving. I wanted to see my father, but mother would neither give me a phone number nor let me see him. It was simply devastating.
My mother's cruelty knew no bounds and she gave me her final blow a few days later. Silver had developed kidney failure for he was, by now, an old cat. She knew we had grown up together and that I adored him. Instead of having the understanding and compassion a mother should have, and being kind enough to go with me to the vet, she coldly ordered me to take him and have him put down. That afternoon I walked two miles with Silver in my arms to the vet. The old cat instinctively knew that his day had come and that this was the final goodbye.
I arrived back at the house with red eyes, a swollen face and choking with agony. I went up to the bedroom and threw myself on the bed and buried my head in the pillow. Later that evening, mother came up to go to bed and all she said was, 'Stop that crying and pull yourself together.' As she was about to turn the light off she eventually said,

'Goodnight Clare.'
I went into the bathroom shaking and sat rocking backwards and forwards with my arms hugging myself, trying to alleviate my indescribable pain. Mother took me shopping and bought clothes. I remember very little, except being told to try this on and that on and walking about like a zombie. It was of no consequence, importance or anything else, what she wanted me to take to Spain.

Chapter 8

Mother had friends who were cousins of a well-known sherry family in Spain. It was through this connection that it was arranged for me to go out to Jerez and live with them as family for a year. Arriving in Gibraltar by plane, and then crossing the border into Spanish territory at Algeciras, I found a restaurant cafe and tried to order something to eat. The waiter didn't speak a single word of English, nor I Spanish! After plenty of miming, which was quite hilarious, and making chicken noises, an omelette was produced.

My first experience of a Spanish bus travelling over a rough track full of pot-holes with dust flying through the windows was quite frightening. We got seated and all the luggage was thrown on top of the roof and secured to collect a thick layer of dust. The afternoon heat was intense. Every time the bus swerved round a corner I got thrown halfway on top of a rather buxom country woman who reeked of sweat and garlic. Next to her was her daughter and they were both dressed in black with small black veils pinned to their hair. The old Spanish custom is that once a country woman is widowed, she will wear black for the rest of her life.

As we gathered speed, with one tyre going into a pot-hole every other minute, the driver would put his whole hand on the horn and blast anything that was obstructing his way. We passed the peasants walking with their children in skimpy clothes with straw hats on. Goats and donkeys wandered about in the middle of the dirt track while

chickens strutted about clucking and flapping their wings, running for cover as they were hooted at. Woe betide any animal that didn't move, for this yellow bus full of passengers would just drive on as if it didn't have any brakes at all! Quite tired, hot, thirsty and bewildered, I arrived at Jerez's bus station. There Cristina's husband was waiting to meet me and take me to their home.
Everything was so strange with all the buildings white-washed, donkeys everywhere, few cars and literally hundreds of motorbikes and bicycles. After being used to wallpaper, carpets and central heating, I found it all rather clinical with the stone floors, white-washed walls and cow-skin mats. The household consisted of Cristina and Julio, their two sons, Gabriel, Daniel, and a daughter named Maria, Nanny who had been there many years and also a housemaid, cook and messenger boy. They all made me feel very welcome and the children were a delight. Every day I would walk to Cristina's mother's house, through the cobbled streets with the two boys aged three and five. Nanny would follow a little later with Maria, who was at that time only one-and-a-half years old.
The grandparents' house was cool inside with an indoor patio and the garden was very pleasant with enormous palm trees. Nanny would settle herself down and get on with piles of mending and sing to Maria. Meanwhile, I would give the boys their English lesson and then we would have lunch inside. Lunches were always quite delicious, but I was left staring in amazement at the amount of food Spanish children were expected to eat! Nanny would stand there shovelling large spoonfuls of

beans, chickpeas or lentils into their mouths. Then meat or fish would arrive accompanied by French fries, followed by fresh fruit.

I had arrived about a week before the famous Vintage Fair of Jerez de la Frontera, which is held every year in September. The first baskets of grapes are carried by girls in traditional gypsy dress, and tipped into the wine press in a ceremony which takes place outside one of the churches. The men stamp their feet up and down on the grapes in the press until the first juices are extracted and white doves are let out from the belfry. This is the start to the Vintage Fair—La Feria del Vendimia—and the birth of a new sherry year in Jerez. Cristina had a wonderful surprise for me. She had found a gypsy dress, so off I went to the fair. The gentleman who accompanied me rode his horse and I sat sideways on the horse's rump. My right hand went round the gentleman's waist and the left hand gripped firmly onto the leather tail strap. We went cantering down the thoroughfares and I silently made a quick prayer that I wasn't going to fall off.

Next morning, Cristina actually made one of my dreams come true. She had not only found a lovely horse for me to ride, but a complete outfit to wear. This consisted of the traditional Andalucian clothes, mainly worn by the Spanish gentlemen on festive occasions. It consists of a shirt with frills down the front, a black, short, fitted jacket, striped grey trousers, chaps, and the wide-brimmed Andalucian hat. My waist-long hair was gathered into a bun with carnations. While on horseback, the custom is to ride about the fair and then stop at one of the 'Casetas'—

individual huts—where the girls would be dancing Sevillanas. Someone would appear with a bottle of sherry and some glasses, and pour me a glass and hand it up to me while still in the saddle. The refrain in Jerez is: 'Tienes que beber dos, si no te vas coja'. Translated it means, 'you must drink two, otherwise you will go away lame.' So I spent the morning getting blissfully happy on sherry and managed to still stay in the saddle.

A few weeks later, I developed yellow jaundice. I didn't get it mildly, but extremely severely, and spent the next three weeks in bed, very ill. It meant constant medication, daily injections and a whole year on a strict diet. When recovered, I kept religiously to my diet, refusing to be influenced by anyone. It paid off because since then there have been no more problems. Cristina felt that it was time I met a few people and arranged for me to go to a piano recital one evening with the assistant nurse's son. His father had been administering my injections and was an old friend of the family. Having arrived and seated ourselves halfway down the concert hall, little did I know that I was being closely watched by a gentleman in the row behind us. Some years later, that gentleman was to become my husband.

Several weeks later, I was invited to a party at the polo club. Sitting with some girls, who spoke a little English, we were carrying on a conversation. While I deeply concentrated, trying to understand what was being conveyed, two gentlemen were standing nearby. One of them was talking to one of the girls and asked her to introduce me. I politely said a few words, and although the

gentleman in question spoke English, I didn't really want to carry on speaking to him. However, I was taken aback when he said he knew where I lived and had seen me at the piano recital.
One evening, one of Cristina's relatives drove me a few miles out of Jerez to his family's country estate. We drove up the long drive which must have been three quarters of a mile, and arrived at the gates of the castle. We went inside to the sitting room and had a drink. My Spanish was still very limited and it was quite difficult to hold a conversation. After walking about and admiring the paintings and tapestries, we went back into the hall and I assumed that we were going back to the car. I stood there expecting him to unlock the heavy wooden doors but, to my horror, he was making his way up the stairs.
'Come,' he said.
Suddenly, I felt terribly cold and very frightened. He continued up the stairs, getting the message over that he was not taking me back home. Physically shaking, I held my ground and told him in broken Spanish that if he didn't take me home, I would walk back and let the whole of Jerez know about his behaviour. To my utter relief, this tactic worked and he descended the stairs and, in a temper, drove me back to Cristina's house.
One morning, while the children were having lunch at their granny's house, Cristina's sister, Magdalena, turned up and brought with her an English girl who was to live with them as family for a year. Having been introduced by Christian names, we started to chat to each other. After a few minutes Patricia looked at me and said, 'I'm sure I've

seen you before.' She paused and suddenly said, 'Didn't you have long plaits at school?'
'Yes,' I said extremely surprised, and then I realised who she was. Patricia and I had been in the same class at the convent when we had been seven years of age. It was amazing that we should both be in Jerez, and even more amazing to find ourselves with the two sisters. Although each family lived quite a distance from each other we were able to meet up on several occasions.
The most memorable day was when I went out with Magdalena's family to Picao. The family consisted of eight children and so she drove them around in a large blue van. On this particular day, Magdalena's husband took the wheel and we all piled in to seat ourselves amongst the picnic hampers. We passed through glorious countryside, arriving at a typical Andalucian farmhouse known as 'Cortijo'. Picao is famous for breeding bulls and I was able to go out on horseback with the country men, riding with them, as they rounded up the cattle. Of course, there is always an element of risk where a large herd of bulls are concerned. Everything was going well as we crossed the vast wasteland where they were. About fifteen minutes later one of the bulls with particularly long horns put its head down and charged straight towards me. It was a matter for extremely quick thinking. I turned my horse round and made for a river nearby and this fortunately stopped the bull from attempting to wade through the water. The men congratulated me, shouting, 'Courageous woman, bravo, bravo!'
When the bulls had been rounded up we then returned to

a lovely picnic lunch of potato omelette, meat and crusty bread. Patricia and I spent the afternoon playing with the children and riding about on donkeys. We returned home to a glorious sunset with Nanny singing to the children and everyone tired but happy.

By this time I felt quite settled and was getting used to the Spanish way of life. Jerez gets unbearably hot in the summer so we moved to a little country house the family owned on the outskirts of the town, some four miles away. It was an absolute haven for children and I loved it. I will always have fond memories of the summer there, for it was great to be away from the hustle, bustle, noise and heat. There was a small swimming pool and the children and I would spend many happy hours in it. Nanny would stand by with a towel, getting more and more frustrated, trying to get the children out of it.

A few weeks before we moved to the country I bought two ducklings from the market. It was explained to me that I must give them peppercorns to keep them warm or they would not survive. When in Spain do as the Spaniards do! So I did just that and named them Peter and Paul. While still tiny, I had them in a cage. At night I would let them run around my bedroom and there wouldn't be a mosquito left. I was very grateful to the ducklings because being out in the country we did get a tremendous amount of mosquitoes and they certainly knew who to bite!

The family owned a horse and two ponies. Because of my love of riding, I was given the opportunity to ride whenever I wanted, and to break in the ponies which no one had ever ridden. This brought about teaching both boys to ride, so when the ponies were trained and safe, we started the riding lessons. My horse was named 'Brownie', the ponies 'Violetta' and 'Downstairs'. I am, at this point, trying to remember why on earth we named one of the ponies 'Downstairs', but it eludes me completely. I vaguely remember some joke we had about upstairs and downstairs and the boys' decision to give the pony this name because they liked the sound of it in English. It was certainly different anyway.

Some mornings while the family slept and the dawn was coming up, I would take Brownie out. There would be a wonderful temperature before the heat of the day and it was so peaceful galloping across the countryside. One such early morning while riding, Brownie took fright and reared up into the air. Underneath him in the middle of the track was a large snake curled up. My first thought was to stay on Brownie, as the snake hissed. I was so thankful for the Andalucian saddle because, had I been sitting on an English saddle, I would have been, without a doubt, thrown off. Brownie then bolted and I held on for dear life, until he decided to calm down and come to a halt.

I used to take the boys out and had a leading rein for the younger one. They took to the saddle as if they had been born in it and became extremely good at riding. On many such occasions, Peter and Paul would waddle off down the driveway to see where we were going. Peter would often sit up on my shoulder, pecking my ear, making quacking noises and even go for rides too! By this time they had turned into two beautiful ducks.

Halfway through the summer I developed quinsy with a dangerously high temperature. I was taken seriously ill and had to have umpteen different antibiotics, suppositories and injections. I was in extreme pain and could hardly open my mouth to speak, let alone swallow anything. The high temperature raged and I drifted in and out of consciousness. Eventually, after two weeks, it started to ease, but left me feeling very weak indeed. In September we returned to Jerez and I left Peter and Paul behind to be cared for, along with the chickens and other animals, by the country couple who looked after the farmland.

Chapter 9

A year had slipped by very quickly and mother had already arranged for me to return to England. Cristina would have willingly had me stay on but mother was in a threatening manner and reminded me, in no uncertain terms, that I was under age. After a tremendous amount of persuasion from Cristina, it was agreed that I could return to Spain on the condition that I went to Madrid to learn Castellano Spanish. The farewell from Julio and Cristina's family was very sad and, once on the plane, I burst into tears. It had been my first chance to be independent, to calm down from the nightmare I had been through for most of my childhood and teenage years. The climate had been a tonic in itself, despite the way of life being years behind other countries. I was already missing the sound of the maids in the early mornings whooshing water from their buckets onto the steps outside the houses and sweeping vigorously; donkeys trotting along the cobbled roads, carrying the daily milk which would be measured out at the door step and then taken to the kitchen to be boiled. Laundry was all washed by hand in a huge sink with grooves, designed for this purpose. On wash day the laundry woman would roll up her sleeves, immerse clothes into water and literally scrub them up and down with a bar of green soap. It involved a lot of banging, rinsing and squeezing. The whites would be put into a huge tub containing bleach to soak, before the whole performance was done again! I never understood where these women managed to get their physical stamina from, but they were

desperately poor and needed the money.
There were no clothes shops in the year 1958 and, indeed, little else as we know it today. You would go along to a material shop and choose what you liked, then find a dressmaker to make up the garment you required, and then explain the design you wanted. She would take measurements and make it up with no pattern at all. It was unheard of for a woman to wear trousers and I remember the stir it caused along the main street when I wore a pair. It kept the shop assistants and everyone in conversation for weeks after. There were very few women drivers and it was very much a man's world at that time.
When on the beach we had to wear bathing costumes. Bikinis were totally illegal and not allowed under Franco's regime. In fact, many women kept their dresses on and just paddled. It was also forbidden by law for women to ride astride a motorbike. Of course, without wearing trousers it was virtually impossible to sit in such a position without being indecent. The idea of showing a knee would have been a scandal! It was an extremely dangerous and uncomfortable way to sit on a motorbike, but virtually the only form of transport if you couldn't afford a car. I always seemed to have one leg that didn't have anywhere to put itself. By the end of the journey, I was left trying to get both legs into a walking position again.
The shops that existed were old fashioned with mosaic tiled walls and stone floors. Massive high wooden counters would stretch from wall to wall while the hum of a ceiling fan could be heard as it moved the hot air around.

Despite the summer heat, the shops were cool inside and customers were always greeted with a genuine smile and a 'Buenas dias' or 'Buenas tardes'. Nothing was too much trouble to oblige, even if it meant turning the shop contents upside down. A ladder would be produced and the stacks of boxes on shelves up to the ceiling would all be opened to find whatever the customer required.

The Spaniards are extremely respectful, patient and obliging when it comes to giving assistance. This also applies to the genuine service and friendliness of the people working in the market place.

Entering into the old building, there would be around thirty fish stalls. Massive sword fishes would be displayed, waiting to be cut into fillets. An abundance of octopuses with their long suckered tentacles would be piled on thick crushed ice along with every conceivable seafood imaginable.

Upstairs was the usual market buzz of conversation, shouting and hand gestures. Here, one would find all the meat products and vegetables. People would be gathered around a stall rather like a rugger scrum—for queuing was unheard of—whilst the butcher chopped meat or chicken on a tree trunk.

Stray dogs would roam about scavenging for anything that they could find to appease their hunger. The gypsy women wearing long skirts and grubby aprons would wander about balancing big baskets on their hips selling garlic and herbs. Invariably pregnant, they carried babies wrapped in dirty rags and suckling at the breast. Clinging to their skirts would be two or three small children scantily dressed and

many times barefooted.
The fruit and vegetables were very fresh and quite delicious having been allowed to ripen naturally by the sun. I often wondered how anything could grow in such a dry, hot climate or indeed how the cattle survived in the parched dessert fields with no shade at all in the searing heat.
One day I had an opportunity to see for myself the simple but effective irrigation system that is used in Andalucia. The farmers leave furrows in between the crops when planting. Early morning or evening a trap door is lifted to let the water flow from a small reservoir. This enables the water to gush down the furrows and keep the crops irrigated.
It has often been remarked by those travelling around Spain that they are totally confused by the various uniformed police. Spain has three main police forces:

Municipal Police:
This police force wear dark blue uniforms and are armed with revolvers. They deal mostly with traffic control, enforcement of municipal laws and minor crime.

National Police:
This police force wear brown uniforms with berets and also have plain clothes police. All are armed with revolvers. They deal with serious crime such as drug dealers, theft, controlling demonstrations, etc. This force also have police guarding embassies, army barracks, etc. and they are armed with submachine guns.

Civil Guard:
This police force wear light green uniform and caps—which have replaced the black patent-leather tricorn hats—and are armed with revolvers. They patrol rural areas and highways dealing with road accidents. They act as frontier guards and immigration officers and are always on duty in pairs, travelling by motorbike or landrover.

Chapter 10

Mother, by this time, had gone back to her nursing and as yet hadn't bought a house, so we stayed in an hotel in Seaford. The weather was wet and cold, the sky was grey and all in all it was terribly boring and depressing. The two weeks back in England seemed like three months. There was only one happy day, when I was able to see my father. He drove me back to the place where he was staying for lunch and tea. It was lovely to see him and we enjoyed each other's company so much. Eventually, I packed up the little I had brought over to England and headed back to Jerez.

Cristina had arranged for me to go to a family in Madrid. It was all very strange and lonely. The family had one daughter aged eleven and I had to accompany her to and from school with a uniformed chauffeur. Late afternoon and weekends were taken up with English lessons. The easy-going and friendly atmosphere of Julio and Cristina's family was definitely missing. I had grown extremely fond of Gabriel, Daniel and Maria. On my days off I took the opportunity to visit the Prado Museum and found it absolutely fascinating. It has an amazing collection of Spanish paintings, dating from the twelfth to the early nineteenth century. On various occasions, I returned to see the glorious paintings, particularly the ones by El Greco, Velasquez, Murillo and Goya.

After three months in Madrid, Cristina and I managed to convince mother that I would be far better back in Jerez. So it was with great excitement that I packed and got on the train. Everyone was very pleased to see me again and I them, for it was like a second home—or should I say the only home I knew at that time. There was an hotel in the main street called 'The Swans'. Here, all the social gatherings took place, there being little where else to go, except the local bars. Walking through the hotel, you could sit outside in a delightful courtyard full of climbing plants and flowers. Beyond this was an indoor garden with two swans swimming about in a pond. It was on one particular evening that the man who had followed me after the piano recital and spoken to me at the Polo Club reappeared. His name was Marcos and he had spoken to me on several occasions whilst walking in the street. He invited me for a drink, and I discovered that he spoke very good English with an American accent. We started to go out with each other. As the weather got warmer, we would go for a ride on his motorbike, or go to one of the surrounding villages.

Summer fast approaching, Jerez was getting stiflingly hot, but we didn't move to the country house due to the boys needing extra tuition. Occasionally, we would all go to the beach and stay most of the day, enjoying the cool breeze and warm water. The boys and I would play on the golden sands, while Nanny, fully clothed, would lift her dress just a fraction from her ankles and paddle with Maria's little hand in hers. Meanwhile, the ice-cream man would appear walking along the burning sand, carrying a great big wooden container selling choc-ices. A few yards behind would be another man with a white cap, carrying a large basket. Crabs, shrimps, salted lupin pods and packets of sunflower seeds were for sale. He would roll a piece of grey paper into a cone and fill it with whatever you wanted. A primitive summer bar on the beach would provide green peppers, olives, fried fish and crusty bread. This could be washed down with a glass of ice-cold sherry or lager.

Mother had decided towards the end of the summer to come to Jerez to meet everyone, and also to take a holiday with me in Malaga for two weeks. It was a total disaster from beginning to end. She met Marcos and decided that I was to return to England at the beginning of September. When we took the bus from Jerez for our two weeks away, it broke down up in the mountains, miles from anywhere. It took two hours for a replacement bus to arrive and meanwhile all the American and English tourists that we had collected on the way got drunk on free drinks at a very primitive bar. It was late at night when we arrived amidst the drunks to the Alhambra Hotel in Granada. We spent the next morning wandering around the Alhambra Palace and gardens. In the afternoon we continued on to an hotel halfway up a mountainside with magnificent views of Malaga. Mother was promptly taken ill with a temperature and had to see a doctor. I sat and had my meals in the restaurant alone, or sat for hours in her bedroom; so consequently, we never saw Malaga at all. Mother returned fully recovered to Jerez and stayed a few more days at The Swans Hotel. She was quite adamant about me returning to England and even threatened me with the police.

It was another very sad farewell to the family and back to

England. It had been arranged for the plane's arrival to coincide with catching the last train down to Sussex. When I arrived at Heathrow airport, I had to go through Customs. I was asked if I had anything to declare and innocently said no. As I was passing along the queue, one of the Customs officers decided to get stroppy and said, 'Are you wearing a wrist watch?'

'Yes,' I said. It had been given to me by Marcos as a present.

'It's a Swiss watch and hasn't been declared.'

'But I haven't come from Switzerland. I've come from Spain. This was a present and I've had it for over six months.' I was tired, hungry and had to cross London to catch the last train.

The Customs officer continued, 'I want all your luggage opened.'

I just couldn't believe it. There he was throwing every article out of my suitcase, all over the place. People stood and watched as bras, knickers and all my personal things were strewn about. He then went through a lengthy procedure to see if the suitcase had a false bottom. It had taken me hours to pack and I stood there in total disbelief. I had nowhere to stay the night in London and started to panic about my train connection. Having spent over three quarters of an hour putting me through all this, he then said, 'You'll have to pay for the value of the watch.'

'I haven't got much money and I need it to get a train,' I replied.

'Well,' he said, 'either you pay, or we keep you here.'

I was devastated and in a real state by this time. 'I won't

have enough money for my train fare.'
'That's your problem madam,' he replied, quite unperturbed that it was late at night. I handed over my money and by this time was totally exhausted. I had to hassle with my luggage, retrieving items of underwear and trying to get the suitcase shut again. I got out into the fresh night air and stood almost in tears. What on earth was I going to do? The bus had already gone ages ago and, besides, I had no money for a taxi or my train fare. Suddenly, out of the blue, appeared a gentleman who was in a hurry. As he dashed past I hailed him and said, 'If I give you my home address and sign a piece of paper, would you lend me some money?'
He handed me a lump sum and said, 'Keep it.'
'No,' I shouted. 'Please give me your address so I can return it,' but he had disappeared into the night. It was such a lovely gesture and I have never forgotten his generosity to a stranded lady in the middle of London late at night. I shall always be grateful to that gentleman—whoever he was!
I had enough money for a taxi, so jumped into one and got to Victoria just in time to catch the last train.

Chapter 11

Mother had rented a flat in a place called Chatsworth Gardens in Eastbourne and I was to start a year's secretarial training at the College of Further Education. Meanwhile, mother had gone back to part-time nursing. Nothing much happened during that time and it meant really getting on with the course. We had a super teacher and she was very good at her job. I must admit it was enjoyable and, on completion, I obtained a diploma with credit. I was exceptionally lucky to find a job almost immediately and went to work for the RAF at Watling. I was employed as a secretary along with another girl and a WRAF. They were both pleasant girls and we had a cramped office all together.

During the period of training and working, I joined the local Scottish dancing club. It was a way of getting to know a few people and away from the atmosphere with mother. The general idea was that, after dancing, we would take it in turns to invite people back home for a hot drink. Having warned mother that it was my turn, I told her that if she heard noises not to worry. I was by this time twenty years of age and expected mother to give me a little independence and privacy. A group of about eight came back with me on an extremely cold winter's night for hot chocolate. To my utter amazement, there was mother, sitting bolt upright in her armchair. She stretched her hand out to each individual so that they could shake it, as if she were royalty. She then took over the whole conversation and left everyone saying 'yes' or 'no' for the rest of the

evening because they couldn't get a word in edgeways.
By this time, I had met a few people and would get invited out occasionally. Any gentleman who came back to the home was immediately bombarded with twenty questions and it really was very embarrassing. The moment they had gone, she would criticise them from every angle and eventually they wouldn't invite me out again. The other thing which she did would be to stand at my bedroom door and say, 'Oh! Are you going out?'
'Yes,' I would reply.
'So, you are leaving me here alone?'
It was a continual mental strain to make me feel guilty.
Life got very difficult in every way. I used to go to work at 6.30 a.m., walking, in all weathers, to the station—it was a good mile and a half—returning home again in the dark. We had no washing machine, so weekends were mostly taken up in going down to the launderette, shopping and domestic chores.
My twenty-first birthday arrived and, on that morning, mother appeared at my bedroom door and just said, 'Happy Birthday. You'd better have this now you are twenty-one.'
She handed me a letter with the address and signature cut off. It was the saddest, most moving letter I have ever read. It hit my deepest inner feelings. The letter had been handed over when I had been adopted. My natural mother had written explaining that she was unable to keep me. Her letter was one of intense pain as she wrote '............ and this baby which is mine and now has to be yours.' She finished the letter by saying she hoped, above all else, that

I would be brought up a good Christian, and be gentle, kind and loving. I sat staring at the piece of paper and felt completely torn to pieces. There was no one to talk to. Shortly after my birthday, mother and I had an extremely bad row over something. She told me to pack and leave. I had nowhere to go. I was still working for the RAF. A Spanish couple that I had met several times on the bus came to my rescue and I moved in with them. They were so kind and had me for two months. Mother turned up one day completely unannounced and said, 'You are coming back with me.'

I couldn't impose anymore on the hospitality and friendship of this couple, so I moved back to the flat with mother. I could no longer trust her and wasn't prepared to be left with no roof over my head again. Something had to be done about it, so I took action.

An assistant matron was required at a boy's prep school in Seaford, so I applied for the job. It was quite ironic that the headmaster and his wife, Mr. and Mrs. Cartwright, had known my parents ever since I was a little girl. I went to see them and they were only too delighted to have me. I went back and told my mother that I would shortly be leaving to take up a living-in job. She was simply furious and couldn't get rid of me quick enough.

The year I spent from 1963 to 1964 at Tyttenhanger Lodge was, without a doubt, the happiest time of my life and if the school hadn't closed down I do sincerely believe I would never have left. The prep school had eighty boys and was very homely, with a wonderful family atmosphere. The Cartwrights, having had no children of their own, were dedicated to all the boys and Valerie, as Matron, was a lovely person to work with. It was a happy time, sadly to be short-lived, and also a time to see my father again on a regular basis. I had two afternoons off a week and father would come and fetch me. We would go out to tea and dinner, taking a drive out in the car to the countryside.

By this time, father was out of his 'digs' and had bought a house in Rottingdean. He had continued during all this time to keep up his meetings and charity work. While in digs, father had been attending the Church of England Men's Society. It was at one of these meetings that he met a gentleman who was to give him a lot of support, help and advice and become a loyal friend right up to father's death. At the time of their meeting, Kenneth lived with his mother.

I met him on several occasions at father's house and, in later years when Kenneth married, met his wife.

In father's years at the nursing home, Kenneth would always keep in contact by phone or visits. It was a comfort to know that father had someone, while I was so far away. I shall always be extremely grateful to Kenneth for his true sincerity to my father.

Mother left Eastbourne and came back to a house she had bought in Seaford some years previously. She had it turned into two flats, renting one of them out. That Christmas, mother and I went to Austria for a holiday. We had no sooner arrived and unpacked, when that same evening, there was an urgent phone call from mother's brother. Granny had died. The funeral was in the morning. I threw our clothes back in a suitcase, while mother made a phone call to the airport. We arrived at 3.00 a.m. at my uncle's house in Staines, and lay half-dressed under an eiderdown waiting for the dawn to come up. The hearse arrived and behind it a car for the family. As I got into the car to sit by mother, uncle Henry said, 'Irene, she's not one of the family. She'll have to get out and go in the car behind.' But mother was having none of that. When we got to the church, uncle Henry wanted me out of the family pew, but mother wasn't having any of that either. To be quite honest, neither mother nor uncle Henry had shed a tear. They were void of any emotion or feeling for their mother's death.

We went to the cemetery and I put some earth on my beloved granny's coffin. I stood with uncontrollable tears pouring down my cheeks, because I had really and truly loved her very much. Father too was fighting back his tears. He stood swaying backwards and forwards in the cold bitter wind, with his hands clasped behind his back. He also had been very fond of her. We all went back to the house and, while people were talking and drinking, uncle Henry called me into the kitchen.

He showed me two rings and said, 'I know my mother would have wanted you to have one of these rings.' I chose an octagonal Victorian ring with a cluster of pearls and diamonds.

Later, father drove me home, while mother stayed another night at her brother's house to sort things out. Before I knew what had happened, Christmas had gone and I was back for the Easter term. Granny had left some money to

me in her Will, and father added to this so that I could buy my first car.
I chose a pale blue Mini and was absolutely thrilled with it. I was now able to get around and be more independent. I took up Scottish dancing again on my Thursday evenings off and was mobile to get over to father's house. During the holidays I used to take living-in jobs with a family that needed extra help with their children. I always made sure that they had horses, so that we could ride in the afternoons.
One morning during term-time, I was called downstairs and told that there was a gentleman who wanted to see me. Imagine my utter surprise when I got to the front door to find uncle Henry on the doorstep. He had in his arms a cardboard box of things which had belonged to granny and thought that I might like them. Having enquired as to my well-being, he then departed. Going through the box, I discovered that most of the things were either broken, needed expensive repairing, or were best thrown out. However, despite large holes in the silver design of a hairbrush, mirror and two crystal pots with silver tops, I decided to keep these. They had always been on granny's dressing table. There were also two brass bowls which had sat on her sitting-room mantelpiece. They had been polished so much that the engraved design work had partly disappeared.
The letter that reached me during the summer holidays was a shock. Mr. Cartwright was extremely unwell and, as nobody wanted to take on the school, it would sadly be closing at the end of the year. Our Christmas term was a

very sad one and everyone was unsettled, wondering what they were going to do next. It must have been quite devastating for the Cartwrights who had been at Tyttenhanger Lodge for many years. After our farewells, I went back home to spend Christmas with mother.

I decided it was time to go and meet Larry and his family in Ireland. He was the son of one of mother's step-sisters and with whom I had never had any contact. Larry and his wife had found a doctor's family who required someone to help out with four children and ride in the afternoons. So it was all arranged that after Christmas I would go over to join this family. Having only been home a few days, recovering from the term's work, mother walked into my bedroom one morning with a telegram. Although quite clearly addressed to me, she had had the audacity to open and read it. The telegram said: 'COMING TO ENGLAND ON FLIGHT IB 253 ARRIVING HEATHROW 28TH DECEMBER AT 2.30 P.M. PLEASE MEET ME. MARCOS.'

I had been back three years and we had written to each other, but life had been busy with work. Looking carefully again at the telegram, I suddenly realised that the date of arrival was the next day. I went to Heathrow to meet Marcos and we travelled back home for a late tea. One evening we drove out to the countryside to a lovely village pub. It was bitterly cold with snow falling thick and fast. When we got back to my car we had difficulty seeing where we were going. I went into a large mound of snow by the road and got stuck. The engine revved and the wheels spun round and round. Eventually, after what

seemed an eternity, we managed to get the car moving again.
On New Year's Eve, we went to a dinner-dance at Alfriston. It was here, after dinner, that Marcos asked me to marry him. He handed me a box and inside was a gold and pearl bracelet. My reply was, 'I'll have to think about it.'
I did think about it and paced up and down at home for two nights, making endless hot drinks! It was all so sudden and unexpected. I didn't know if I could cope with going to live abroad for the rest of my life. One thing I did know however was that I was deeply in love with Marcos. The evening before his departure, we became officially engaged. Mother was not impressed. I had to do some frantic packing because I was off to Ireland, spending the night at father's house. Then we were driving up to Fishguard and he was seeing me off on the ferry. I had no difficulty in finding the doctor's house and Larry lived only a few miles away.
On my first day off, I went over to meet Larry's family. They all made me feel so welcome. At that time his wife Ann had three children and seemed to spend her time shovelling food into mouths. I felt an instant warmth and lovely friendly atmosphere and spent nearly all my free days with them. Due to my engagement, I was to stay with the doctor's family for three months until the end of March, which gave them time to find a replacement. It was bitterly cold and, apart from the usual Irish rain, we did get heavy snow as well. The children were spoilt, so therefore disobedient and quite a handful, although I must

say, by the end of three months their behaviour was better. Their parents usually went out in the evenings, so all in all, it did get rather boring and my only comfort was when I could escape to Larry and Ann.

The day for departure came and I found myself back on the ferry. Father, always so reliable, was there looking anxiously for me and we stopped on the way back for a nice lunch. Driving along a main road, a cat suddenly leapt out in front of the car. Had I slammed on the brakes, without a doubt, my father would have been thrown against, or through, the windscreen. Split-second thinking—father or the cat? It hit the front of the car with an almighty thud and the sound made me feel physically sick. I stopped the car and went back to make sure the cat was dead. My only consolation was that it had been killed instantly. There was nothing more I could do with not a house in sight. It upset me, more than I could have imagined, and I spent several nights worrying about it, reliving the thud, but there had been no alternative.

Back at home, mother and I went up to London to buy my wedding dress, clothes and bed linen. By this time, mother had had time to come to terms with my forthcoming marriage. Although thoroughly against it, she did decide on this occasion that she would only get one opportunity to enjoy shopping for my wedding dress. On arriving at Victoria Station, we always followed the same procedure and that was to dive into the Grosvenor Hotel to go to the loo. After an extremely hectic morning, we had lunch at Claridges as a special treat. Then we roamed about London, in and out of taxis and shops, as if there were no tomorrows. It had been decided that I would go out in two weeks' time and stay with some friends of Marcos at their country house. We would then decide on the wedding date and get everything planned, invitations out, etc. etc. The wedding was to be in Jerez, because my future in-laws refused to travel on a plane and didn't speak a word of English. Mother went into hysterics over the whole thing, but there really wasn't much option. I embarked on an exhaustive packing procedure and eventually banged the last nail into the last tea-chest. Suitcases were at bursting point, as I bounced up and down on top of them before setting out on a round of farewells. Before leaving, I managed to get a few days with father. We would take drives out to the countryside and stop somewhere to have a cream tea.

The days flew by and soon I was being met by Marcos in Gibraltar. We drove back through the dusty track that I had travelled on for the first time five years previously. We stopped at a country inn and sat in the open-air courtyard, surrounded by plants and flowers. A wonderful Spanish salad with olives, tuna fish, hard-boiled eggs, peppers and large ripe tomatoes appeared on the table. After lunch we continued on our way to Marcos's friends and I was made very welcome. Marcos lived with his parents and his brother Alberto in a country house about two miles out of Jerez. There was a large garden with acres of fruit trees and vegetables. A small bungalow was being built a few yards from the main house for us to live in. Marcos and I went to a local antique dealer to choose some furniture and, while in the shop, he saw a pair of twin beds. They were rather beautiful with large oval headboards in mahogany, inlaid with lighter wood. He insisted on having them and I, at the time, thought that because of the intense heat in the summer months, this was the reason for not wanting a double bed.

Although twenty-two years old, I was extremely naive. Convent school had meant being imprisoned within high brick walls, where the real world was non-existent. For years I had had it drummed into me that if I wasn't a good Catholic and committed a mortal sin, I would be condemned to hell for all eternity! Mother was a strict Roman Catholic and anything that should have been discussed in the way of sex education was taboo. She had brought me up with the rigour of Victorian times. It was my total innocence that never made me think that there was anything unusual in him wanting twin beds.

Marcos worked at his father's factory with his brother. It was a family business, having been handed down from his grandfather. The factory made all the plastic tops and corks for the sherry industry. I started to notice quite irrational behaviour from Marcos, but put it down to work, the soaring heat and nerves before our wedding day. On returning from a picnic on the beach, he would argue about something quite insignificant and become really unkind, dropping me off at his friend's house and then not seeing me for two days.

In my innocence, I suppose I thought that the way Marcos treated me was part of Spanish life. Evenings, he would come and fetch me from the house and then drop me off early. His moodiness and bad tempers were upsetting,

especially when he just left me waiting for him and never turned up for an evening. I returned home at the end of July to see my parents and fetch my wedding dress. Marcos and I were to be married on 20th August. The bungalow had been completed, so I moved in.
Mother had arranged to arrive two days before the wedding. I booked her into The Swans Hotel. After she had unpacked and changed, we took her back to the bungalow. There was a searing heat-wave, so we sat outside by the swimming pool. We chatted away, while we had a quiet drink waiting for Marcos's parents to join us. It had been arranged that we would drive mother out to a famous seaside restaurant in San Lucar, to have a fish dinner. I took mother to show her our wedding presents, which were all on the dining-room table. She sniffed after a minute and waved a hand over our presents, remarking 'If you had been married in England, you would have got far better presents.'
I was very upset because, in actual fact, people had been extremely generous and we had been given some really lovely things. I tried to take no notice and while she seated herself outside on the terrace, I went to put some lipstick on and comb my hair. The next thing I knew was mother hysterically saying, 'Get me a taxi. I'm going back to the hotel.'
'What on earth has happened?' I asked Marcos. He just shrugged his shoulders.
'He's been rude to me,' said mother, her voice going up into a crescendo.
'But what has happened?' I repeated.

'Are you calling me a taxi or shall I walk?' cried mother. By this time Marcos's parents were standing outside, wondering what all the commotion was about. I went inside their house to phone and was about to ring for a taxi when Marcos slammed the receiver down.
'If your mother wants to leave, she can walk.'
'She can't walk back. It's two miles to the hotel,' I replied. I went out to the garden but mother had disappeared. By this time, my future in-laws and Marcos were all trying to compete in conversation and nobody was listening to anyone. I sat in a chair thinking it was all a bad nightmare. Surely this couldn't happen just before my wedding day. Eventually, when everyone had calmed down, Marcos told me that I could take his van to find my mother. As I approached her, I slowed down and opened the window.
'Mother, do get in,' I said.
'No,' she replied, marching along as if she had a herd of elephants behind her. 'Is he with you, because if he is I'm not getting into that vehicle,' she said, still marching along.
'No, Marcos isn't with me. Now do get in and we can talk about it.'
Mother stopped and got in and said, 'I want to go to the hotel.'
When we got to the hotel lobby and I had asked for her room key I went upstairs with her. She stopped at her bedroom door and I said, 'Mother, let's talk, please.'
She looked at me and said, 'Goodbye Clare. I shall be leaving tomorrow morning and I shall not be at your wedding.'
With that, she shut her bedroom door leaving me in the

corridor.
Next morning I went to see mother and asked the receptionist, 'Is my mother upstairs in her room?'
'Oh no,' he replied. 'She has left.'
I was busy the rest of the day because father was arriving late afternoon with his cousin, Alan. Neither of them had met Marcos, so that evening we all went out to dinner. I told father all about the saga with mother and we came to the conclusion that it was best to give the matter no more thought.
Father and I had decided that because of the heat he would wear his morning dress for the church and then Marcos's brother would drive him back to the hotel to change into a light suit. Marcos's father had made arrangements for the seating in the church. As is customary in Spain, the bride's mother has a special pew in the front of the church as a mark of respect. Of course, when I announced that mother had left the hotel, the pew was removed.
On 20th August 1965, I got up at 6.00 a.m. to have a leisurely bath. The hairdresser arrived to comb my waist-length hair and make the most attractive bun, interweaved with individual white violets. My dress was satin damask with shoes to match.
The wedding ceremony was to be at 10.00 a.m. and just before 9.00 a.m. Marcos's father appeared to tell me, 'Your mother has just rung to say she is coming to the wedding.'
Father arrived shortly after looking absolutely the part, beaming with pride and joy on seeing me in my wedding dress. By this time I considered that nothing else could

possibly go wrong to mar the day—but how wrong I was. Father and I alighted from the official car and Marcos was at the church door with his parents and brother. Guests awaited the bride sitting in their pews and we started to walk up the aisle towards the alter. My full attention was on father who was leaning heavily on my arm, so there wasn't time to see where mother or Alan had been placed. After Mass, Marcos and I went to sign the register and walked out of the adjoining chapel to descend the alter steps. As we were proceeding down the aisle, mother suddenly cried hysterically and before we had got out of the church had managed to get several pews of people in a turmoil. She apparently had also made a fuss on arriving at the church to find her pew had disappeared. Mother didn't want to sit in the same pew as Alan, because she didn't like him, and didn't want anything to do with father's relatives at all. However, Marcos's father, not speaking a word of English, had seated her next to Alan and this had annoyed her no end.
While the guests got themselves to The Swans Hotel, Marcos and I had gone back to his parents' country house to have photos taken in the garden. Afterwards, we joined our guests. As we walked in, a thoughtful waiter handed me an ice-cold lager which I gulped down while I held a large fan in the other hand. The heat was tremendous and I was melting in my wedding dress. Mother refused to speak to me and I tried to introduce her to friends. She wanted nothing to do with me and kept well away. Father bravely fought the heat and spent most of his time with me, being introduced to people. Although unable to speak

a single word of Spanish, he never failed to leave an outstanding impression on all that met him. Ten years after my marriage, the Jerezanos would remember him and always say, 'Clare, how's your father?'

After opening telegrams, listening to speeches, drinking champagne, cutting the cake and sampling it, we said our goodbyes. We went back to the bungalow to change and fetch our luggage for we were catching the afternoon flight to Majorca for our honeymoon. My parents and Alan were waiting outside as we put our suitcases into the van. Father gave me an enormous hug and I knew how much he was going to miss me. Alan said goodbye with a kiss, one on each cheek—Spanish custom—and then I turned to mother and went to put my arms around her. She flung her arms out in front of her and said firmly, 'Now you are married I never want to see you again, and as for going away in a van, at least you could have had a car!'

With that, she turned around and moved away, totally ignoring me. I was very hurt and didn't deserve this kind of treatment for I had always been very loyal to my parents and had never given them undue upsets of any kind.

Chapter 12

It almost seemed that from the moment we were married I was destined for many years of total hell. No sooner had we boarded the plane than Marcos shattered our honeymoon.

'Of course, you do realise that we are not taking a honeymoon, but going to Mallorca to negotiate business for the factory,' he declared.

The hotel was extremely basic and had no character to it at all. We arrived just as the dining room was closing, but after the staff realised that we had just got married, we were allowed to order dinner. The bedroom had two beds and was fairly sparse, but there was a bottle of champagne with the compliments of the proprietor. That night Marcos was quite gentle with me for I was a virgin. In the morning I was in quite a lot of pain and found walking difficult. I spent the day relaxing by the hotel swimming pool. Meanwhile, Marcos went to make numerous business calls which took priority over my company. Our second night of marriage will never be forgotten. Marcos wanted to have his satisfaction, but I was still very sore and could not relax. He turned really nasty and got into his bed. I lay awake, wondering whether this was a husband or a beast. I loved him so dearly and longed for him to just hold me in his arms. I whispered this to him and was told to shut up. I was so hurt and had all the doubts in the world about him. How could my husband behave like this if he truly loved me? I cried bitter tears and lay awake, frightened and alone. Marcos ignored my sobbing and got

himself off to sleep and was soon snoring.
In the morning I was told by Marcos to hurry up and get myself ready to meet a family downstairs. I was to spend the day with the wife and her three children while Marcos went to talk business with her husband. It went on the rest of the week and, to my disbelief, we even went out with them in the evening. Only one morning did we manage to go and see the Monastery, where the women were sitting outside in traditional Mallorcan dresses. There was a lovely boat which was anchored out at sea and at night it was lit up by what seemed to be hundreds of lights. People were dining on board and it looked so romantic. But Marcos wasn't interested; in fact, we never saw Mallorca at all.
A week later we were back at the bungalow and Marcos at the office factory. My in-laws had decided that we would eat lunch with them on a daily basis, so that I had time to settle down to this new way of life and learn the Spanish cuisine. My father-in-law had also decided that he was keeping a key to our bungalow. Had he respected our privacy, it would have been fine. It had taken me two or three weeks to get things shipshape and I had just finished getting the furniture into the right places and the wardrobes sorted out. One Saturday, we went out somewhere and on arriving back I stood in amazement. My in-laws had been into the bungalow and rummaged through wardrobes and cupboards. They had had the audacity and nerve to move every single piece of furniture in the sitting room to a completely different area. There was little I could do except put everything back to its original place. Marcos's father owned the land, the

bungalow and factory. We were dependent on his father for everything.
Marcos had a motorbike and on rare occasions his parents would lend us their car or we would be able to take the van, which was mostly used for the factory business. I found it desperately lonely and looked forward to seeing Marcos, but father and son were always at logger-heads with each other. Meals were a source of continual upheaval with very few peaceful moments. Seldom did Marcos come back with me to the bungalow to have coffee after lunch. By the time he had eaten, he was heading out of his parents' house straight onto his motorbike, roaring off at full throttle due to yet another argument with his father. Never did he think of my anguish, nor the fact that I spent all day alone. I had no way of escaping, even to do some shopping. We were a good two miles from the town centre. Once a week I used to have to go shopping with my mother-in-law to the market.
My father-in-law and both his sons had nasty tempers and could get extremely violent. On one such occasion, I happened to be in my in-laws' house while Marcos and his father were having a heated debate. Marcos brought his fist down on the glass top of the dining room table. His father picked up something and threw it at the glass door, which smashed into great splinters. I was terrified, having never seen such behaviour and thought about my father who had always been the perfect gentleman. It upset me so much I went back to our bungalow shaking. To think that we had been married only a month.

There was no escape because I had been into Jerez to see the doctor, who confirmed that I was expecting a baby. I waited patiently until Marcos came back from work and told him we were going to be parents. We went to give the wonderful news to Marcos's mother and father and thought they would be thrilled. I remember walking into the sitting room and announcing the pregnancy. There was complete silence and I wondered if they had heard me. The normal custom would have been to have given me a kiss and tell me they were delighted. Instead my father-in-law said nothing and my mother-in-law remarked dryly, 'It's much too soon to be expecting.' I knew then that all that mattered was to make my marriage work and perhaps things would settle down when Marcos was a father himself. I had little comfort from him because he seldom wanted to touch me and often didn't even bother to say goodnight. He would get into his bed and turn the light out. I had been through so much misery with my parents' failed marriage that I was determined that I would do everything possible for the sake of the baby I was carrying. Despite all that had happened, I was truly in love with Marcos and, what is more, he knew it. I vowed there and then that no matter how unkind or cruel he was going to be, I would put up with it all. For the first time in my life, I was going to have a human being of my own flesh and blood.

A few weeks later, Marcos announced that he was going on a business trip for a month. It would have been a chance for me to see other parts of Spain, but he made it very clear that I wasn't going with him. What is more, he refused to tell me where he was staying either and, during that month, he never called me. He would ring and speak to his secretary or his brother and get them to ring my mother-in-law. She in turn would let me know he was alright. The day he was due back was a Saturday and I had prepared a special dinner to welcome him home. Marcos turned up at 1 a.m. He made the excuse that he was exhausted from work and travel. On looking at him I knew he had been living it up at night and had clearly been drinking and smoking far too much.

Next morning, Marcos said that he was going to go to the football match that afternoon and asked me if I would like to go. Anything, I decided, would be better than sitting alone in the bungalow another day. Apart from everything else, I wanted to be with my husband. We climbed a flight of stairs and seated ourselves halfway up on the concrete seating. We had a good view of the pitch and soon the match had begun. A few minutes after play commenced Marcos said his eyes couldn't focus on the ball. I said, 'You are very tired, so why not put on your sunglasses and close your eyes and rest them.' He did this and five minutes later he was shouting, 'I can't see, I can't see. I've gone blind.'

'It's alright,' I said taking his arm. 'I'll lead you out.'

At this point as I held on to him, two gentlemen who had heard Marcos shout came to my rescue. 'Señora, please let us help.' They took an arm each and guided him down to the steps. As they all reached the last step, Marcos's eyes went white. He foamed at the mouth and his whole body went rigid. It was exactly the same as an epileptic fit. I was screaming at the top of my voice, 'Doctor, doctor, doctor!' Marcos was being carried towards the Red Cross hut and two doctors who were at the football match were running towards us. They all went into the hut and the door was locked, leaving me outside. I thumped on the door and said, 'Open the door. I'm his wife.' It was total chaos and I was almost crushed against the door because a mass of people were all trying to see what had happened. Suddenly a gentleman we knew was pushing past everyone and told them to let us in. Marcos was unconscious, so an injection had been administered and he was being carried on a stretcher to an ambulance. At this point, someone in the football stadium had told Marcos's father that his son had been taken ill. We followed the ambulance back to the bungalow. Marcos remained unconscious for three quarters of an hour. The doctor told me Marcos would be alright and to give him nothing else but fresh orange juice during the night. When he regained consciousness, I was seated by his bed holding his hand.

He spent the rest of the night drifting in and out of sleep. His parents walked off back into their house, locked their door and went to bed. I could not believe that they weren't worried about their son. I had no access to a phone and not only was I under shock, but pregnant. I stayed up all night and have never squeezed so many oranges in my life.

Next morning, a chauffeur-driven Mercedes appeared in the driveway. A lady was walking towards our bungalow. My mother-in-law came out to greet her but got called away to the phone so I walked out to welcome her. After

explaining to her what had happened to Marcos, she took my arm in hers and said, 'Of course, it doesn't surprise me, because you know that there are several cases of mental instability in the family.'
I had no idea what this lady was talking about and it took all my physical and mental control not to breakdown. As I stood in our bedroom amidst the background chatter, I uttered the appropriate 'yes' and 'no' as required. My mind was racing and my thoughts went to my unborn baby, and I felt quite weak. At this point, my mother-in-law joined us and stated to us all that the cause of the unconsciousness had been due to a digestive disorder, nothing more! I insisted that Marcos should have an electroencephalograph and my mother-in-law immediately said that that wouldn't be necessary.
'All he needs is to see a doctor about his stomach,' she said very quickly. Later when Marcos was alone with me, I convinced him to have an electroencephalograph. Possibly due to feeling weak, he agreed. We went to see the doctor and the EEG showed an irritation on the left side of the temple. Marcos was told that he radically had to stop all alcohol and stop smoking. After two or three weeks, Marcos was back drinking and smoking, ignoring the doctor's orders. He went back to his usual outbursts of temper and irrational behaviour.
By now, I was getting quite fat and had the most embarrassing cramp which would come on with no warning. It would leave me gripping on to whatever was near me, or leaning against a wall, unable to walk with acute pain shooting up and down my legs. I just had to

wait until it subsided before I could put my feet into motion again. As the pregnancy advanced I could feel the baby kicking and it was so lively that my tummy would suddenly go sideways. Apart from these minor details and my continual hunger for food, everything was going along fine. Surprising really, because I used to get down on my hands and knees to clean the stone floors. There were no such luxuries as floor mops in those days. Monday morning was laundry day and I dreaded it. I had a washing machine that had to be filled with buckets of water and it would then churn the clothes about. The machine would only take one single sheet at a time and then it had to be manually wrung out and put in a bath full of water. Bending up and down rinsing several times was a back-breaking performance.

Father wrote cheery letters, almost on a daily basis and I missed him more than words can describe. He was overjoyed at the idea of becoming a grandfather. I had written a long letter to my mother, but there was no news from her at all. Marcos had arranged for me to see a gynaecologist who was a friend of his, so I thought I was in good hands. Little did I know what was in store for me. I'd been examined and everything seemed quite normal. The baby was due on 12th May. That date came and went, and so did the whole month of May. Five weeks went by and the gynaecologist did nothing!

On Sunday 19th June, Marcos and I went to have a drink at The Swans Hotel. While there, I felt unwell and asked to be driven home. The waters hadn't broken but I was in pain, so off we went to the Red Cross Clinic. By this time, it must have been 1.30 p.m., I lay on the bed in one of the rooms while Marcos sat on the other bed and later my mother-in-law joined us. The pain just got worse and worse without abating. It was quite indescribable. I gritted my teeth for I had been on the bed now for three hours and wanted to scream. The gynaecologist had decided not to give me a pain-killer despite my pleading. The midwife was nowhere to be found and Alberto had to drive fifteen miles to find her amidst a packed beach. Meanwhile, the pain was taking over my whole body. I gripped the sides of the iron bed frame with my hands until I almost cut the skin. The pain was so excruciating that, had someone given me the option of dying, I'd have gladly taken it. No one was doing anything to help me, the problem being that there was no dilatation taking place at all and baby wanted to be born.

At around 7.00 p.m. I was taken up to the operating theatre. Marcos did hold my hand and I gripped it thankfully. Although weak with pain, I tried to think about the baby that had to be delivered and tried to push but I wasn't dilating, and the gynaecologist didn't know how to do a Caesarean. Due to being summer time and a Sunday, most of the doctors were miles away on the beach. It was obvious that drastic measures had to be taken. I was fully conscious and heard the gynaecologist say to Marcos, 'Who do I save, mother or baby?' There was no hesitation in my husband's reply. 'Baby,' he said. That answer will stay with me always—we had only been married just over ten months.

There was severe cutting and forceps were used but to no

avail. The baby had discharged excretia inside me, so there was no time to lose. The gynaecologist took another pair of larger forceps and managed to pull the baby out at 8.00 p.m., leaving me with a ruptured rectum. I could hear the midwife patting my baby's back. No one in the operating theatre spoke, there was a deathly silence. I didn't dare ask whether it was a girl or boy because I knew that my baby hadn't screamed. The seconds seemed to be running out. Suddenly, there was an almighty scream. My baby filled her lungs with air and went on screaming and screaming. She was brought to me by the midwife as I lay on the operating table and then taken away for a bath. I shall always be truly grateful to God for giving my daughter her life. She tried for so long to be born that it was a miracle she survived. Meanwhile, I was stitched up in raging agony and eventually reunited with my baby daughter. Every mother thinks their baby is the loveliest of all. Paloma was born with a beautiful face and her features were perfection itself. But the forceps had left the back of her head longer than the average baby. Her skin was completely dehydrated due to my ten month and nine day pregnancy. I was totally exhausted, feeling very weak and wanted to try and sleep through the pain. But my room turned into a continual coming and going of nurses and doctors, due to their fear of me developing septicaemia. I was unable to get out of bed due to the stitches and incapable of feeding myself. Food had to be spooned in and drinks given from a cup with a spout. A nurse had to give me assistance to turn over while I gripped the iron headrail with one hand in sheer agony.

Thirty-six hours later on Tuesday morning the gynaecologist came to examine me. 'Stitches all have to come out again tomorrow morning,' he announced and, with that, departed. I lay there in disbelief and was simply terrified at the idea of another ordeal in cold blood. The nurses were all very kind at the clinic and when I remarked to one of them what the gynaecologist had said, she told me she was not surprised. 'Most women stitched up by that gynaecologist have to be taken back to the operating theatre!'

When Marcos arrived I implored him to hold my hand and stay with me next morning. There was no compassion at all and he replied, 'Oh, I've got business to see to, so I'll tell my mother to come.' Next morning he got up, gave me a kiss on the cheek and walked out of the room.

The nurses came to fetch me and it was exactly the same as being taken off for the torture chamber. No other words can describe the pain the gynaecologist and his assistant put me through. My mother-in-law arrived and was allowed into the operating theatre. She watched what they were starting to do to me and she was visibly shaken. Paloma had been left unattended and I started to worry. It was wrong for her to be alone and I asked my mother-in-law to go and sit with her.

The stitches had not been stitched tight enough, so all of them had to come out. They were pulled out while I was fully conscious and in complete agony. When the gynaecologist had finished, I had had a total of forty stitches in thirty-seven hours.

Chapter 13

Three days later I was told that I could go home. My mother-in-law and Marcos got me to my feet, which was an agonising procedure. I was far too weak with pain to do anything and the dress I had arrived in was put over my head. I couldn't walk but shuffled painfully, slowly, out of the room. We went down in the lift and the movement nearly made me sick. My mother-in-law was holding Paloma, but Marcos wasn't holding onto me at all. I walked three paces and crashed unconscious onto the stone floor in the hospital entrance. I remember so clearly, as I opened my eyes, thinking that I was lying back in the operating theatre and that they were going to stitch me up again. I was simply terrified and a nurse kept saying, 'It's alright, it's alright.' Some drops were put in my mouth and I recovered sufficiently to get to the standing position again with the aid of three people. A rubber ring had been provided as I was quite incapable of sitting on a car seat. The journey back was excruciating, with every bump magnified a thousand times over.

I was completely helpless and extremely frail. I wondered whether I would ever walk again. For three weeks I had to sit on a sun lounger, or lie on my bed. My mother-in-law and her maid would come in to assist and look after Paloma. My long hair hadn't really been combed since I went into labour, so I tried myself. It was just too exhausting and physically I was unable to cope. In the end, I asked Marcos if he wanted to brush my hair and because it was knotted he started to complain that he hadn't got time. I had delivered this beautiful daughter of ours and all Marcos cared about was himself. He would grumble at night because Paloma would cry when she was hungry. I was unable to get out of bed and Marcos would have to pick her up from her cot so that I could feed her. His selfishness was soul destroying. One afternoon I made a great effort to try and brush my hair. Imagine my horror when it fell out in handfuls, filling a waste paper basket. Taking the advice of my doctor, I had no option but to have my hair cut off to strengthen the roots, or go completely bald.

After Paloma's bath I would cover her in baby oil and creams, because her skin was very dehydrated. It was so hot that she was dressed in a light top and nappy and put in her Moses basket, with a mosquito net, underneath a large tree by the swimming pool. She would spend many happy hours blissfully asleep, or try to put her feet in her mouth making gurgling noises. She was a good baby and gave me no trouble, but it was at the price of being unpopular with my in-laws and visitors. No one seemed capable of just admiring a baby, while it was sound asleep or awake. The immediate reaction was to pick baby up and jiggle it about, bounce it up and down, or the irritating habit of moving the pram backwards and forwards. I was having none of it. Firstly, I wasn't strong enough to cope with holding a baby all day. Secondly, once a baby gets used to these habits, it will cry every time it's awake, in order to be picked up.

When Paloma was five months old, I found myself pregnant again and it came as rather a shock because it

was totally unexpected. When confirmed by the doctor, I can truthfully say that I spent the whole pregnancy simply petrified at the thought of another birth. This time I insisted on personally finding the best gynaecologist in town and he turned out to be simply marvellous.
A long, extremely hot and exhausting summer followed. To give you an idea, it was like wearing a fur wrap around my tummy with soaring heat in the nineties. I got a craving for ice-cream, which normally I would never bother with very much. To be honest, there is nothing worse than being pregnant during the summer months in a hot climate. The baby was due in the first week of October. Father, on hearing the news, wrote to mother telling her that I had been extremely ill having Paloma and that she should have been there to help me. He added that she ought to come for the second birth in case there were any difficulties. Meanwhile, as I grew fatter, I found looking after Paloma and keeping up with washing nappies in a primitive washing machine and rinsing in the bath more and more difficult. I was on my swollen feet all day and it was very taxing in the heat.
Around the month of August, we employed a young girl as a nanny and Anna turned out to be a godsend. I grew very fond of her and she had infinite patience. She loved playing and amusing children. She was also company and someone for me to talk to. Anna soon got into my routine with Paloma. I felt perfectly happy about leaving her with Paloma, when the time came for me to go to the clinic. The Moses basket on wheels was put in a corner of the sitting room and a doll placed in it. I explained to Paloma

that this was going to be for the arrival of a real baby, but at the moment it was growing in mama's tummy.
One Sunday afternoon in September, Paloma was lying in her cot and I was bending over playing 'peep bo'. There was no warning at all as she grabbed one of my screw-on pearl earrings and swallowed it. She started to choke because it had got stuck in her windpipe. I thumped her back but to no avail while Anna rushed to help. Paloma was fighting for breath and we were completely alone in the country. Everybody was out and we had no phone or car. Not that anyone could have done anything in the circumstances anyway. I thank the Lord that on what must have been her last breath, the earring dislodged itself down into her stomach. Ten minutes later Marcos arrived and bundled us all into the car driving at eighty miles an hour to the surgery. By the time we got there, Marcos was in a lather and Anna was carrying Paloma and looking very worried. I was having visions of the earring obstructing the intestine and doctors having to operate. Meanwhile, Paloma hadn't a care in the world and was, by this time, giggling and clapping her hands as we waited in the surgery. She was thoroughly enjoying all the fuss and attention. The doctor took one look at Paloma and said to me, 'Don't worry, it should come through the other end, let me know if it doesn't.' Anna and I had to take rotas with strict observation on Paloma for the next twenty-four hours. It was quite hilarious when eventually my earring appeared again. Anna shouted, 'Señora, the earring, I've found it.' Celebrations and a big sigh of relief all round. Granny came over and said, 'Thank God for that.'

There had been no news from mother, except a short letter to acknowledge the fact that I was going to have another baby and that she hoped I wouldn't have any more! Father was extremely worried about my pregnancy and the fact that I might have another dangerous delivery, so he arranged to travel out with his cousin, Molli. They arrived at the beginning of October and we all waited and waited—but nothing happened. So on 21st October my gynaecologist had me into his surgery and told me he was delaying no longer and was going to induce the birth.

On Sunday 22nd October, we took father and Molli to see The Sound of Music at the cinema. Father sat blissfully unaware of what was happening to me. During the film I hissed at Marcos that the contraction pains had started and gripped his arm. I had got to the state of being so terrified I didn't want to be taken to the clinic. Eventually, Marcos said he thought we ought to leave the cinema. 'No,' I answered, 'I'm alright.' I managed to see the end of the film, which I enjoyed very much, and then, while I didn't have a pain, started walking very quickly out to the street. I managed to get to the car while another wave of pain hit me. We all got back to the bungalow, with father getting very worked up and puffing away on his pipe.

I decided that I was going to have an omelette and stood in the kitchen beating eggs; stopped to endure a pain and then carried on! In actual fact, as the pain kept coming and going, I found it nothing to fuss over. After the indescribable pain of over six hours with Paloma's birth, this was hardly noticeable. Lying on my bed, I ate my omelette and waited for the gynaecologist to come and see

me.
'My goodness, I've been watching the football match on TV,' he said to Marcos on arrival. 'You didn't tell me your wife was this advanced. Get her to the clinic at once.'
There was a mad scramble as the gynaecologist left in his car, followed by Marcos and myself. Bringing up the rear was Alberto with father and Molli. I was wheeled straight up to the operating theatre and the gynaecologist kept his promise to me. No one was to do anything until I had been put to sleep.
I awoke to find myself back in bed with a baby boy in the cot beside me. Carlos had been born at 11.00p.m. Both my children were born at night and on Sundays. Father and Molli crept in to kiss me and take a peep at baby Carlos before retiring. Marcos was sleeping in the bed next to mine.
Carlos cried and then cried some more, while Marcos just got angry. The more our son cried, the angrier Marcos got. I spent the night ringing the bell and different nurses came in, all with different explanations. They'd pick him up and say 'He's probably got wind,' or 'He's probably got a tummy ache,' or 'He probably needs another nappy,' and so it went on. But to my way of thinking, there was something terribly wrong with a baby that had cried almost continuously since birth. I told Marcos I wanted the family doctor to examine Carlos. He was more interested in himself and the fact that he had been unable to sleep.
'The baby's alright, nothing wrong with him. It's me that isn't having another night here,' and with that he left the

room. I grabbed the phone from the wall and spoke to the family doctor about my concern over Carlos. Motherly instinct told me that whatever was wrong with my baby, it was urgent.
Having examined Carlos, the doctor phoned a specialist and asked him to come straight to the clinic, as it was an emergency. Carlos had been unable to empty his bladder since his birth due to having no orifice. Had his condition been unattended a few more hours, he would have died. The specialist had to perform a minor cut, there and then, to enable the bladder to empty. He explained that he would circumcise Carlos in the early morning and would have to use general anaesthetic. Marcos returned at mid-day and brought with him his mother to see her grandson. I wanted our son baptised before the operation in case anything went wrong. Carlos would only be thirty-three hours old when they gave him a general anaesthetic. As his mother, I was under an obligation to see that he was baptised.
Marcos's and his parents' behaviour was really vicious, cruel and unkind. I couldn't believe what they were saying to me. 'Look here, nothing is going to happen to the baby. Do you, as a foreigner, think that here we just throw some water over it's head? We are going to have a big celebration with a party later on and have the baptism done properly. Our grandson is not going to be baptised now.' They reduced me to tears and marched out of the door.
'You know perfectly well that our son should be baptised before that operation. I want to see a priest, Marcos.' He

walked out of the room as if he hadn't heard me. I made a silent prayer and told God that there was nothing more I could do.

I awoke from a restless sleep at 4.00 p.m. that afternoon to a knock on the door. In walked a priest from one of the local churches. 'I hope I haven't disturbed you,' he said, 'but Marcos asked me to come and see you.' I told him about my urgency to have my son baptised and the opposition I was up against. He looked at his watch and said, 'Ring your in-laws and tell them the baptism is at 6.00 p.m. If they protest, then there is no need for them to come. Don't worry, Clare,' he said 'you are quite right. Your son must be baptised today.'

I rang my in-laws and they started to make excuses, so the priest made things rather clear over the phone and put the receiver down. Having spoken to Marcos, it was arranged that when his mother came to the clinic, she was to bring my father with her for the baptism. He was overjoyed at actually being able to attend his grandson's baptism and, at the required time, stood waiting by our bungalow door. Molli had taken a lift in the car with Marcos and was dropped off at the clinic in case I needed anything or to help with Carlos. Mother-in-law arrived next, plus one of her maids and placed the Christening garments on the bed. 'I'm not doing up a single button on that baby,' she announced.

Molli bent over my bed and said, 'Don't worry, Clare, I'll gladly dress him and I shall carry him to the church.' I was so grateful to her; she was so sweet and like a second mother. Marcos arrived with his father and the

commotion that evolved was unbelievable. His parents were simply furious. Suddenly Marcos turned round and said, 'Where's Clare's father?'
'Oh,' said my mother-in-law, 'I left him behind. There's no point in bringing him. He doesn't understand Spanish anyway!'
Marcos went off in the car to fetch him. Anna later told me how she had seen my father outside the bungalow, reduced to tears. He had stood there leaning on his walking stick as my mother-in-law walked past him and got into her car, driving off without him. It was despicable to upset my elderly father when he was such a kind, gentle person. After the baptism, family and relatives filled the room, standing about drinking and eating. My father-in-law seated himself next to Marcos on the spare bed. In a loud voice he addressed his son and said, 'Well, she's got him baptised, but God only knows if it's yours!'
I was truly thankful that neither my father nor Molli understood what foul language had been uttered by my father-in-law. There was a deadly hush in the room and no one could believe what they had heard. Had I been able to get on my feet, I would have had no hesitation in hitting him across the face.
When everyone had left, I cried uncontrollably. A nurse came in and she put her arms around me and said, 'Please don't upset yourself anymore, for the sake of your baby.' But it had been a gruelling day and tomorrow was to be yet another one. The specialist arrived at 8.00 a.m. and had the nurses scurrying in all directions. I gave my son a kiss and off he went to the operating theatre. I spent my time

praying for his safe return and an hour-and-a-half later, he was carried back and put in my arms. He was a smaller baby than Paloma had been at birth and didn't have her robust health. Due to everything my in-laws had put me through, the emotional upset had taken its toll and I was unable to breast-feed at all. Carlos had lost a lot of blood and needed plenty of nourishment and extra care.

Father and Molli stayed until I came out of the clinic and then they had to fly back to England. I had to take things easy and two days later the gynaecologist turned up to see how I was feeling. To his utter amazement and mine, my in-laws walked into the bungalow to say they were off for a holiday and had their suitcases in the car.

'You're joking of course,' said the gynaecologist. But they weren't and, with that, they drove off.

Anna offered to bath Carlos, but I preferred to look after him myself. The dressing would stick to the wound and the stitches would stick to the nappy. It had to be dressed and kept scrupulously clean, needing time and patience. Anna was a blessing and would take Paloma down through the fruit trees for walks, while I looked after Carlos.

Paloma was fascinated with her baby brother and would constantly peer into his Moses basket. For many years, she always called him Carlito—little Charles.

Chapter 14

We were very cramped for space now in the bungalow with two children and Anna, so it was decided by Marcos's father for us to move into an old building belonging to him in the main street near The Swans Hotel. The bottom flat had been rented for many years to a married couple and their grown-up children. We were to occupy upstairs. It was simply horrible and I hated the place, but I had no choice in the matter. My father-in-law had renovated some of the stone floors and left the others with extremely old tiles. It didn't matter how often you cleaned and mopped the floors, they always gave the impression they were dirty. A new bathroom suite had been installed but my father-in-law had decided to renovate only half the pipes in the primitive plumbing system. This meant that I could put on the immersion heater and get hot water from the bath tap, but not to the wash basin. I had to keep a bucket permanently in the bathroom to fill the wash basin. The kitchen sink had two taps, but no hot water either, so I just learnt to wash up with cold. I had one metal wall cupboard to put things in and two long wooden shelves in a recess. Here I would keep the saucepans and kitchen clutter. It was just like going back to medieval times.
The entrance to the building had heavy wooden doors, which were shut and bolted at night. An old wrought-iron gate had to be negotiated before leading up a long flight of white marble stairs. They were diabolical to keep clean, showing every mark, and had to be scrubbed by hand using a powder cleaner and scourer. There were twenty-

one steps to negotiate with one small child, a baby and a pram. These had to be carried down and up again every time I went out.

Shortly after moving into the flat, we nearly had a major tragedy. Paloma had got to the stage when she had to touch and pick up everything. I'd even had to put strips of Elastoplast over the electric sockets to stop her putting her fingers in the holes. I'd bathed Carlos, fed him and tucked him into his Moses basket in a corner in the sitting room. I went through to the kitchen and cut up some onions and put them in a pan to fry. It was difficult to smell anything else, but after a few minutes, Anna said to me, 'I can smell gas.' We rushed out of the kitchen to find that Paloma had opened the black clip on the top of the butane bottle for the gas heater. Carlos was profoundly asleep, so we opened every window in the flat and let the fresh air flood in.

*   *   *

Father's cousin, Doris, had never married and had lived with her mother in a large three-storey house in Eastbourne, but when her mother died, she decided to move into a smaller place. There were three grand pianos to be disposed of and, with no warning at all, she had one shipped off to me, being the only member of the family who played the piano. It resulted in being a complete nightmare, to say the very least. When I received the news by letter, the piano had almost arrived at the port of Cadiz. We had had no time to prepare for the arrival of a

baby grand and we had none of the essential documents to enable us to get it through Customs. What was even worse was the fact that we had no idea on what ship it was arriving or when. Marcos did get hold of an official at the port and managed to sort something out, and was told that we would be informed on its arrival. We had been having torrential rain for when it rains in Southern Spain it comes down like a monsoon. The roads turn into rivers and the drains are unable to cope with the flow of water. On such a morning as this, Marcos and I had to go to the Cadiz port to sign documents. The piano was standing on the quayside in a wooden crate awaiting Customs clearance. When we arrived we discovered, to our horror, that the piano had arrived ten days previously and the wooden container was surrounded by enormous puddles. The fuss and commotion that ensued was just unbelievable. We wanted to remove the container immediately but the Customs official decided that they wanted more documents—the Spaniards just love paper work and rubber stamps. You would have thought we were smuggling diamonds into the country. However, after quite a lot of messing about, endless discussions and time-wasting, Marcos paid what they required. We signed some more papers, and then there was a lot of rubber stamping which made them all happy.
Having got the piano installed, it was time for the arrival of my father who was to stay for three weeks. I never told him about the way Marcos was treating me and how lonely I was because I wouldn't have upset him for the world. Besides, I had married Marcos and for the sake of

my children I had to carry on, no matter how much I had to suffer. But father could see the way Marcos treated me and that I was a walking skeleton and very frail.
My mother-in-law, on her occasional visits to see the grandchildren, would say, 'I keep meeting people in Jerez and they keep asking me if there is anything wrong with you because you are so thin.' She would continue, 'I really don't like people asking me.' I would look at her and continue bathing Paloma. My mother-in-law knew perfectly well what was wrong and, of course, didn't want the people of Jerez to know the way her son was treating me. In fact, one afternoon, just as I had let the doctor in, my mother-in-law arrived to see her son who was ill in bed. I remember how the doctor looked at me and then looked at Marcos and said, 'I think it's your wife that needs the medical attention, she's far too thin.' My mother-in-law replied very quickly, 'Yes, people keep on remarking in Jerez, but I really cannot imagine what is wrong with her!' The doctor looked at Marcos and there was a slight pause before he said, 'I'm telling you to be careful with your wife, because in her state of health another pregnancy would kill her.'
Little fear of that, I thought to myself. Marcos wanted nothing to do with me. On the occasions that I had tried to cuddle down next to him in his bed, I would be told, 'Get out and get back into your bed. Go to sleep and leave me alone.'

Chapter 15

I always made sure that whatever happened, lunch was ready when Marcos came home. It took just a few minutes to heat the meal up or take it out of the oven when he arrived. As babies cannot be programmed, sometimes he would appear as I was at that precise moment changing a nappy. All hell would be let loose and he would start demanding his food. I would reply, 'It's all ready. It only needs heating up, but I'm just seeing to Carlos.' Then the shouting would begin. 'Don't you forget I come first, before anything else!'

Marcos had been jealous of the attention Paloma needed but with two babies, only fourteen months apart, he was unbearable. Everything was demanded, there was no respect or feeling for me at all. It was totally humiliating and I was treated far worse than a servant. There was never a 'please' or 'thankyou', or 'would you mind doing this or the other for me?' It was always 'Clean this, bring me that,' etc.

Carlos was on dried baby milk and both babies needed a variety of items from the chemist. Marcos had decided some time back to have an account at a chemist across the road. One morning he started to shout at me and complain about the bill. I told him to read the account and he would see that the list consisted of food and medicine for our children. Marcos announced that he was sending out a circular letter to all the chemist shops in Jerez, informing them that his wife was expressly forbidden to buy anything, unless a form had been signed by him giving

permission. He came back that evening with a pad of printed forms and locked it in his gun cupboard and took the key. I was always very careful never to run out of dried milk for Carlos or anything that the children required from the chemist. There was another even greater problem and that was that Marcos would give me very little money to manage on. He had money for cigarettes, his car, expensive clothes and going out drinking, but I had to do miracles every week to cope because he was so mean. I didn't have a bank account and had no way whatsoever of getting money in an emergency.
Countless times, either Marcos was in a bad mood or, worse still, a temper about something, and would literally refuse to sign a form or leave me any money in the house. I would be left at the door repeating yet again, 'Marcos, I have to feed Carlos and I haven't got enough tinned milk.' Time and time again, I would run out of milk and food for the babies because Marcos would decide not to sign a form. It was a complete nightmare and, while Carlos would be crying because he was hungry, I would have to go and ask my neighbour downstairs to lend me some money yet again. This was only the beginning of what I was to endure and, looking back, I wonder how I found the strength to continue, but a mother's love gives you an inner strength like no other and, above all else, I was determined to protect and look after my children.
Marcos had no time for me, Paloma or Carlos at all. He had taken to coming home demanding his lunch and, later, coming back demanding his dinner. He would then change into a suit and go out for the evening, slamming

the front door, returning at two, three or four o'clock in the morning. I would sit for hours unable to sleep and, in time, started to lose my appetite through sheer exhaustion and worry. It was slow torture and I was well and truly trapped. Sometimes, I would pace up and down the flat until I was worn out and then go and kiss my sleeping children and lie in bed.

I soon discovered that whatever I did I would be tormented. If I spoke to Marcos he would tell me to shut up and mind my own business, so I would pretend to be sound asleep. There was, of course, no consideration and, on arriving back, all the lights would be switched on in our bedroom. Having stumbled into bed, throwing all his clothes on the floor, Marcos would torment me further. 'I know you are not asleep. Why aren't you sleeping?' he would say. If I continued to pretend to be asleep the lights would go on again and I would be grabbed and shaken. 'It's none of your business where I go, I'll do what I damn well like. I've told you to go to sleep when I go out and you are going to obey.' I would cry through sheer exhaustion and he would usually turn over and go to sleep. But sometimes, when he had been particularly nasty to me and I couldn't stop the tears from flowing, he would continue, 'You're going mad. I shall have to send the children away because you are becoming mentally unbalanced.' This would terrify me and I would lie in bed trembling with fear that he would try to take my children away from me.

One morning, Marcos asked me to buy him some shoelaces. I explained that, as usual, I hadn't even got a peseta in my purse, but if he would give me some money I would see that they were bought. He left the flat leaving me no money.

At mid-day, Marcos returned for lunch and demanded the shoe laces. 'You didn't leave me any money,' I said. He lifted one of the dining room chairs over his head with the intention of cracking my skull open. By the grace of God, the chair legs went through the ceiling and when Marcos managed to bring the chair crashing down, I had had time to move. The chair hit the stone floor with such force it was broken into bits. He then left the flat.

When Marcos returned that evening, he angrily told Anna to take away my cutlery and table mat from the dining room table. 'My wife will not be eating there anymore,' he announced. Marcos then ate his meal and disappeared into our bedroom, closing the door. I took my food to the dining room table and wearily sat down. I had just picked up my knife and fork and was about to eat when the bedroom door opened and Marcos came towards me. He threw my plate of food on the floor shouting, 'You are not having supper here.'

I walked into the kitchen and poured some milk into a saucepan to have a warm drink. Marcos appeared and hit me across the face so violently that I lost my balance and fell against a glass shelf. The corner of the shelf cut my head and the pain was so excruciating that I turned round in self-defence and slapped him on the cheek. He stood there in disbelief and said, 'No woman has ever slapped me before.' I replied, 'And I have never been hit by a man before either.'

The side of my head was so painful and the blood was running down my face. I felt so weak I thought I was going to pass out, so I walked through our bedroom to the bathroom to rinse my cut head with cold water. Marcos had stopped and opened the door of his wardrobe. I assumed that, as usual, he was going out for the evening. I quietly said, 'Yes, I think you'd better go. You've done enough.' He replied, 'That's what you'd like isn't it, for me to go?' He took a leather belt from the wardrobe door. I quickly shut myself in the bathroom but, to my horror, he got through an internal window, adjoining our bedroom to the bathroom. 'If you don't get into bed right away, I'll thrash you to bits and disfigure your face.'

Trembling, I got to my bed and lay in it with my knees up to my chest, shaking with fear. Marcos started talking. 'Tomorrow morning, you will get up at seven o'clock, next day at six o'clock, next day at five o'clock and so on every day. You are going to obey me.'

Next morning the alarm clock went off and Marcos said, 'Get up at once. It's seven a.m. And run me a bath and prepare everything.' I'd had no lunch and no dinner the day before and my body shook as I made my way to the bathroom. I was totally incapable of bending over to put the plug in the bath. Everything was spinning round and I knew I was going to have a black out and crash to the floor. Holding onto the furniture, I managed to return to the bedroom and sit on a low chair and bend my head down.

'Get up at once and do what you are told,' said Marcos. 'I

can't. I'm ill,' I replied. Marcos went to the bedroom door and locked it and then took out a leather belt. I was thrashed heavily across my back. I screamed in agony, but down came the leather belt again, and again, until I thought he would kill me.

When Marcos decided to stop, I was huddled in a heap on the floor and there I stayed totally motionless. Meanwhile, he calmly had his bath and, while dressing, announced that things were going to get much worse.

'You are forbidden to leave the flat under any circumstance,' Marcos said. Unbolting the bedroom door, he called Anna and said, 'You are to catch the afternoon bus back to your village.' Marcos then removed a piece from the telephone, so that it was disconnected, and left the flat.

Anna rushed into the bedroom and put her arm around me and assisted me back to bed. I only had a night-dress on and was stone cold from pain and shock. My back was one mass of weals where I had been thrashed and I was so thin that you could clearly see the bones in my spine and rib-cage. Anna went to get me a warm drink and when she came back I said, 'We haven't much time. Get me my portable tape machine.' As I lay back in bed I recorded on tape all the recent incidents. 'Get a shopping basket and put the machine in it and cover it up so that if Marcos sees you he'll think you are shopping,' I said. 'Go to Marcos's cousin's house and make sure you hand the machine to Susana.' Anna did this and when Susana had heard the tape she went to her husband's office. They were so horrified that they went straight to my in-laws for them to

listen to it.
Anna returned having completed her mission and was worried about leaving me. I promised that I would call her back as soon as I was able and with that she went to catch her bus. I really don't know how I got through the day, but I knew I had to because there were two babies who needed their mother. Marcos did not return to the flat all day and after I'd put Paloma to bed and Carlos in his cot, there was a ring at the flat door.
I opened the door to find Alberto's girlfriend standing there. She came in and said, 'Marcos's mother is coming to see you, but has sent me on ahead to stay here with you. Let me have a look at your back.' I turned around and lifted up my blouse and Lucia gave a gasp of horror. 'Oh, my God. What a brute!'
We sat chatting and Lucia told me that she and Alberto were going to get engaged, but she wasn't sure whether she was doing the right thing, because she had doubts about Alberto. 'Perhaps I ought to leave Jerez and get a job in another part of Spain,' she said wistfully. I replied, 'Leave, please leave, don't stay with Alberto, because I'm having a hell of a life and you, no doubt, will too. For God's sake, go before it's too late.'
My mother-in-law arrived and said, 'No man is going to hit a woman, not even my son. I'm taking you back with me to the bungalow.' It was 24th December. I wrapped Paloma and Carlos up in blankets and carried them out along the streets to the car. We spent an uneventful night in the bungalow.

Chapter 16

Next morning, Christmas Day, I was sitting in a bath in my in-laws' house, when I heard footsteps pounding through the back entrance. It was Marcos shouting, 'Where's my wife?' His brother and mother were trying to calm him down, but he pushed them aside and burst open the bathroom door.

'You had better get out of that bath and get back to the flat, or you will have hell to pay.' His parents and his brother were incapable of doing anything. Everyone seemed afraid of Marcos and I was driven back carrying Carlos and holding Paloma's hand tightly. I was locked up in the flat all day with Paloma and Carlos, barely having enough food to feed my children. Meanwhile, Marcos, Alberto, Lucia and the priest that had married us were all seated at my in-laws' table eating turkey and celebrating Christmas Day!

On entering our bedroom, I discovered an empty bottle of champagne and two dirty glasses, so I just left them there. Marcos came back in the evening and told me how worried he had been the night before to find the flat empty. He suddenly remembered he had forgotten to remove the Champagne bottle and glasses, trying to make out that he had bought the Champagne for us to drink as a peace offering. It was such a deliberate lie, because firstly, I hate champagne and secondly, on finding the flat empty, he had immediately rung his mother. She had told Marcos that I was in the bungalow with the children. So it didn't take much intelligence to work out what had been

going on in my absence.
Life carried on. Anna returned and a new year commenced. As the old saying goes: 'A leopard doesn't change his spots.' All too soon, Marcos was back to his shouting, being rude and treating me with contempt, regardless of where we were.
Unbeknown to Marcos, I went to see a doctor about my health and to show him what had been done to me. I asked him, in his capacity as a doctor, to make sure he wrote a report about the physical and mental cruelty received, in case I ever needed him as a witness. I also asked him to do a test on my mental condition, which he found to be one hundred per cent normal, because I was terrified with the threats Marcos constantly made about taking the children away from me. I no longer trusted Marcos, which wasn't surprising. His unbalanced behaviour was extremely frightening. The doctor was very kind and prescribed a strong tonic containing iron, vitamins and minerals, and a course of injections because he was appalled at the state of my health. The doctor saw me again two months later and, although under continual stress, my physical condition was improving.
When Carlos was six months old, he developed severe otitis which nearly perforated his ear drum. It took a long procedure to cure and continued for weeks on end. He was so tiny and I hated seeing him with such pain. During the day, when he cried, I would pick him up and cuddle him, but at night the pain seemed to get far worse. Having gently laid him in his cot, within ten minutes he would scream. I'd pick him up and walk up and down, endlessly,

from one bedroom to another, backwards and forwards, until sleep overtook him. No sooner had I settled back into my cold bed, when he'd scream again in pain. I got so tired that I got to the stage when I was almost falling asleep while carrying him over my shoulder. I was worried that sleep would overtake me and I would drop him! He would catch his breath several times and make little snuffling noises because of his pain, while his little head rested against my shoulder. Some nights were so bad that he could not be laid in his cot. I would end up sitting on the floor in his bedroom playing with him until the dawn appeared. Marcos did nothing but grumble, saying, 'I wish that child would shut up!' Thankfully, after many weeks, his ear infection cleared up and Carlos never had any more trouble with it.

Chapter 17

A new club had opened up on the outskirts of Jerez called Club Nazaret and it was a lovely place and had facilities for tennis, indoor sports and swimming with a restaurant and bar etc. It was the first of its kind and a great novelty in the area. One evening we were invited to a dinner there. It was the custom, at that time, to sit next to your husband or wife but as we were about to be seated, Marcos went off to the opposite side of the table and seated himself next to a young single girl. He used to take tremendous pleasure in humiliating me, ridiculing me, being rude to me and showing off in public. It was very offensive and I used to suffer in silence. Marcos spent the whole dinner chatting up this girl, oozing with false charm and totally ignoring anything I happened to say. He would hand his packet of cigarettes round and when I put my hand out to take one, he would pronounce in a loud voice, 'Oh no, you are not having a cigarette, these are mine.' His behaviour was obnoxious time and time again.

Having seen the club, Marcos decided that we would become members, as he considered it to be ideal for business contacts. As I was feeling physically stronger, I rummaged around in a cupboard and brought out my old tennis dress and racquet. It would be an opportunity to meet other people, for I had been shut up with the children far too long. Anna would come too and enjoyed walking around the pathways underneath the trees or sitting with Paloma and Carlos. I had been invited to play singles on one of the courts. When we were about to leave the club, someone came up to me and said, 'You play a good game of tennis. We need people like you here. Will you come and play a doubles next weekend?' I said that that would be lovely, so a time and day was fixed and Marcos decided to come along as well. He sat and watched while I played and then we went on to the terrace to have a drink.

Marcos had never had any interest in tennis, so I was extremely surprised to hear him say, 'I want you to teach me to play.' I spent quite a few weeks teaching him how to hold a racquet and the basic techniques of the game. It soon became apparent that he was jealous and wanted to stop any more invites that I might get to play tennis. He made quite sure that I was excluded from any more tennis games and derived so much pleasure from goading me on to teaching him how to play.

One afternoon, we had just arrived at the club and, by this time, Marcos thought he could play tennis. He suddenly spied a gentleman who he wanted as a customer, so he turned round and said to me, 'I want you to be extra nice to this gentleman because I consider him very important as a business client.' He marched up to the gentleman in question, slapped him on the back and asked him to play with us.

Lorenzo had been waiting for a partner who hadn't turned up, so he came over to our court. Marcos immediately decided to take one side of the court, leaving us on the other. The balls went flying over the net from our end and Marcos kept missing them, getting few returned. One of the strings on my racquet suddenly broke and I made a

remark to Lorenzo, who stopped playing and said, 'Clare, please have my racquet, and I'll play with yours.'
Marcos started asking rudely, 'Are you going to play or not?'
'Lorenzo has very kindly offered to change racquets over,' I explained. 'Mine has broken.' We stood in amazement, as Marcos started to bawl at the top of his voice in front of all the players and spectators, 'How dare you answer me back. Get off this court at once and get into the car.' I went off to the car park and sat in the car. About twenty-five minutes later, Marcos appeared and said through the open window, 'You can come out now and join us.' I followed him to the open-air bar and Lorenzo immediately got me a drink.
Marcos never learnt what good manners were and would leave the company he was with and go off to talk to someone else! It was something he would do constantly and he would often leave me alone standing by myself. Marcos suddenly saw some people, who were seated outside on the terrace and off he went, leaving Lorenzo and myself at the bar. Lorenzo leant forward and said quietly, 'I just couldn't believe it when Marcos sent you to the car. In fact he was going to leave you there but I told him that it was no way to treat you.'
'Thank you very much,' I replied. 'I'm very grateful.' We had no time to say much else, because Marcos was on his way back to us.
The incident on the tennis court and my broken racquet put an end to playing. It also put an end to any social life and I became a prisoner once more. In fact, after an

appalling incident, to which Molli was witness, it put an end to everything at the Club. Molli had decided to come and stay. Over the years, she came on six different occasions and I loved her visits. She was like a mother to me, sympathetic and kind. Her visits kept my sanity and were the only times when I could laugh and giggle with her. We took Molli to have dinner at the Club Nazaret. It was a lovely summer's evening and we strolled round arm in arm whilst I showed her the facilities. Marcos had seen a group of people having drinks on the terrace and had immediately dismissed us and made his way to their table. On returning from our walk, we made our way towards the table where Marcos was still seated. Two gentlemen got up and offered us their chairs and I was just about to introduce Molli, when Marcos said in a loud voice, 'No, they are not staying.' Then, while looking at me, he waved us away, saying, 'Go and sit at another table.' It was blatant rudeness. We turned round and seated ourselves at a distance and I ordered drinks for us both. When the head waiter served us, Marcos beckoned him over and said something to him. The next moment the head waiter was coming over to our table looking very upset. 'Señora, your husband has told me to send you into the dining room to start your meal, but the other waiters and staff are finishing their meal in there and we don't serve until they have finished,' he said most apologetically.
'Please don't worry,' I said. 'We will wait and have our drinks out here until you are ready.'
Molli and I were commenting on Marcos's appalling behaviour and drinking our sherry when, suddenly,

Marcos got up from his chair, threw it on the ground and made a beeline for the head waiter.
'I told you,' he shouted, 'they were to go and have their drink in the dining room.' The head waiter tried to explain, but Marcos was shouting again. 'When I give you an order, it is to be obeyed at once!' The Club was quite full by now, with people sitting at tables, standing on the terrace or at the bar, and everyone was looking. We went into the dining room and discussed the menu and had already got through our starters before Marcos made an appearance. He had accomplished, yet once more, to do what he most enjoyed—drawing attention to himself and humiliating me in front of everyone. The evening had been ruined for Molli too.
On another of Molli's visits, this time with my father, it was decided to take them out somewhere one evening. We all changed ready for departing and got into the car. Marcos started up the engine and then turned round and said, 'Where are we going?'
'I really don't mind,' I replied.
'Well, if you don't mind, we won't bother to go anywhere.' With that, he turned off the ignition. None of us spoke, so he finished by saying, 'Well you can all go upstairs again.' I was determined that under no circumstances was I having either my father or Molli upset further, so I quickly said, 'Oh, darling, don't be like that. Let's go to so and so.'
'No', he replied. I tried again and every time it was 'no'. Marcos made us all sit in that car for over twenty minutes. He had no consideration for two elderly people at all and it was yet another totally unnecessary performance of his

irrational behaviour. Suddenly, without warning, he revved up the engine and shot out into the road, and took off at such a speed that father's hand went out to steady himself, while Molli sat well back in her seat. I knew that if I asked Marcos to reduce the speed, he would do just the opposite!

As the years passed, father would come out and stay for a month at a time. He could see that I was desperately unhappy but he was afraid that if he said anything to Marcos he would forbid him any more visits. Father knew how heartless Marcos was and for this reason didn't dare rock the boat.

Chapter 18

As I have explained previously, I had great difficulty in making ends meet with the household money, and even greater difficulty when the children needed clothes or shoes. I'd worry for days before broaching the subject of money for I dreaded the usual outburst that followed. It was always the same torment to cause me stress and he'd always make out that the factory was doing badly financially. Therefore, rather than be antagonised further, I often went without real necessities for myself. I was seldom told to go and buy a dress or had the fun of going to buy material and take it to a dressmaker. So bad was the situation that I spent nine months pregnant with only two dresses to wear. One in the wash and one on. The only time that was important to Marcos was when he wanted to impress other people. So when a party came up at one of the Bodegas—premises where wine is matured and stored in casks—I was told to go out and buy a cocktail dress.
I managed to get to Sevilla and bought a black crepe dress with white organza sleeves which were decorated with white embroidered flowers. It was very elegant, and I was simply thrilled with it. I put the dress on for Marcos to see and put it back in its box ready for the party in two weeks' time. I might have guessed that anything, however small, that gave me the slightest joy or happiness would be short-lived.
Two days later, Marcos had one of his moods, ending in a temper. 'Fetch me the box with that dress at once, because it's going back to the shop.'

'Please Marcos, don't send it back,' I pleaded as I tried to fight my tears.
'I said it was going back and you are going to wrap it up now.'
He sat down, lit a cigarette and there was a smug expression of satisfaction on his face as he watched me tie the box up and hand it over to him. It wasn't the first time that I had been told to get dressed to go out and then persecuted over and over again. I would be waiting to go out somewhere and then suddenly for no reason he would turn around and say, 'Go and change, because you are not going out.' Then he would slam the front door and leave, coming back in the early hours of the morning to have another verbal attack at me. I soon hated any celebration, because I knew, months beforehand, that Marcos would find a way to spoil it by a punishment or something unpleasant. Often, of course, he would punish the children as well. I dreaded Christmas, Easter, birthdays, Saints days, and the May and September fairs.
Anna was a godsend and was just marvellous at sitting on the floor and playing for hours with the children. She really did enjoy their company, and loved them both, but because she had arrived before Carlos's birth, she had an extra special place in her heart for him. Besides, he was not as strong as Paloma, who had developed into a robust little girl with a strong will of her own and a temper to go with it.
Some months later, a circus came to town and I persuaded Marcos to let me take the children. They were thrilled and clapped their little hands as they sat watching everything. I

noticed Paloma's cheeks were getting rather flushed but took it to be the excitement. It wasn't until we were leaving the circus that I realised Paloma was far from well with a high temperature. She had developed chickenpox. I was so worried that she would scar her beautiful face from scratching—because of the intense itching, she was intent on not leaving it alone. I made mittens out of face flannels with tape tied round her wrists, so she couldn't pick at the spots. I plastered her in Calamine lotion at least three times a day, until she was well again. Three weeks later, I awoke to find both myself and Carlos covered in spots. We both got chickenpox very badly, far worse than Paloma's. Out came the mittens again and with enormous bottles of Calamine, I carried Carlos into bed with me, so I could look after him. Anna was having the afternoon off and had to be back by 10.00 p.m. Marcos arrived back from work, had his dinner and put Paloma to bed. Both Carlos and I had a temperature and were far from well. At 10.00 p.m. Anna hadn't appeared. Apparently, she had been talking to her newly acquired boyfriend and had suddenly realised that she was nearly a half-hour late. Marcos opened the door and, in a totally unnecessary manner, asked her if she knew the time. He then told her that he thought it extremely inconsiderate when his wife was ill in bed. Anna unfortunately said, 'Well, I'm only twenty minutes late.'

I sat propped up with pillows, feeling extremely ill, with Carlos lying beside me. I shall never forget what happened next. Marcos was shouting and told Anna that she was sacked from her job.

'You will leave first thing tomorrow morning.' I lay there in total disbelief at what was happening and pleaded again and again for him not to dismiss her. How on earth did Marcos think I was going to cope with an extremely severe case of chickenpox, Carlos so ill as well, plus Paloma who was already very difficult to cope with? What about meals? Feeding the children, bathing them, etc. etc.? Surely Marcos couldn't leave me in this situation without Anna. I had no family to help me. Besides, Anna had been with us for over two years. She had been very loyal, had a sweet nature and had been dedicated to Paloma and Carlos. Nothing was going to change Marcos's decision, and in the morning Anna stood there with her suitcase, said goodbye and left. For years after I missed her. I'd lost my only companion and life could only get worse from now on. I never forgave Marcos for getting rid of her. It left me devastated.

There was nothing for it, but for me to get out of bed and stagger into the kitchen to feed the children. I would get Paloma sorted out, feed them both and then collapse into bed again, incapable of doing much at all. Carlos and I got intense itching and it was unbearable. It seemed to get worse at night and we both developed a nasty array of spots all over the face and body. The itching got to the stage where Carlos and I could stand it no longer and we would sit in a bath, together, in the middle of the night to alleviate our condition. During the day I would nurse Carlos, cope with Paloma, cook meals and muddle through the absolute necessities. I was far from well and standing about on a stone floor in a dressing gown,

shivering from the cold, soon took its toll.
Two weeks later I developed bronchitis. Marcos's mother came some afternoons and would bring cooked food. Despite my condition, I had to look after the children. I dreaded the nights, because I spent most of them sitting on the edge of my bed with fits of coughing and fighting for my breath. The tears would roll down my cheeks from the pain in my chest. The coughing, sleepless nights, and trying to cope during the day were totally exhausting. Not only did I have Marcos's constant outbursts of temper, moods and cruelty, but Paloma too was becoming more and more difficult to cope with. From an extremely early age she developed a strong will, terrible temper and was determined not to obey. By the time she had learnt to walk, if she didn't get her own way over something, she would get down and bang her head on the stone floor and kick her little legs in a temper.
Some months later there was an epidemic of mumps, so I had both children vaccinated. This prevented them from getting it badly. My main concern was Carlos, because of its danger to boys. They sailed through the mumps still on their feet with almost no ill effects at all. The trouble was that I had not had it as a child. So, three weeks later, I went down with mumps with severe swelling, earache and temperature.
One morning, during the beginning of a hot summer, Paloma came into the kitchen, while I was having a cooking session. This involved putting on an old dress, pinning my hair up and slaving over a hot stove. I discovered that one way of keeping Paloma in my sight

and amused was giving her two saucepan lids. She loved banging them together and I could get on with the cooking. I'd just got two pressure cookers hissing away and was in the middle of preparing another dish, when Paloma grabbed a big knife. I retrieved it quickly, saying, 'No, that will hurt you.' The next minute she had bent down to start kicking on the floor and as she went down she hit her head on the side of a saucepan which was on a low shelf. I turned round in horror to see the little white dress she had on turn red. She had blood gushing from just above the eyebrow so, picking her up, I carried her to the bathroom to fetch a towel. There was a trail of blood and I knew that I had to get her to a hospital quickly. I rang Marcos, leaving Carlos downstairs with my neighbour, and was about to get a taxi when Marcos appeared. He put his handkerchief out of the car window and hooted and all the traffic got out of our way. This is customary in Spain when there is a real emergency and it is an extremely sensible idea. We arrived with Paloma and myself saturated in blood and both looking a right mess. It was decided that she must immediately have four stitches and it took five of us to hold her still. She was kicking the doctor and the nurses and screaming at the top of her voice. It ended by each nurse firmly holding a leg, Marcos and myself each holding an arm and another medical assistant keeping her head still. The doctor did a marvellous job and within a few days she had forgotten all about it. Luckily, as she grew older, the scar disappeared into the hair line and didn't leave a mark on her face.

Chapter 19

It was going to be a long, hot, tedious summer, stuck in the flat with two small children. So father suggested that we travel to England and have a holiday at a Devon farm. Father had a wonderful time organising the itinerary at his end, while I had chaos at my end, packing clothes for four people for a month, plus one-hundred-and-one other things that the children would need during our stay in England. It was no small task.

It would take three days to get up to Bilbao in order to arrive in time to embark on the ship for Southampton. I could not imagine, in the searing heat, how I was going to manage with two small children travelling in a car all day. I could visualise that every ten minutes either one or the other would want to stop for a wee-wee, a drink, feeling sick or arguments between sister and brother. Having to contend with that lot, plus Marcos in a continually bad mood because of his lack of patience with the children, wasn't worth thinking about. Eventually, I came up with a brainwave. We would travel by night with both children asleep so that we could have a peaceful journey and take it in turns to drive, stopping during the day.

We set off with Paloma sleeping on the back seat and Carlos on his cot mattress on the floor. The only problem was that, apart from taking on a good deal of driving while Marcos snored, he wouldn't help with the children at all during the day. He left me to amuse and feed them, while he disappeared to a hotel room to sleep. When we arrived to drive onto the ship, I had gone eighty-two hours with no sleep. Paloma was full of energy, with no signs of tiredness whatsoever. We looked for our cabin that evening but it was rather complicated to find, so we did quite a lot of walking up and down corridors, passing people struggling, likewise, with luggage and peering at cabin numbers and bumping into passengers which occasioned a lot of apologising. Eventually, we found our cabin and I sat Carlos on a bunk bed. I could leave Carlos anywhere and he would stay put which was a blessing to say the least. I had just peered out of a port-hole, because we were on the move and had started to sort out an overnight bag, when I realised Paloma was missing. Marcos stood at the cabin door while I charged off in search of her. She certainly was nowhere to be seen in our corridor, so I tried an adjoining one.

Everyone was installed in their cabins with people having a wash and change before having something to eat. Meanwhile, Paloma was in her element, having started at one end of the corridor she was opening every single cabin door, regardless of what people were doing inside. By this time, several people in various degrees of undress, were peering out of their doors. I grabbed Paloma, just as she had opened yet another door, and heard a lady scream. I got back to our cabin to find Marcos lying down and looking rather pale. 'I feel sick,' he announced. I took the children off to eat a snack and put them to bed. Marcos spent the whole journey in the cabin, which meant that I had to look after the children and him.

We drove off at Southampton to find father and Molli waiting for us. Paloma and Carlos adored my father, who

they always referred to as 'Grandpa from England', and Molli as 'aunt Molli'. Father was tired so I took over the driving, taking the children with us. Marcos, Molli and the luggage brought up the rear. That evening, father's cousin, Molli's brother Alan, arrived to join us, so that made seven.
The following morning Marcos started the day by getting annoyed because he had to wait to get into the bathroom. There were other guests staying at the farmhouse. We had all managed to arrive at the required time to the breakfast table and were half way through our eggs and bacon when Marcos appeared. He wasn't at all pleasant to anyone, and started grumbling about the smell of eggs and bacon.
'It's cold anyway,' Marcos said and called Mrs. Stokes over to our table. 'I want this heated up.' The farmer's wife took the plate back to the kitchen. Father was cringing while Molli quickly started talking to Alan. Marcos had lifted the lid of the teapot and let it drop in disgust, remarking, 'I'm not drinking that. I want coffee.' Mrs. Stokes came back and placed the cooked breakfast in front of him. 'Would it be possible to have some coffee for my husband please?' I said quickly, before Marcos could be rude again.
We had all nearly finished our breakfast and were waiting for Marcos. He poured a cup of coffee, took a sip and said, 'I'm not drinking this revolting muck. You English call this coffee?' he asked in a loud voice. By this time, he had everyone in the dining room in a hushed silence watching our table. He had to have an audience, no matter where we were, and he had to be rude. My father didn't

have a lot of money, but had generously invited us to the farm as a treat and because he knew I needed a holiday. The very least Marcos could have done was to behave in a civilised manner. It never occurred to him to consider anyone else. He was one hundred per cent selfish to the extreme and didn't care a damn whose feelings he hurt. We all spent the rest of the day putting up with his bad temper. Marcos made no attempt to be nice to me or the children and his cruelty knew no bounds. Father was visibly upset.

Next morning we all went our different ways. Marcos wanted to go into town to buy some clothes; Molli and I decided to potter around the farm with the children, while father and Alan sat in the lounge reading newspapers. I'd had a word at the kitchen door with Mrs. Stokes to apologise for Marcos's behaviour and asked her where we could go on the farm with the children. Mrs. Stokes said that they could go and see the animals, play in the hay loft, or ride a pony.

Paloma had been led about on the pony and then I mounted, putting Carlos in front of me, leaving Molli to keep an eye on Paloma. Carlos had loved animals ever since he was born, and his little face was all smiles, saying, 'More, more mama'. As we returned from our ride around the farm, I saw Molli at a quick march through the farmyard with Paloma firmly held by the hand. Molli disappeared into the house with Paloma—something was amiss! I found Molli upstairs telling Paloma that she was a very naughty little girl. 'You are not to do that again,' she said. To this day I still laugh at Paloma's quick reaction to anything. She was always doing something she shouldn't be doing and once her mind was made up, she was as quick as lightning. She had discovered some ducks which were housed in a shed and, out of aunt Molli's vision, she had not only let the ducks out but was having a marvellous time throwing eggs against the shed!

That evening Marcos and I went out with another couple to have a drink at a pub. On returning he started grumbling again, saying, 'There's nothing to do. I don't like England.' He had been in a mood ever since we arrived and now he started a verbal attack and, with no warning, threw a suitcase on the bed.

'What are you doing?' I asked.

'I'll tell you what I'm doing. I'm leaving early in the morning,' he replied.

'But we've got a month's holiday. What about the children?' I asked.

'You can stay here with them. I'm going to take the car and go back to Spain.'

He had picked up all his clean, folded clothes and was throwing and stuffing them into suitcases.

'How am I meant to travel back with two young children and all the luggage we have brought in the car?' I asked.

'I'll take what you don't need back with me,' Marcos replied. 'You'd better hurry because I'm going to load the car up,' he shouted. 'I've had enough of your father, you and the children,' he bawled. He threw the return tickets on the bed for the three of us.

'But how on earth do I get back from the port of Bilbao to the south of Spain?'

'You can go and get some air tickets for Madrid, then get another plane to Sevilla, where you will be met.'
My heart was pounding, my mind was racing and I didn't know what I was going to say to my father. I surveyed the children's clothes, wellies, macs, toys, etc. etc. and decided that with such changeable weather and a whole month on a farm, they could not go without the essentials. So, I reduced my things to a minimum and hurriedly packed up another suitcase. By this time, Marcos had been up and down the stairs several times, back and forth to the car and it was 2.00 a.m.
'I really cannot physically cope with the rest of this luggage and two tiny children back to Spain. Marcos, please be reasonable and stay,' I begged. He stood there for a minute, his face red with anger, 'I'm not standing another minute of this. I'm going now.'
'You haven't left me any money,' I said. Marcos gave me some money in an envelope and, as he handed it to me, he said, 'That's all you're getting.' He left and never even bothered to go into the adjoining room to see Paloma and Carlos.
Next morning, I went into town with father to sort out the air tickets and discovered that, after I had paid for them, Marcos had left me with barely enough money for travelling. Father didn't make a big issue out of Marcos's disappearance, firstly, because he was extremely hurt by his selfish behaviour and total lack of responsibility as a husband and a father, and secondly, he'd only had to look at my face at breakfast to see that I was very pale and suffering from shock.

Molli and Alan left later that afternoon. Father drove them to the station, while I played with the children. That evening father and I made a decision to drive about for the next few days and see if we could find another farm. We eventually found an ideal place, not too isolated, where a young couple ran the farm. The husband's parents lived in a bungalow nearby and did bed and breakfast. They welcomed us with open arms, loved children and gave us wonderful home-cooked food.

Chapter 20

Having unpacked yet again, I took the children for a walk around the farm. We had a delicious high-tea and, while I was putting the children to bed, the phone rang. It was Marcos who had rung the other farm and Mrs. Stokes had given him the new phone number. After a bombardment of verbal abuse as to why we had moved, I eventually managed to get a word in edgeways.

'I've sent you a long letter with our new address and all our news,' I said.

'Well,' said Marcos, 'my parents are forwarding all my correspondence because I've met an English couple on board and am on my way to Portugal for a holiday with them!'

Instead of feeling rejected and abandoned, in actual fact, I felt that I could relax and, although the children had to be constantly watched, everything took on a much calmer outlook. Father was loving every minute with his grandchildren and having me around for a whole month. It was very peaceful and, to my surprise, Paloma gave no trouble at all, for the first time in her short life. Father had a special place in his heart for Paloma because physically she was the spitting image of me as a child, and father would always remark, 'It's as if I were looking at you again at that age.'

At breakfast one morning a letter arrived. 'Oh good, there's a letter from Marcos,' father heard me say, as I opened it. The letter, basically, accused me of changing addresses in order to be nearer old friends. This, obviously, could only mean one thing—to have an affair while he wasn't there! Father had seen the horror and disbelief as I read the contents of Marcos's letter and left the breakfast table. He did come along to my bedroom later and said quietly, 'Is everything alright?'

'Don't worry,' I said. 'Marcos has written some very nasty things and it's upset me.'

'Well,' said father, 'keep your pecker up and let's take the children out for a picnic.'

We had a lovely day and, while I clambered about on the hilltops, father sat in the car with the door open puffing away at his pipe and reading the newspaper. Suddenly, I would see his hand go up to wave and from far away I would wave back. Father had always been such a comfort and I was so grateful to be with him.

We had about ten days left of our holiday when another letter arrived from Marcos. It was quite obscene and literally said I had been unfaithful and that on my return I would have hell to pay. It went on for pages and ended by saying—'you are nothing but a loose woman and not fit to be a mother.' I sat at the breakfast table and froze. How in the world could he write these things when I did nothing else but dedicate my life to him and our children. It was the first time that I had ever seen my father interfere with a personal letter, or get so angry. Father didn't ask to see the letter, he said 'Give me that at once.' I handed the paper over and he read the whole letter.

'How dare Marcos write such a letter to my daughter. I will not have such cruelty.' Father continued, 'Clare, you are not to answer, because I'm writing to Marcos.' That

put an end to that saga!
The days flew by and soon I was trying to cram things into already bulging suitcases. The children sat on them and bounced up and down and thought it was great fun. Both father and I were fairly quiet driving back to Southampton. He knew now just how cruel Marcos was to me and I was leaving the father that I adored and being parted from him by thousands of miles. It always went through my mind that it might be the last time I ever saw him. Father gave me a big hug and a kiss saying, 'Keep your pecker up.' As the ship moved away from the quayside, father was frantically puffing at his pipe. I waved from the deck with the children and knew that the tears were rolling down his cheeks, as they were mine.
Never in my life have I had such a nightmare journey as that journey back to Andalucia. I vowed afterwards that I would never, ever, travel with the children again, except by air. We'd found our cabin and Carlos was exhausted from the long day, so I put the children to bed. It took me ages to get Paloma to sleep and I was getting very hungry. Eventually, in the knowledge that they were asleep, I went to the other end of the ship to find myself something to eat. There was a long queue of passengers, all with the same idea. After what seemed ages, I sat down feeling very weary with a hot cup of tea and a plate of food. Before I could even contemplate my tea, a loud voice came over the Tannoy.
'Would the mother of a little girl please return to Cabin 237 as she is calling for her.' Back I went through endless doors, miles of corridors to the other end of the ship.

There was Paloma wide awake and bright as a button. Meanwhile, Carlos was sound asleep. I took off her night clothes and went through all the performance of dressing her again. Off we went back to the restaurant to a stone cold cup of tea and a congealed plate of food. Repeating the queue once again, I sat down to drink my tea and Paloma promptly fell asleep on my lap. Trying to carry a heavy little girl, falling all over the place, and, at the same time, opening swing doors wasn't the easiest of operations.

Next morning we trundled off back to the restaurant for breakfast. Carlos was happily getting on with his eggs and bacon but Paloma wasn't feeling very well and was sitting next to me. Luckily I had just explained what the paper bag was for and—whoosh—Paloma was very seasick. That was the end of my breakfast but Carlos calmly carried on with his!

Later, I took the children to the upper deck where there was a small dance floor. Three men were entertaining all the children and one of them said, 'I want any child that can sing a song to come up here to the microphone.' I had taught Paloma and Carlos many songs in English and Spanish. Not only could they sing in tune together, but were both naturally talented in gestures too. I pushed them towards the stage and Paloma, as always, held onto her little brother's tiny hand. They really looked so cute together and whatever Paloma did her baby brother would follow suit. They sang and performed and everyone clapped.

Shortly after this, the men retired and it became a lounge

again. I had settled Paloma down with her book and crayons which Grandpa had given her. Carlos was on the floor playing with his present which was a red double-decker bus, and I went over to a table to retrieve a newspaper.
Suddenly, the fire alarm went off and, swinging round to grab the children, I found Paloma in the process of getting down off the wall-seating, having pressed the button. Within a matter of seconds there was complete chaos and total bedlam. One of the officers was telling everyone not to panic, whilst doors were closing and stewards were enquiring as to where the fire was and who had set the alarm off! I disowned Paloma momentarily; you never knew what she was going to do next. Eventually, everyone settled down and I decided to take the children for an early lunch, before they could get into any more trouble.
That afternoon there was a film show and I thought that if the children were seated, they would be easy to cope with. We launched ourselves into a pitch dark room. We'd been there about a quarter of an hour, when I discovered that one of Carlos's shoes had come off. I groped about on the floor in the darkness, found it and fastened it back on. When I sat up again, I realised that Paloma had slipped away. We struggled to get out for the back of the room was jam-packed with standing parents. Having firmly gripped Carlos's hand, I now wondered which way to go and started off not knowing where we were heading. I eventually decided to go and report to reception and, whilst on our way there, the Tannoy was making an announcement.

'Would the mother of a little girl called Paloma please come to reception to fetch her.' Flustered and dragging Carlos, we arrived to have Paloma handed back. I apologised profusely and thanked the lady behind the reception desk. She gave me a stony look, putting her nose in the air to gaze at me through her glasses. I knew what she was thinking—irresponsible mother!

Both children, being so young, they soon got bored, endlessly fidgeting, and they were extremely exhausting. Today, tomorrow and the next day, there would be no rest, for there was only fourteen months between them. I took them back to the cabin and got some toys out, but they wanted to play on the upper deck so off we went. While helping Carlos to climb the steps, I looked up and Paloma had disappeared again. I bumped into a couple round a corner and stopped breathlessly to ask them if they had seen a little girl with plaits.

'Yes,' they said, 'she went that way,' and started to point out directions. During this conversation, Carlos had decided that he wasn't holding onto Mummy's hand anymore and had wriggled free. Thanking the couple, I went to grab Carlos's hand but he was nowhere to be seen. It really was a living nightmare and, by this time, I really didn't know what to do.

Rushing off as directed, I found Paloma watching a shoal of dolphins leaping in and out of the sea. She had managed to get the upper part of her body through the railings and, as I grabbed her, she got a good smack on her bottom. Worried to the extent of feeling sick with a pounding heart, I began frantically calling and searching

for Carlos.
Over the Tannoy came the message, 'Would the mother of a small boy, dressed in a white T-shirt and short blue trousers, please come to reception.' I went through another embarrassing procedure, retrieving my child, and made a final decision. Marching back to our cabin, I firmly locked the door and told them to play with their toys, while I lay on one of the bunk-beds to recover.
Later, when we went to the restaurant, I put one child on each side of me, with their little hands gripping firmly onto Mummy's dress. I made it very clear that under no circumstances were they to let go. It was a brilliant idea and for many years after I kept to this routine.
The ship was due in at 5.30 a.m. and we had to be off by 6.30 a.m. Once our luggage had been dumped on the quayside, I was completely immobilised! Although the children could grab my dress, leaving me with my hands free, I was carrying a heavy shoulder bag from which dangled a collection of things. On the other shoulder was a large handbag weighing a ton and bulging to bursting point. Fortunately, I spied a rather grotty cafe a few yards away which had just opened its doors. An assortment of workmen were making their way to it to have their coffee and toast. Leaving the luggage, I made a beeline for it, seating the children at a rickety table and dashed out for the luggage. We sat for over an hour-and-a-half having toast with olive oil and coffee, until it was a civilised time to enable me to put my plan into action.
Having hailed a taxi, we were driven several miles into town where, struggling with the suitcases, I walked into a

travel agency. I explained that our flight to Madrid didn't leave until the afternoon and could I leave my luggage with them. 'No problem, Señora, we will put it at the back of the office,' replied one of the staff.
I found a large store called El Corte Ingles and headed straight for the playroom to leave Paloma and Carlos under supervision. We had just gone up on the escalator and were crossing the shop floor when, without warning, Paloma put her hand out. She touched the display model dressed in fashionable clothes on a platform. The model swayed dangerously and lost her hat as she was about to crash to the floor. I battled with her, standing on the platform with my handbag entangled round one of her arms, while we embraced each other! Thankfully, an assistant came to my rescue. I got back to the children and was, by this time, at the end of my tether. Paloma stood looking at me with such innocence and then, finding herself in a playroom, immediately started to sulk. We managed to linger over lunch to kill time in the store's restaurant and then had to go back to the travel agency before they shut.
We got a taxi to the airport and then found that as the flight wasn't until 3.30 p.m., I couldn't get rid of the suitcases! The weather was fairly hot, so I found a table outside on the terrace and ordered some lemonade. Later, I gave strict instructions to both children to stay seated, as I was just going to check in. I staggered in carrying the lead-weight luggage, got our air tickets confirmed and dashed back to the terrace. Carlos was sitting with his hands clasped round his glass of lemonade but Paloma

was nowhere to be seen.
'Where's your sister?' I asked.
'She went,' explained Carlos.
'But where?' I asked.
'Don't know,' said Carlos, shrugging his shoulders.
We had exactly half-an-hour before take-off and by this time the airport had suddenly filled with people to-ing and fro-ing. I'd just grabbed Carlos's hand when an announcement was being made that flight IB 173 from London was about to touch down at Bilbao with destination to Madrid. I pushed people out of the way and made for a taxi rank outside, asking the taxi drivers if they had seen her. I then asked two Civil Guard policemen if they had seen a little girl with plaits, wearing a pink and white dress. The Civil Guards came into the airport and started to look for her. Some fifteen minutes had gone by but it seemed like fifteen hours. It was quite impossible, dragging Carlos about and trying to find Paloma amongst a mass of moving legs and arms.
An announcement came over loud and clear: 'All those passengers for flight IB 173 destination Madrid, please make your way to Exit 3 to board your plane.' That's it, we are going to lose the flight, I thought in a panic. Oh my God, what am I going to do if I can't find her? Thoughts were racing through my brain and, with every second, I was terrified at where Paloma might be.
Suddenly I had a brainwave. Could it just be possible that she was in the ladies' WC? I opened the door and there stood Paloma, drenched from head to foot, like a drowned rat. She was having a marvellous time, pressing

taps and squirting water everywhere. I was in such a state by this time that I lifted her off the floor by the back of her dress and got her out of the Ladies. Poor Carlos was totally exhausted because his little legs were tired so I couldn't hurry him anymore. As we got onto the tarmac, I could see the last passengers going up the gangway steps. I got to the plane and could have gladly collapsed through nervous and physical exhaustion. The air hostess was a young woman and she stood impeccably dressed at the top of the gangway. She had no intention of moving or assisting me with the children and just looked down at me, laden with hand luggage. Physically, it was impossible for either Paloma or Carlos to climb the steps and, almost in tears, I said, 'Can someone help?' Two gentlemen were disappearing into the plane and heard my plea. I bless them to this day. 'Oh Señora, allow us to help.' They rushed down and one picked Carlos up and the other Paloma. They even belted the children in and stored my luggage away.

Soon we were touching down, struggling all over again, as I entered Madrid airport. Suddenly, Paloma and Carlos were swept off their feet and my hand luggage was taken from me. My neighbour's daughter and fiancé were staying in Madrid and had come to meet me. It was simply wonderful because we had three hours in Madrid before the next flight and I had been dreading it. The children were taken off and thoroughly spoilt, and I sat over a drink and chatted until our next plane was due. When we eventually arrived at Seville, Marcos and my in-laws were there to drive us back to Jerez, where we arrived at 11.00

p.m., completely shattered.
The novelty of having us back only lasted a few days before Marcos went back to treating me like a slave. 'Bring me this, do that,' he would demand. He even had an argument about a shirt he wanted to wear and couldn't find in his wardrobe.
'Marcos, if you remember, you wore it the day before yesterday,' I explained.
'Well, why isn't it back in the wardrobe?'
'Because it's in the linen basket,' I said.
He turned round and shouted, 'Your holiday is over and just remember that I come first and don't you forget it. I want that shirt for tomorrow!' With that he slammed the door and left. Marcos's irrational behaviour and tempers got worse and for a time he would finish his sentences with, 'You're going mad.'
Not only did he torment me mentally, but his cruelty to our small children was unbelievable. He would say, 'Mummy is going away because I'm sending her to England and she won't be coming back again.' Paloma and Carlos would cry, running to put their arms around me. I would kiss and reassure them that I would never go anywhere without them.
Another incident was when Marcos appeared with an air ticket which he put on the dining room table, saying, 'You're going.' Having eaten his lunch, he left. I went across the road to the travel agency and returned the ticket, with the apology that there had been some mistake.

Chapter 21

One afternoon, I had taken the children out shopping, and we were climbing the stairs to our flat. My neighbour, Catalina, suddenly opened her front door and screamed, 'Fire, fire, help me! The butane cylinder has caught fire and I don't know what to do.'
Without thinking of my own safety, I reacted like lightening, knowing full well that a bottle of gas could explode like a bomb at any minute. I turned to Paloma and said, 'You must obey mama, this is very serious. I want you to hold onto your brother's hand and run to the plaza and sit on a bench.'
I evacuated Catalina and her daughters, who were all hysterical, into the street. I ran up the steep stairs, two at a time, unlocking the door and grabbing my fire extinguisher off the kitchen wall. I knew that within minutes there could be an explosion. My heart was pounding as I dashed into Catalina's flat to see the gas cylinder in flames that almost reached the ceiling. I sprayed the flames full blast and eventually managed to extinguish the fire. It was the most frightening experience and, once the danger was over, my reaction was to run out of the flat and down the stairs. My legs turned to jelly on the bottom step in the street and gave way. As I sat there in severe shock, Catalina appeared, having gone across the road in a panic to fetch her son for assistance. On arriving back to the entrance, I was almost carried up the stairs as my legs refused to operate. Having been seated in a chair, I was given a large brandy. For once, Paloma had obeyed

and was still clutching tightly onto her brother's little hand when one of Catalina's daughters rescued them.
Some weeks later, there was to be another frightening experience. We had a massive, heavy, free-standing wardrobe along one length of our bedroom. I awoke one night to see this big wardrobe swaying and tilting forward towards our beds. The fact that the ceiling obstructed it was the only reason that it hadn't crashed on top of us. For a few seconds, I thought I was dreaming, and then I heard the tea trolley in the sitting room going backwards and forwards across the floor.
I shook Marcos and said, 'Quick, there's an earthquake!' The whole building was shaking, but the children slept on. It soon stopped and we decided that we wouldn't evacuate ourselves, but stay put. Meanwhile, chaos was reigning in the street with people coming out of houses and blocks of flats by the hundreds. I have never seen such an assortment of nightwear. Most families went to sit in their cars, which was quite ludicrous. Had there been a prolonged earth tremor, they would have been crushed by the buildings. A large majority wouldn't go back to their houses until it was well and truly daylight.
When Alberto married Lucia I had high hopes that we would become close friends because I longed for a sister-in-law. My life entirely revolved around my children, whom I adored above all else, but I felt desperately lonely and very isolated. Unfortunately, Lucia was distant, independent and jealous. Whatever she was going to do she did with her mother. Frankly, she never bothered about me at all and I was deeply hurt.

I rarely saw Alberto either, although we had never had a disagreement and he had always been quite agreeable when we had met. Therefore, what I am about to relate came as a complete shock, to say the least. Alberto and Lucia were, at the time, living in the bungalow, at my in-laws' country place. They were having a birthday party for one of their sons. Paloma and Carlos had been invited to their cousin's party but Marcos suddenly decided, at the last minute, that he wasn't attending. So I took the children, arriving just as Lucia was driving out of the gates to fetch her mother from Jerez.

On the table was an enormous birthday cake covered in deep meringue. I sat down and chatted to Alberto while we waited for everyone to arrive. Suddenly, one of his sons put his finger in the cake and ran off to plaster the wardrobe mirror with meringue! He came back a few minutes later to do it again and, to my amazement, Alberto suddenly said, 'Okay, if your mother can't be here in time, then all put your fingers in the cake.' His baby brother started as well and they were getting meringue everywhere. My children had been taught to behave themselves and stood hesitant.

Alberto repeated to my children, 'Go on, put your fingers in the cake as well.' They both looked in disbelief and, although not very old, knew that this kind of behaviour was totally out of order.

'No,' I said, 'you are not going to put your fingers in the cake.'

Alberto rose to his feet and shouted, 'I told them to and when I say something they do it.'

'I'm sorry, but my children do not do that kind of thing,' I said firmly.
At this point, my mother-in-law had walked into the room. Alberto had picked up a dining room chair and, as he was about to bring it down on my head, his mother held his arm in the air, shouting, 'Clare, run, please run. I can't hold him.' I ran out to the car getting the children in and drove off as Alberto came out of the bungalow. It proved to me that, fundamentally, both brothers had the same irrational behaviour.
It was around this time that we decided to take a weekend away, up in the Sierra Cadiz mountains. Paloma was constantly getting inflamed and swollen tonsils with extremely high temperatures and the continual antibiotics were doing her no good. Carlos, although fair with freckles, looked extremely pale and was a notoriously bad eater. All in all, the children were, without a doubt, lacking fresh air and a country environment. So off we set to look at the surrounding whitewashed villages.
Paloma did suffer from car sickness and she used to dread travelling in a car driven by her father. Marcos would drive too fast and I would sit clutching the seat, gritting my teeth together, as we roared round bends with one wheel almost over a precipice. He would then light up a cigarette and this, coupled with the speed, would make her feel very ill. As usual, Marcos would be most unsympathetic, making the whole situation worse. I used to have to implore him to stop and put up with his horrible temper in order to get Paloma out of the car. I found that if we walked briskly and eventually ran back to the car, it filled

her lungs with oxygen and alleviated the sick feeling.
We stayed at a very basic bed and breakfast in a mountain village and spent two days wandering about seeing different places. The food in these villages was the best you could ever wish to taste. It was all home-cooked, with broth from their own free range chickens. The food in general was far tastier than any first class hotel. The water was crystal clear with no added chemicals and the fresh mountain air was a tonic bringing rosy cheeks to us all.
Looking at our map on the final day, we decided to go and see a rather remote village called La Huelta de Benamahoma, nestling between mountains with no through road. We left El Bosque village and made our way up the steep rough mountain road. After lunch we took a stroll down a track full of dust and pot-holes on the outskirts of the village. By a waterfall, we discovered an old building. It had been abandoned some thirty-odd years and had seen better days! The roof was caving in, the shutters creaked as they swung backwards and forwards in the wind, and there were large puddles on the mud floor.
A few yards further up the track was a clearing with a massive weeping willow, by a small reservoir where the mountain water collected.
Over a small wall the water gushed down some sixteen feet, cascading crystal clear into the river, which led down to a small steep path to the baker's house. It belonged to two brothers who would bake bread at 5.00 a.m. and deliver it by donkey to the villagers. They had no modern equipment to assist them and would pull a heavy chain up from the stone flour, setting in motion the water wheel.

Clanking and creaking, the machines would slowly go into action and start to grind the wheat, producing fine floor. The dough would be weighed out on a huge weighing machine using heavy brass weights. The oven was high up in the wall, previously having been lit with firewood, then emptied, ready for the dough to be baked. The bread was a hundred percent natural country bread and one slice would give you plenty of energy.
Imagine my utter surprise when Marcos suddenly announced, 'Shall we buy this dilapidated building? It will take a long time to renovate and we'll have to do it bit by bit,' he continued.
'Well, can we afford it?' I asked.
'It'll go for a song. Nobody will want it as it is,' said Marcos. 'Let's go back to the village and make enquiries.'
Some weeks later, Marcos had sorted everything out and the place was ours. Paloma and Carlos clapped their hands, jumping about, asking when we were going to see the broken house again. By now we were into winter and it was getting quite chilly in Jerez but up in the mountains it was bitterly cold. Marcos arranged to have half of the roof removed because it was extremely dangerous and about to cave in. We would spend the weekends at night in sleeping bags on the wooden floor in what used to be the hay loft. We could look up and see the stars through immense spaces in the rafters, and would listen to the nearby waterfall.
The villagers took me and the children to their hearts and I became very fond of them. They were simple, poor, mountain people who did not possess even the bare

necessities of life, but would willingly give you their last piece of bread if necessary. They had no malice and were kindness itself, as I experienced on more than one occasion. They gave willingly, not expecting anything in return. It was quite impossible for me to walk through the village without being hailed with a genuine smile and a 'Good morning, how are you and the children?' or 'Come in and have a coffee,' or 'Sit yourself down and eat.' The villagers would have a bowl of chick peas, sausage, potatoes or lentils with a spoon in one hand and a chunk of bread in the other. They would be genuinely hurt and very offended if you didn't accept what they were offering. When the villagers heard that we had bought the house and were there at weekends, they would turn up with hot coffee, bringing a tray of burning charcoal to keep us warm. While huddled around the embers, we would discuss the future projects and what name we were going to give the house. The children had asked one day, 'Are we going to live in this broken house?' Every weekend they would say, 'Are we going to the broken house?' and so it officially became known by that name, 'La Casa Rota'. Paloma continued to get severe tonsillitis and I decided that she ought to see an ear, nose and throat specialist. He said that although the tonsils were not infected, they were extremely large, leaving little space in her throat. Paloma had had months of high temperatures and I was now afraid she might get glandular fever if it continued. The specialist came to the same conclusion and so they were whipped out, and from that day on Paloma hardly had a day's illness.

Now that the children no longer lived between stuffy classrooms and the flat but had wonderful mountain air at the weekends, there was a visible improvement in their health. They both had lovely rosy cheeks and played all day outside, regardless of the weather. When all the school went down with an epidemic, or flu, Paloma and Carlos were the only children who never caught any of the illnesses.

Chapter 22

Molli came to stay several times and she was such a loving, supportive person, full of energy and interested in everything. She was the loving mother I had never had and was a tower of strength in my moments of desperation. Molli always had a hearty appetite and, mercifully, would eat anything I cooked. She was also very complimentary and would always say, 'It's delicious.' Paloma and Carlos adored her and would talk about their 'Tia Molli'—aunt Molli—for months after her visits. There was one thing the children would imitate and it always brought a smile to my face—'It's delicious,' giggle giggle. Marcos could not tolerate the idea of either my father or Molli staying because anything that gave me a little bit of happiness would make him jealous. The moment they had gone, Marcos would be very unkind making hurtful comments and leaving me night after night, month after month, sitting alone. The only reason that made me put up with this miserable life was my children. They were the only human beings that I had ever known of my own flesh and blood. Under no circumstances was I going to leave the most precious gifts that God had given me.

Added to this was the fact that mother hadn't kept in contact with me, nor had she come out to stay or taken any interest in being a granny to Paloma and Carlos, or given me the love I longed for. So, on one of father's visits, when we were alone, I broached the subject of my adoption. Father, apparently, could shed no light on the subject because after agreeing to the adoption, mother had

arranged everything else. My birth certificate had no information on it as to my natural mother's surname or, indeed, the Christian names she had given me.
At the time, English law stated that if you were adopted, you had no right to know anything about it. However, father did get some investigating done and discovered that my real mother's surname had been Stapleton, but the Judge would divulge no more. Since that terrible evening, when I had been six years old, it had haunted me and, on receiving my natural mother's letter at twenty-one, it had torn me apart. I thought that after marrying and having my own children the constant urge to find and see my natural mother would have subsided. It hadn't and was always tormenting me at the back of my mind. There was no love from either my husband or mother and I dreamt of the day when I would find my natural mother and we would run into each other's arms.
Marcos would go off for three weeks at a time on so-called business trips. I would continually ask him to let me know where he was staying in case there was an emergency. He refused to let me ever have any way of contacting him. He would leave me in the flat and never ring to find out how the children and I were—it was as if we didn't exist. Had it not been that Paloma and Carlos needed their mother to look after them, I would have left my unbearable and lonely existence. Marcos only needed me as a skivvy, running about to his every command. There was no love from him and many a time when I attempted to get into his bed at night, he would tell me to 'Get out at once!' The mental anguish was unbearable and

I blamed myself time and time again. I felt inadequate, rejected and completely belittled.

One lunch time, Marcos walked into the flat and told me that he had met a school friend who had married a Swedish lady and that we were all going out that evening. Marcos spent the whole evening making sarcastic remarks and even telling me to shut up on several occasions. Greta and I immediately became firm friends, for we had had the same kind of education and had many things in common. She could see by Marcos's unkindness that I was having a terrible life with him and was horrified at the way he treated me. Although Greta lived in Madrid, we met again in Jerez about a year later and have been friends ever since. She's a lovely person and I have always treasured her friendship.

Weekends were spent at The Broken House and, as Marcos refused to buy saucepans or even basic necessities, I was obliged to transfer umpteen things with me. Woe betide if I forgot anything, no matter how trivial. There would be hell to pay and he would refuse to speak to me for two or three days.

'Bring me this, do that,' and so it went on. 'I come first and don't you forget it,' he would bawl at me constantly.

When Carlos's milk teeth were developing, one of his front ones had a brown stain on it. It was jokingly referred to as the 'Bovril tooth' and Carlos would point it out with his finger proudly showing everyone. I was relieved when his second lot of teeth appeared with no Bovril marks and the normal colour!

There were many childhood incidents but one of the

funniest happened late one evening. Having said goodnight and turned out the bedroom light, I went off to the kitchen to prepare Marcos's supper. Unbeknown to me, Paloma started doing head stands on her bed while Carlos watched this performance with interest.
'Come on Carlito,' aid Paloma. 'You try to do one.' The next thing I knew were almighty screams from Carlos and I rushed into the bedroom. 'Cure me, cure me, mama!' cried Carlos, as I looked in horror to see his head stuck one way.
Thoughts raced through my brain—spine connected to head—spinal injury! I rang the hospital and was told to bring my son immediately for X-rays. Meanwhile, the specialist we required had just left the clinic for his home and had to return to the hospital. It was now 10.00 p.m. Leaving Paloma downstairs, I got in a taxi with Carlos. His head was fixed in one direction; it was well and truly stuck. Rushing into the hospital in a real lather, we sat for a while, and were then ushered into the X-ray department. At this point Carlos's neck returned to normal movement. Although very relieved and delighted to see my son alright, it really was embarrassing when he announced in a loud voice, 'What are we doing here mama? I'm perfectly alright.' We left with profuse apologies to the medical staff.
It was time for the children to have some animals so I managed to get a white hamster for Paloma and a brown one for Carlos. Never have I seen two hamsters so different in character. The white one never became tame and would constantly give painful, voracious nips, so he

had to stay in his cage. But the brown hamster settled in, took stock of everything, hurrying along the skirting tiles. He was very friendly and tame.

After baths, the children, in dressing gowns, would have their supper. While sitting at the table we would chat about what they had done during the day. Suddenly, a little head would appear from Carlos's dressing gown pocket and I would mutter, 'What are you doing with that hamster when you are having a meal?'

'Please mama, he's not doing anything,' Carlos would say with all innocence. The hamster never got out of his pocket but would sit bolt upright with bulging cheeks and a cheeky grin, and proceed to wash his ears. He always made us laugh and was so entertaining. After a few months some children came to play one afternoon and the hamster disappeared and was, sadly, never found again. We never did find out what happened to him.

We also had a Goldfinch which would fly onto the breakfast table and perch himself on the edge of a plate, pecking away at bits of toast. He spent most of his time with the cage door open flying about and then returning to land on my finger.

Marcos continued all during our twelve-year marriage to make me scrimp and scrape, doing miracles with the little money he gave me. But, in actual fact, the business was progressing at a steady pace, enabling us to start renovating The Broken House. The place that had stabled the animals was made into a large sitting room. It already had a wooden ceiling with heavy beams, so a huge brick fireplace was built, as this was to be our only source of

heating. The floor was tiled in red brick.
When the summer holiday arrived and the intense heat started, the children longed to get away from the awful flat, so we went to live in the sitting room at The Broken House. Looking back, I now wonder how on earth I managed that summer. We had no electricity, no running water, no phone and no loo! I had a small, two-ringed, portable cooker on a window ledge attached to a gas cylinder and did miracles with a frying pan and pressure cooker.
I kept milk bottles, butter, etc. in jars, surrounded and weighed down by heavy stones, in the icy cold river. I had a leg of smoked ham hanging from a rafter along with a string of garlic and dried peppers. Fresh mountain rabbits were occasionally given to me in return for grazing goats in our garden. The old boy who used to bring the rabbits taught me how to skin them. Sometimes, he would bring me honey which he had collected straight from the bees up in the mountains.
Fish was unattainable, so Carlos took up fishing from an early age and taught himself. He would go and sit under a large weeping willow by the bakery with his straw hat on and his feet dangling over the river bank. Carlos became extremely clever at catching river trout and would return with his little face beaming with pride as he handed over his catch. Sometimes, we would put some stones together, building a fire to smoke them, then eat the fishes and green peppers with our fingers.
In the afternoon, I would leave the children's baby bath filled with river water, placing it in the sun. Later, both

children were lathered all over and rinsed in the bath. I washed clothes in the river, the same as the village women had done for years. They had no running water in their houses and did their ironing by heating the irons on a stove. Occasionally, we would return for a day in Jerez and then I would put the washing machine on and have a blitz. Loaded with piles of wet washing and a stock of food, we would return to our haven in the mountains.

The view was breathtaking, surrounded by mountains and olive trees. The goats and cattle grazed peacefully on the other side of the river, accompanied by the ringing of their cow bells. Paloma and Carlos loved the freedom away from the continual town traffic, playing with other children and living like gypsies.

During all that summer, Paloma gave me no trouble, but on our return she started being stubborn and disobedient with the usual temper tantrums. Children sense much more than we give them credit for and Marcos's domineering way and unreasonable behaviour made her rebel. But I was not prepared to accept her temper and knew that it had to be controlled while she was still young. So, for many years, I had a battle royal which taxed my health and drained my energy. Not only had I to contend with continual physical and mental cruelty, and all that went with it, but a child that was not going to conform under any circumstance. We very seldom got through a day without some tantrum or other. In desperation, I took her to a psychiatrist who, after various tests, considered that she was highly strung and, for a while, she was put on medication. If she didn't get her own way, she would

throw herself on the floor, banging her head whilst kicking her legs up and down. If I tried to pick her up, she became a dead weight and would scream blue murder.
In desperation, I would put her in a room where she would proceed to try and kick the door down. I would tell her through the screams that while she went on I was not opening the door. It took a lot of guts to do this and made me feel guilty, but in the end Paloma realised that if she stopped behaving in this manner, the door would be unlocked. Only then would I give her a cuddle.
Carlos was the complete opposite and was self-amusing most of the time. But I simply dreaded mealtimes, especially when there was meat. A piece would go into his mouth and stay there. When I said, "Swallow it," he would pass it from one side of his cheek to the other. It was frustrating and time-consuming to say the least. Carlos could happily spend an hour or two sitting on his bed, trying to decide which sock to put on which foot! Nothing really bothered him much, time was of no essence in his little world. The real difference was that if Carlos wanted to do something, he would come and ask permission first. Paloma was the total opposite—do it first, get punished later!

Chapter 23

By the end of the winter, more renovations had been completed on The Broken House. By summer, we were able to spend the holidays in a more civilised manner, but it was very basic and hard work to keep clean due to the dust flying about on the rough track outside. The floors had to be mopped down every day and the sitting room floor alone was forty-eight feet long by thirty-four. When, eventually, late evening came with the children asleep and the kitchen cleared, I would put my feet up on the sofa to relax. I no sooner had done this than Marcos would start ordering me about.

'Get up and bring me a glass of water.' If I said I was tired, I would be severely punished. The punishments consisted of all sorts of different ways to make my life as unbearable as possible. He would tell me to arrange a baby-sitter because we were going out for the evening. Having got dressed and organised someone to baby-sit, Marcos would get in a mood, slam the front door and leave me standing there.

He would take great pleasure in picking up an ornament I treasured and threatening to smash it. Just when I thought the threat was over, he would throw it in my direction saying, 'I'm going to disfigure your face.' Marcos enjoyed seeing me struggling, day in and day out, with insufficient household money. I dreaded asking him for extra for the children's clothes, because it would end with one of his tempers. I gave up asking for anything for myself unless it was completely essential. I would get a torrent of verbal

abuse and he would derive so much pleasure from forcing me to grovel at his feet.
Father came for his monthly holiday and would sit outside in the garden when the heat had subsided, wearing his Panama hat. He loved being with the grandchildren but I knew that he worried about me.
One weekend, after having had dinner, father and Marcos went into the sitting room while I cleared the kitchen. I came in to sit down and father asked, 'Clare, would you please bring my tobacco pouch from my bedroom?'
'Yes, of course I will papa,' I replied. On my return, father lit his pipe and then disappeared out of the room. After a few minutes, I asked Marcos, 'Where's father gone?'
'I don't know,' replied Marcos.
I went and knocked on father's bedroom door and walked in. Father was sitting on the bed, bent forward with his hands on his head and the tears rolling down his cheeks. I knelt down in front of him and said gently, 'What on earth is the matter? What has upset you papa?'
Father looked at me with such compassion and said, 'When you went to fetch me my tobacco pouch Marcos said 'Dudley, if you want something you do not ask Clare, you command her.' Father paused and continued, 'What a brute. He doesn't deserve to have you.'
After father's departure and Marcos was back in Jerez during the week, I decided that it was time to give upstairs a good clean out. It had been a hay-loft in its day and had long rafters across the room where the saddles etc. had once hung. The room was above the sitting room and had the same dimensions. Two village women and myself

spent a whole afternoon scrubbing the wooden floor boards with soap and buckets of water. We put the children's beds on one side and ours against the opposite wall in the large bedroom.

Some weeks later, I went upstairs to get ready for bed. I had just kissed Paloma and Carlos and was standing looking at the two angelic little faces fast asleep, when I saw something moving near our beds. Looking in the dim light, I realised it was a very large scorpion. I froze and watched. It was exactly the colour of the floor boards and I knew that if I lost track of its whereabouts it, more than likely, would finish up in one of our beds. My heart was pounding and my eyes were staring at it for fear of losing it. It had its tail high up above its back and had started to move about. I really didn't know what on earth I was going to do. It ran underneath our beds to the other end of the room and I strained my eyes focusing on it. I kept telling myself not to lose sight of it.

After a while, it scuttled back again underneath my bed and for half-an-hour I was motionless, just watching this venomous arachnid. If I left the room and went downstairs to get something to kill it with there was always the possibility of it getting into the children's beds. The other problem was that there was a massive floor area for it to run about on.

Hardly moving, I very slowly put on arm behind my back, not taking my eyes off the scorpion as it ran backwards and forwards. I caught one of Paloma's feet at the end of her bed and gently pinched it and said, 'Paloma, it's mama, wake up but don't move, and listen to me. There's a scorpion in here and I want you to go out of the door and run to Diego's house and tell him to come,' I whispered. 'Wait until I say 'now' and then run.' The scorpion was on the move again and away from the door so I whispered 'now'. Paloma was very brave because she was only six years of age. She ran barefooted in her nightie out of the house and down the road. Within minutes, she reappeared with one of the village men called Diego. He had great big boots on and, having cornered the beastly scorpion, he brought his heavy boot down on it.

Due to the fact that a scorpion's sting can be so deadly, most of the villagers kept a remedy to stop it being lethal. It consisted of frying a dead scorpion in olive oil, then keeping that olive oil in a bottle and applying it to anyone who was unfortunate enough to experience the venomous sting. There was no doctor in the village and only one public telephone which spent its time out of order. Therefore, I learnt many extraordinary things from the villagers. Herbs and plants were collected from the mountains and infused in boiling water. A glassful would cure flu and a raging temperature. The village children seldom got ill, but if they did get tonsillitis, it would be cured by feeding them with a wooden spoon carved from the bark of an ivy plant.

One of Paloma's big toes became infected and I discovered that it had pus underneath the nail and was very swollen. Having no medical assistance in the village I put into practice what the villagers had told me. Once Paloma was in bed, I placed her toe in a warm tomato and bandaged it up. By morning the tomato acid had drawn all

the pus to the surface and the pain had gone!
In the old part of the building, which had been the living quarters, I came across a large heavy bell. When the renovations took place, I got the builders to cement it into the wall outside the kitchen door. When a meal was ready or the children were required to return home, I would ring this massive bell. It would be heard everywhere and would echo across the mountains. Paloma and Carlos were allowed quite a lot of freedom but I did have certain rules and there were specific places that were strictly out of bounds.
One weekend I rang the bell as usual for lunch. Shortly afterwards, Carlos appeared but no Paloma. Marcos asked Carlos where she was. 'I saw her playing in one of the villagers' houses with some children,' said Carlos. Paloma turned up when we were finishing our lunch. With no warning at all, Marcos started shouting at her and then he took off his leather belt. Paloma ran through the house and I shouted, 'For God's sake, stop it Marcos.'
He turned on me and said, 'Shut up at once, it's not your business.'
In a blinding rage he lashed out with his leather belt and hit Paloma. She screamed and ran and I followed. Marcos had managed to corner her and had brought his leather belt down across her back several times while she screamed, 'No papa, please no papa.' Marcos had his arm in the air ready to thrash her again, but I managed to shield Paloma by getting myself in between the two of them. Marcos said, 'Get out of the way at once or I'll thrash you across the face and disfigure you.'

I stood my ground and said, 'Do what you like but you are not touching Paloma anymore.' He stood for a moment looking at me and realised that nothing in the world was going to make me move. A mother protecting her children is a very powerful force. He turned around and walked away.

Paloma was a mass of nerves, shaking all over. I took her downstairs, made her a drink and sat while she ate. Later, when Marcos had left the house, I looked at Paloma's back and was simply shocked. She had weals of inflamed burning skin and I gently covered them in cream, but I knew that I could do nothing. I was battling against all odds and no one was going to take any notice of me at all.

During the summer we had the annual village party. It was a grand affair with a band playing and everyone dancing in the village square. I'd spent the afternoon with the children watching a procession and a traditional fight between the Moors and Christians. The fight would end with all the men throwing each other into the river. So by the time all this had taken place, the children were ready for bed.

A married couple who kept in touch, called Margarita and Ramon, were coming over to spend the evening with us. They had four children and on various occasions we had all gone out together. Margarita was about my only contact and I was so pleased at the prospect of seeing her. I'd just spent considerable time in getting ready and was wearing a smart dress for the occasion, when I heard a crash downstairs. I found Marcos in the kitchen surrounded by wine on the floor.

'The bottle dropped as I was trying to open it,' explained Marcos. I went to get a broom to sweep up the glass. Meanwhile, Marcos had grabbed the mop and, as he grabbed it, the mop head parted company with the pole.
'Why haven't you seen to this?' asked Marcos.
'It was alright this morning when I used it,' I replied.
'How dare you answer me back,' Marcos roared. 'You are going to pay for this.' He was red in the face as he continued, 'You are not going anywhere. Go and take that dress off and get upstairs until tomorrow.' I implored him to let me go out that evening. He swung round, hitting me, and I ran upstairs.
At this point, Ramon and Margarita arrived and, having sat down with drinks, I heard Margarita say, 'Where's Clare?'
'She's upstairs in the bedroom,' replied Marcos.
'I'll go up and see her,' said Margarita.
'No, you won't. She's punished. She's not going with us,' said Marcos.
'Oh, you can't do that,' said Ramon. 'Come on Marcos, call her down and we''ll all go out.'
Marcos continued, 'If she dares move from this house she will be locked out of it and never set foot in it again. I'll have her reported for abandoning the children.'
Meanwhile, I had been sitting on the edge of my bed in the last hope that these friends would make Marcos change his mind. The physical and mental cruelty had been going on for seven years. I could take no more and screamed at the top of my voice. I had decided to throttle myself and end the hell. So when Margarita arrived I had

both hands around my throat. She couldn't release my locked hands and had to be assisted by Ramon. While he went to fetch a glass of water, Margarita gently laid me back against the pillows.

'I don't want to go on. I've had enough,' I repeated again and again. Margarita sat on my bed stroking my forehead.

'You must go on, if only for your children,' she said softly.

I felt completely drained and exhausted. Margarita went down to make me a hot drink and meanwhile Ramon was saying to Marcos, 'Go up to see your wife and give her a hug.'

Marcos said, 'She's just hysterical. Leave her alone up there and let's go off to the fiesta and have a meal.' Ramon and Margarita refused to go anywhere and left soon after. The moment their car had gone Marcos slammed the front door and went off to the village, coming back in the early hours of the morning.

God gave me the strength to continue and so the dawn came up on yet another day. Marcos spent most of the morning in bed because he had drunk too much and when he did get up, he went off back to Jerez.

I must have got to the stage in my life when my nerves were at snapping point. It was, I kept telling myself, my children that needed me and therefore I had to go on and look after them. However, the continual strain was taxing my health and a few weeks later I was taken very ill. It was total exhaustion, and I suddenly had no strength at all. My legs would no longer hold me up and I couldn't get to the bathroom without gripping onto another person. My blood pressure was extremely low making it almost

impossible to feel my weak pulse.
Paloma went and told one of the villagers that mama was ill in bed. Within ten minutes there were several women walking down the track towards our house. On arriving, one of the women went back to the village to ring Marcos in Jerez and also the nearest doctor at El Bosque—some six miles away. Someone went to prepare a hot drink in the kitchen for me while another woman took both my children to her house to give them lunch. These village folk were kindness itself and I was very grateful. That afternoon the doctor arrived and prescribed a course of injections. Marcos's car could be heard outside and, as he came upstairs, the doctor turned and said, 'Your wife is very weak. She must be looked after and not left alone in this house.' Marcos smiled at the doctor and said, 'Of course. I shall stay here until she is better.'
Marcos stayed that night and put the children to bed. Next morning he opened the door to a lady who, on hearing I was ill, had very kindly brought some toast and a jug of hot coffee all wrapped up in a clean tea-towel. I heard Marcos say, 'Well I'm off to Jerez.'
'You're not going to leave your wife here alone, surely not? She needs you to look after her.'
'I've things to do in Jerez,' he replied and drove off. The villagers were truly marvellous looking after me and the children. They didn't want to leave me alone at night and even offered to stay, but I insisted that I would be alright. Gradually, the injections started to take effect and I grew stronger by the day until I could carry on with the daily routine.

Chapter 24

Carlos had been born with a large raised mole on his back, very near to his spine. It happened to be exactly where the elastic went round his waist and with the heat Carlos had started to scratch because of the intense itching. So, on our return to Jerez, I decided to take him along to a skin specialist. The mole was not malignant but it was giving him a lot of discomfort. I personally believe in getting ailments seen to whilst a child is still young, so the specialist gave Carlos a local anaesthetic there and then, burning it out.

Father wrote to say the he would prefer to visit us during the cooler months of the year having found it too hot during his last stay. So it was arranged for him to come for Christmas and he would sail to Algeciras, bringing his car. Marcos and I drove down to meet him and watched everyone driving their cars off with a steady flow of passengers disembarking down the gangway. Father was nowhere to be seen and I started to worry. We waited and waited, wondering what had happened. Suddenly, the last car appeared and there he was. In father's excitement he had been the first car on board, thinking he would be the first off. The back seat and boot were laden with Christmas presents for the grandchildren. Paloma and Carlos had a marvellous Christmas and had never seen so many toys.

In January we were given a smooth-haired, black and white mongrel and we named him Tiny. He grew and grew and went on growing to a large size! He would pull me down the cobbled streets at high speed and people would say to Marcos, 'I saw the dog taking your wife for a walk today.' Tiny developed a skin problem and I took him along to the vet. Unfortunately, in those days, vets dealt mainly with cattle and were a far cry from what we know today as vets for domestic animals. The skin problem became chronic and the vet suggested that I should send Tiny away to a special place in the country where there was a natural sulphur river. I had no choice but to take Tiny to spend two months out there. He was looked after by the cowherd who would take him down to the river everyday to have a swim.

When the summer came we picked Tiny up from the farm and took him with us to spend the holidays at The Broken House. His bald patches seemed to be improving and I really thought he was on the mend. After a few weeks I realised that Tiny was getting nasty oozing sores and his condition was steadily getting worse. My fears were confirmed on asking one of the old men in the village to have a look at him. It was ringworm and highly contagious. There were no vets and immediate action had to be taken for, without a doubt, if I didn't, the children would have contracted the disease.

At the crack of dawn, I slipped away leaving Marcos and the children fast asleep. I fetched the old boy with his gun from his home. We drove up the mountain road far above the village and let Tiny out. He bounded off to retrieve a stone and ..... bang, bang. He died instantly and we buried him up there. I turned to the old boy and howled as he said very gently, 'We had to do it. He was a danger to you

and your family.'
'I know,' I cried. For the next week I stood cooking meals with tears streaming down my face, but I knew I had done the right thing, for it was my duty to protect my children above all else.
Mother had not bothered with me since my wedding day and had only written a couple of times. I did write to her occasionally and tried to make everything sound normal. She had never made any attempt to come out to see me or her grandchildren during all those years. So, imagine my surprise when mother suddenly announced that she was coming to stay.
Mother arrived in all the heat and dust, having not seen me for eight years. She was introduced to Paloma and Carlos who found it difficult to see their connection with Grandmother. Father, on the other hand, had come out frequently and kept in contact since the children had been babies.
While mother was staying, she suddenly appeared upstairs while I was pottering about in a night-dress. She made a comment about how thin I was. She also noticed the bruises and that my night-dress was falling to bits. Mother gasped and said, 'He didn't do that to you, did he?'
I bluffed off the bruises, saying that I had knocked into some furniture and fallen. Mother recognised the night-dress which we had bought before my marriage.
'Do you mean to say that Marcos hasn't bought you any night-dresses in eight years?' asked mother.
'That's correct,' I said and left it at that. Mother was simply aghast and when she did leave, she gave me some money

to go and buy some new night-dresses.
One afternoon, mother was relaxing in an armchair and I was in the kitchen getting some tea. Suddenly there was a thud and a scream from the sitting room. 'It's a scorpion.' It had made its way down the chimney-breast, run across the floor, while mother had picked up a log and thrown it at the scorpion. It had scuttled over to a pile of logs stacked on the other side of the room and disappeared. Being mountainous countryside, we were surrounded by massive boulders and rocks and this was the ideal terrain for scorpions. They weren't small either, and moved with the speed of lightning. Their segmented bodies have a hard shell-like protection and they are extremely difficult to kill. The only time that they will sting themselves to death is when they are surrounded by fire.
After mother's departure I had a surprise visit from uncle Henry whom I had only seen about four times in my life. He stayed for a few days for he was travelling around Spain on holiday and had decided to drop in to see us. On leaving, he told me that if ever we visited England to go and stay at his house. We said our goodbyes, with the promise of seeing each other again, some time in the future.

Chapter 25

During our last summer at The Broken House, I was rather surprised, on returning from the village shop, to find an eighteen-year-old woman in our sitting room. Marcos introduced her, saying her name was Adela and that she was the granddaughter of an elderly couple we knew in the village. She sat with a skirt right up her thighs, leaving very little to the imagination, while Marcos held forth with lots of smiles trying to impress her. Marcos even had the audacity to tell me to 'Bring some glasses, Adela is staying for a glass of sherry.' I turned a complete deaf ear to this request and left the pair of them in the sitting room. I was sickened by what was going on through my mind—but perhaps I was just imagining things and shouldn't be so silly.

The summer holidays progressed while Paloma and Carlos made friends with a family from Cadiz. Julian and Rosa had seven children and had just had a house built not far from us. The children and I went on several day excursions with the family taking a haversack and climbing up mountains to enjoy the breathtaking views.

Occasionally, if Julian and Rosa were passing our house they would pop in for a chat and a cup of tea. They were a lovely family and I never failed to admire the way Rosa coped with so many children. Paloma and Carlos nicknamed them 'Snow White and the Seven Dwarfs'.

Molli came to stay for a few weeks and we spent our time chatting nineteen to the dozen. She was most interested with the village bakery and, after being introduced to the

two brothers, we got an invitation to watch the whole process of bread making at 3.00 a.m. Arm in arm with a torch, we made our way down the rough track to the baker's house. It was truly fascinating to watch the whole process. Possibly, it was the last mill in Spain to go through such a primitive procedure in producing bread for the villagers.
One morning while I was busy cooking, Carlos had taken himself off for a walk. He would spend hours collecting coloured crystals which lay on the mountainside and was at the age when all insects were of interest. Many a time, I would absentmindedly open a box of matches to light the gas and scream. Inside would be some creepy-crawly that had been added to his collection! As the morning progressed, the heat got intense and apart from a mule resting his head inside the open front door and two goats grazing under the olive trees in the garden, everything was quite peaceful. Leaving two pressure cookers hissing away, I went outside to stand in the track, shading my eyes with my hand from the glaring sun. In the distance, I could see a plaintive little figure sobbing his heart out.
'Mama, mama,' cried Carlos.
'What's happened?' I asked as I ran towards him.
'Well,' said Carlos, 'I got tired and had a rest under a tree.' In between the tears and sniffs he continued, 'Then a goat came along and picked up my straw hat and ate it.'
I laughed and reassured him. 'There are plenty more straw hats in the village shop and we'll go and get another one.'
August came to an end and by this time the family business was financially progressing in leaps and bounds.

One weekend Marcos suddenly announced that he had bought a flat by the sea in Valdelagraña near Jerez. Of course, I had not been consulted and it came as no little surprise.
'What on earth do we want a flat for when we are renovating this house?' I asked.
'It's an investment,' said Marcos. 'We are going to spend a few weeks there.'
So off we all went to stay at the flat in Puerto de Santa Maria. I had no sooner arrived with all the work of packing and unpacking, than Marcos announced that a business associate and his wife were coming to stay for a few days. The couple were from Valdespeñas near Madrid where Marcos frequently visited when travelling and I had met this couple previously on one of their visits to Jerez. On their last evening we had had dinner and were all joking and laughing, which annoyed Marcos who got in a mood and just went off to bed. The three of us had some more coffee, chatting away until quite late. Eventually, Ester's husband said goodnight and when we were alone Ester said, 'I'm sorry to have to tell you this but I really think you ought to know. Your husband has told my husband that when he comes to Valdespeñas he goes to a brothel.' It came as a violent shock but I was grateful to know what was going on.
At the back of my mind there was a feeling of guilt as I constantly blamed myself for Marcos's continual rejection of me sexually. For twelve years I suffered his cruel domination as he belittled and antagonised me. On those nights that he wasn't out drinking or at night clubs, he

would take great pleasure in tormenting me. Getting into his bed and waiting until I was almost asleep, he would then start an argument. If I ignored him and kept silent, I would be told to answer at once or get hit. If I answered him, I would be told to shut up and he would threaten me with a thrashing—I just couldn't win. Having got me into a complete mass of nerves, he would then jump out of bed and say, 'I'm going. I'm not staying here with you,' and having dressed, he would depart. I would cry my eyes out. There was no one to help me, no one to talk to. No one at all.

One particular night, while at Valdelagraña, the hours ticked by and I couldn't stand the uncertainty any longer so I got dressed and sat on the steps of the flat outside in the fresh air. When I heard Marcos's car, I got up and, as he approached me, he said, 'What are you doing?'

'I couldn't sleep. I was waiting for you,' I said. I went to follow him in and, as he got to the top step, he slammed the entrance hall door shut, bolting it from the inside. I called to him but he took no notice and disappeared into the lift. I went round the building to our bedroom window and called, 'Please open the door.'

About ten minutes later the bedroom light went out and I was left in the street. I spent the night sitting in the car and it wasn't to be the only night either! Marcos would sometimes decide that he wasn't going to move from his bed and would order me to get dressed and to leave my house keys on the bed and go and sleep in the car.

Summer came to an end and we returned to Jerez. We never stayed at the flat again and it wasn't rented to

anyone, so I really couldn't see the point of having it at all! When the children went back to school, I went to clean the flat out and fetch things that had been left there. On returning, Marcos demanded my key back and said, 'It's my flat, you don't need a key!'
In October, Marcos informed me he would be in Sevilla all day, so I found a key to the apartment and decided to go and have a look at it. What greeted me on opening the door was not pleasant. The sitting room had bottles of every kind of drink imaginable, along with tinned ham, crisps, olives etc., and the ashtrays were full of cigarette butts. The bedspread was hanging off the bed on the floor along with a pair of Y-fronts. The clean towels had been used and gave plenty of evidence as to what had been going on. It was no use confronting Marcos—he was a born liar. So I kept quiet. Besides, he would have physically assaulted me if he had known that I had been to the apartment.
A few days after this discovery, Marcos announced that he was off again on another business trip. It was all rather sudden, so I knew I had to get information about what exactly was going on behind my back. Marcos's secretary had been working at the office factory for many years and had known me long before I got married. She was a nice person and I decided to make a visit to her house. Alicia was very pleased to see me and invited me in for a coffee. We chatted about the children, whom she had known since they had been born, and then I brought the conversation round to Marcos's journey. Alicia must have thought that I knew what was going on, or at least felt that

it was time someone told me the truth. She spoke of a young woman who was continually ringing Marcos at the office. Alicia told me how her brother had been told by Marcos about an affair that he was having with an eighteen-year-old from Sevilla. I pretended that I had known about it all the time and eventually left Alicia's house. Once in the street, I wondered how I was ever going to make it back to the flat. I mechanically put one foot in front of the other, staring ahead and not seeing the people walking towards me. I was suffering from complete shock.

That same evening with the children in bed fast asleep I must have spent two hours pacing up and down the flat non-stop. The telephone suddenly rang and a woman's voice said, 'Is Marcos there?'

'Who am I speaking to?' I asked. She insisted again that she wanted to speak to Marcos. I told her I wanted her name.

'I don't mean to upset you. Please tell me if your husband is there?'

'No,' I said, 'he's away.'

The voice on the phone then said, 'I'm Adela's mother and I want to know if Marcos's car registration number is CA 325D'.

'Yes, it is,' I replied.

'Well,' she continued, 'my daughter is staying in Tarragona at her cousin's house and Marcos has turned up to take her out. The cousins didn't know who Adela was going out with so they took the car registration number and rang me,' she explained. 'I'm having her sent home tomorrow

to Sevilla.'
'Give me your address. I shall come and see Adela tomorrow myself,' I replied.
Having got the address, I put the phone down. There are no words to describe how I felt. I was numb with pain and it was cutting me through and through. In the end, after what seemed like hours and hours, I knew I had to ring and talk to someone. I phoned Rosa in Cadiz who immediately offered to accompany me to Sevilla the next morning.
Having got the children to school, Rosa and I set out and, arriving at Adela's parents' house, found that Adela was still in Tarragona. I returned alone the next day and confronted Adela. She and her father accompanied me to a Notary and a statement was taken. No sooner had I left, than Adela contacted Marcos to warn him that I had found out about their affair. Marcos immediately sent me a telegram in which it said:

FOR GOD'S SAKE DON'T BREAK UP OUR MARRIAGE FOR THE SAKE OF OUR CHILDREN

A few days later, Marcos returned and implored me to forgive him. He sat and told me about his affair with Adela and how he had been seeing her for over a year. The discotheques, flamenco parties, the drink, the presents and the hotels. It was all explained in black and white and I sat motionless and expressionless. That would have been enough for any wife to hear, but Marcos hadn't finished talking yet! He'd also slept with Adela's mother!

He went on to tell me how he had frequently slept with a German girl while her husband was away at sea. Also, another girl in Malaga and other sexual activities relating to our seaside apartment. I had nothing to say. Something inside me had gone dead and I was completely numb—my world had fallen apart.

I slowly got up from my chair and went to kiss my children sound asleep in their sweet dreams. I stood a long time looking at them and wondered what I was meant to do. My whole body had turned stone-cold and I lay in bed physically shaking until the dawn came up. I hadn't uttered a word since Marcos's return and felt I never wanted to speak to him again.

Father wrote to say that he was spending Christmas at Molli's house and wished that I could be there too. I desperately needed a break from everything and would dearly have loved to have spent time with my father. I hadn't had a holiday for three years and the children were always with me. I hated the old flat we lived in; it was an awful place with small windows and lacking light; altogether it was very depressing. Since Marcos's return the flat had become even more oppressive and it had nothing but bad memories.

Meanwhile, Marcos was terrified that I was going to break our marriage up but it had never been a proper marriage in any sense of the word. Marcos had never been a husband, a friend, a companion or a lover and had never been a loving father either! The ball, for once, was in my court and I decided to take advantage of it. I addressed Marcos that evening and said quite firmly that if we were

to continue, I wanted to leave the flat and go and live in a house away from Jerez. The other proposal was that I needed to get away and wanted to spend Christmas in England with my father to have a rest.
Marcos agreed to both requests but that we all went to England as a family. I was too exhausted to have a discussion over anything so air tickets were bought and we were to leave on 26th December. By this time, we were almost at the end of November, so I was kept very busy organising clothes and presents etc. The thought of seeing my father and Molli kept me going. Paloma and Carlos were getting very excited and I wrote to uncle Henry to ask him if we could stay overnight at his house.

Chapter 26

We left Jerez with Paloma and Carlos for Malaga airport on 26th December 1974. It was a mild, sunny morning and ideal for travelling. On arrival we gave the children lunch while they watched in fascination at the planes which were taking off and landing. At 3.30 p.m. the plane rolled down the runway and took off into the sky. The children were amazed to see a second lunch being served up in the clouds! Carlos suddenly got a second appetite too and solidly plunged his way through everything on his British Airways tray. On landing we expected the freezing cold of an English December but were greeted by the most wonderful mild, calm, warm weather and uncle Henry. We had covered many miles and Paloma and Carlos were very tired so I put them to bed. Uncle Henry had cooked the most superb soup, roast turkey and potatoes, which was accompanied by Gilbert and Sullivan music in the background.

I awoke at 7.30 a.m. to find uncle Henry entering the bedroom with an early morning cup of tea. He stood and told such a hilarious joke that I nearly spilt my tea all over the bed. When uncle Henry was free from his surgery we set off to take the children to see a model village and then on to Windsor Castle. The Queen was in residence and the Queen's guards were parading up and down, ... stamp, stamp, and back to the sentry box. Carlos went to peer up at one of the guards' faces. Very puzzled he returned to my side and said, 'Mama, he hasn't got a key in his back!'

At 4.00 p.m. we said our goodbyes and took our leave for the Isle of Wight. Everything went well until we were five miles from Southampton. The taxi we were travelling in decided to bellow smoke out of its engine and came to a halt. We sat in the dark for one-and-a-half hours while the driver went off to phone for another car. We just managed to catch the last ferry for Cowes at 8.00 p.m. Paloma tried to keep still but couldn't, so spent her time jumping about from one window to another looking at the lights. Carlos, exhausted, had settled down on a sofa in the lounge and promptly went to sleep. On arrival we went straight to see father and Molli before finding our hotel.

We'd had long hours of travelling and next morning I could have slept all day but before 8.00 a.m. there was a lot of giggling and laughing going on. Two little heads appeared round the bedroom door.

'We want cornflakes mama,' was the first greeting. I suggested that they tried to order their own breakfast in English and there was a mad rush for the dining room. After a brisk walk along the seafront, we met up with father and Molli. In the afternoon we took the children to the Osborne Wax Museum, dating back to 1228 A.D. which had once been one of Queen Victoria's houses. On entering there was a glass case with a shrunken human head and this practice was done in secret by the Jivaro Indians in the Amazon. King Henry VIII was very lifelike in one of the rooms and Queen Victoria appeared in gracious state with her foot tapping and breathing deeply. Another room had a skeleton playing an organ which Paloma and Carlos didn't like much and they were glad to

step outside into a pretty courtyard.
The following afternoon we set off with father and Molli to have tea with Ursula and Mike—Molli's daughter and son-in-law. I had been in contact by letter with Ursula for over ten years so it was lovely to meet her in person. Their two children and ours all had a wonderful time playing together. After tea Ursula and I got an opportunity to have a tête-à-tête in the kitchen before saying goodbye.
Next morning Marcos had an argument with the hotel manager over the price of our accommodation. This ended with me having to pack up everything and we moved to another hotel. It was old and rather worse for wear, presumably having once been a private house in its day. However, the manager and his wife were homely people and didn't mind two energetic children bouncing about. We took Paloma and Carlos to see Walt Disney's Peter Pan. They loved every minute of it, especially the pirate's ship with Captain Hook and the crocodile with its 'tick, tock'. Father and Molli had been invited out to drinks to see the New Year in so we stayed put that evening at the hotel. A couple had arrived with two children and so we saw the New Year in with them. We spent a quiet day on 1st January with father coming to have lunch with us and Molli arriving later for a family dinner.
After breakfast next morning we took the children to see the coloured sand at Alum Bay and walked down the eighty-odd steps to the beach. I scooped sand into different plastic bags to take back to Spain. We had tea at Molli's house and did Daddy's packing for him. His

luggage gave the appearance that he had been staying two months—in actual fact, it had been ten days. His car boot was laden with tool-boxes and spare car-parts and we had all our luggage to cram into father's car as well. I left Marcos with the task of trying to fit everything into a Morris Minor! We couldn't all fit into father's car so Marcos had to go by train. We had a pleasant journey and stopped to have lunch just outside Chichester before arriving at Rottingdean. Marcos had arrived before us and was already waiting at the hotel, which was on the seafront a few yards away from father's house.

The following day was hectic with a trip into Brighton. The children accomplished one of their dreams; this was to sit upstairs on a double-decker bus. We had lunch at father's house and then set off to Seaford to have tea with a couple who had known me since I was a child. At 6.00 p.m. we had been invited to have drinks with Mrs. O'Hara, her eldest son, his wife and their four children. We had a pleasant evening catching up with all the gossip. Father's housekeeper had arranged a belated Christmas dinner, so we sat down to an enormous meal and the children had great fun with a box of crackers. At 1.30 a.m. I eventually closed the last suitcase. We seemed to have accumulated so many things that father had to lend us another suitcase.

Next morning we were on our way back to uncle Henry's house and he was delighted to see us again, taking us all out to a restaurant for lunch. That evening I cooked dinner while uncle Henry dealt with an overflow of patients in his surgery. On our final day we had promised to take the children to a pantomime and so, after lunch, we proceeded to Old Compton Street to see Cinderella. Uncle Henry had hoped to take us to Heathrow and see us off but found himself snowed under by a whole crowd of patients. We said our farewells and sat in the airport surrounded by parcels, plastic carrier bags and hand luggage, looking more like a family moving house. We arrived back at Jerez at 10.00 p.m. absolutely exhausted. Father rang at 11.00 p.m. and we had a chat, as I stood amongst half-opened suitcases with utter chaos surrounding me.

Christmas holidays over the children went back to school and weekends were spent at The Broken House. One Saturday morning Marcos got an invitation to shoot and we spent the day at a farm which was on the way to Benamahoma. In the courtyard were a litter of eight-week-old puppies with their mother. Paloma and Carlos had been playing with them while I sat outside talking to the women. By the time we were ready to leave it was late afternoon and the farm owners offered us a puppy. We contemplated the puppies from every angle and, eventually, chose one that was black and white. She had a beautiful head and very pretty markings for she was part English Setter, part Pointer. I named her Flicker because she moved with the speed of lightning.

By Easter, documents were being signed and sealed for a house that we had seen in a residential area by the sea. It was on the outskirts of a small fishing village called Saint Mary's Port—Puerto de Santa Maria. Time had come to pack everything up for moving and, as usual, I did it all single-handed.

The removal van had just departed leaving me standing in the middle of the sitting room, surrounded by tea-chests when, through the open front door, walked uncle Henry.

'I'm travelling about and thought I'd drop in on you and went to the flat in Jerez,' explained uncle Henry. 'On not finding you there I went to see Paloma's godfather at Sandeman Bodega and got your new address.' Uncle Henry sat down and continued, 'Well, I wouldn't have come if I'd known you had just moved today. I'll go and find myself an hotel,' he said.

'Oh, no,' I replied. 'I've got to find some sheets and make up beds so one more won't make any difference.'

Uncle Henry stayed for two nights and on his last night, after dinner, the two of us sat and talked almost until the dawn came up. He left with the promise of us meeting again but that never happened. He had always been a chain-smoker and whisky drinker and died of a massive heart attack two years later in 1977.

Meanwhile, Marcos was being quite civil for the first time in our married life and summer was upon us once again. There was a club called El Buzo which had a restaurant, bar, terrace and swimming pool. It was situated right by the beach and there were miles of glorious golden sand. The club was only four minutes walk from our house. It was a haven for grown-ups and children alike. Being a summer residential area meant that most people had a house there as a second home and only came to stay during the long school holidays. The children loved stepping out of the front door into the garden, swimming in the sea, playing with all the other children and being able to ride their bikes.

We lived in bathing clothes all the summer and took long walks along the beach with Flicker. She would watch us wading into the water and bark excitedly. When she wanted to join us she would plunge into the sea and swim right out to where we were. She was completely fearless and would spend half an hour out of her depth swimming round in circles.

On one such occasion whilst Valerie was staying, we were sitting on chairs on the beach. Flicker had settled down behind us in the shade. We were busy chatting when Valerie's chair collapsed and she suddenly disappeared out of it. Flicker had got bored and had been busy digging an enormous hole in the sand.

One morning I was busy cooking and hadn't seen Carlos for ages. I went upstairs, went outside, came in again and popped my head behind the sofa. There was Carlos on the floor with Flicker and a pair of scissors. Flicker had the feathery tail of a Setter and Carlos had decided to trim some of her hair off! He would sit for ages with her and lift up an ear flap and whisper to her. Great conversations went on between them.

The children were still at their school in Jerez so that meant that, during term time, I had four journeys to do of thirty minutes each way to two different schools. Paloma would get in the car and say, 'Hello mama,' and Carlos would get in the car and say, 'Hello Flicker', and sit with his arms round her all the way home.

Chapter 27

The typical Andalucian gypsy dress is worn by tiny tots right up to grown-ups. It is a tradition to wear these dresses during the May and September fairs and dance Sevillanas. But, sadly, it was one of the many things that Paloma was deprived of as a little girl. Marcos considered it a nonsense and a waste of money. One afternoon whilst visiting my mother-in-law, she asked me what she could give Paloma for her ninth birthday.

'She desperately longs for a gypsy dress,' I replied. So her grandmother and her godfather decided, jointly, to pay for a dress to be made.

I took Paloma into Jerez to choose the material and we bought metres of snowy white lace. We then set off for our appointment with a dressmaker who specialised in making Andalucian dresses. In September we went off to the fair and Paloma looked so beautiful with white carnations in her hair. She's a natural dancer and dances Sevillanas with great art and is a joy to watch.

In the same year that we moved to Vista Hermosa, General Franco's death was announced on 20th November 1975. Two days later, as he lay in State, Prince Juan Carlos was sworn in as King of Spain.

It was the end of an era, where there had been virtually no crime, no drugs and, above all, no violence with the safety of knowing that anyone could walk about at night and not be attacked.

Spain hadn't been used to so much sudden freedom. The horse that for years had been reined in and controlled had

had, without warning, the stable door opened and was now allowed to run wild.
The Spaniard had been taken from one extreme to the other and in came corruption, drugs, violence and all the other things that we today call a free country!
I received a letter from father to say that he would be delighted to come and stay at Christmas. We had placed a large freezer in the yard outside the kitchen, so I decided to prepare things in advance. If you want a turkey that is fresh, then you do exactly that! We drove out to the country and I stood by the pen of turkeys.
'Which one, Señora?' said the farmer's wife. I pointed and she ran after the turkey with a knife and plate.
Although expertly killed, I really had to walk away from the scene. The country folk are so poor that, where food is concerned, nothing is wasted. Hence the plate to catch the turkey's blood, which is then put into a mould. It is then cut into slices and fried ready for eating.
We came home with three turkeys and I then had to sit and pluck them. By the time December arrived I was all prepared and stocked up with everything ready for Christmas and father's arrival.
Another letter arrived from father explaining that he wasn't feeling a hundred percent and felt he just couldn't face the journey. I was very upset and so were the children. We had all been waiting for his visit with such excitement; we hadn't seen him for a whole year. Shortly after this news, Marcos came back one evening and announced that he had booked us into an hotel in Marbella for Christmas.

'What about Flicker?' I asked.
'I don't know,' replied Marcos. So I rang the hotel and was told that as long as she stayed in the bedroom she could come.
We arrived on the 24th and that same night there was to be a grand dinner; full evening dress, no less. Having got the children organised, Marcos took them off downstairs while I got ready. It was a luxurious hotel and the dining room had a wide aisle which seemed to go on forever with dining tables on each side. We had to walk all the way up the red carpeted aisle to the top of the dining room.
Meanwhile, Flicker had been left in the bedroom and had settled down in a corner, quite happily snoozing. On my way down from the third floor, I stopped to tell the receptionist that the dog was in our bedroom and that we didn't need the chamber-maid to go in and turn our bed covers down. The dining room was very busy, full of people all elegantly dressed. Chandeliers glistened and table lanterns flickered as far as the eye could see down the length of the room.
We were sipping our chilled wine and the maître d'hôtel had taken our orders. The prawn cocktails and melon arrived and I had just put a large prawn into my mouth along with some lettuce when the maître d'hôtel returned to our table. He bowed with great dignity and said, 'Señora, your dog.'
In horror, I looked round to see Flicker at the other end of the dining room. Her nose was brushing the carpet aisle and she was trotting along the length of it. Having found us, she stood and looked at me, wagging her tail. I grabbed

her by the collar and braced myself for our departure from the dining room. While people sat staring with food suspended at the end of their forks, I made my way back to the third floor.

Apparently the chamber-maid had not got my message and, on entering our room, Flicker had run out. The animal was certainly very clever because she had negotiated three flights of stairs, a large reception area, walked through several other rooms and down a flight of stairs to the dining room.

Christmas went by without any mishaps and the children were thoroughly enjoying it all. One morning we looked out of the hotel window and found that it was pouring with rain. Not knowing quite what to do all day with two children and a large dog in the car, we decided to drive to Malaga. On arriving there, we all got out of the car and Marcos said, 'Come along, we are going to buy mama a fur coat!'

'But I don't want one,' I said. 'Really I don't.'

'Yes, you do and we are going to choose one now,' replied Marcos.

Quite stunned, to say the least, I stumbled along with the children as Marcos marched off up the street into a furriers. I was made to try on every coat in the shop and eventually ended up with cheetah. Stupidly, I thought that this was Marcos's way of trying to make amends for the past but, regretfully, I found out soon enough the reasons for this sudden lavish expenditure on me.

On our return home Marcos decided to take me out frequently to El Buzo Club where we would meet other people from Jerez. He would insist on me wearing the new fur coat. Sometimes it was quite mild and I would put a jacket on to go to the Club.

'I told you to wear your fur coat,' Marcos would say. 'Go and change at once. I want people to see that I can afford to buy my wife an expensive coat.' The coat became an embarrassment with Marcos showing off in front of people and talking in a loud voice drawing attention to himself and me.

The family business was doing extremely well and, financially, had never been so good. Coupled with this security was the fact that, by now, Marcos was fast forgetting his endless affairs and cruelty. He felt great power in having money to spend and gradually slipped back to his former violence. He would shout orders with physical abuse and make our lives a misery.

Coming up to spring, Carlos started to have dizzy spells and feel unwell. He would be playing outside with other children when suddenly they would come and call me, 'Come quick, Carlos isn't well.'

On one such occasion, Marcos had to carry him in and lay him on a bed. After several of these incidents I decided it was time to take him to a specialist. I took him to a doctor in Cadiz who had treated me in the past for terrible migraines. The doctor spent two hours going through all sorts of tests and taking a stomach X-ray.

Unbeknown to any of us, Carlos had a birth defect which meant that the food he ate would take twice as long to digest as an average child. This explained a lot because Carlos was seldom hungry and I would invent all sorts of things in the kitchen to entice him to eat. He was extremely thin and would get very tired. The doctor put him on several different medicines, all at various hours of the day, and after lunch Carlos had to lie on his right side for an hour on his bed every day. It was to be a long, tedious thing to put right and needed my complete dedication to enable Carlos to fully recover.

I was determined, above all else, to nurse Carlos back to health and we were not going to end up with him having to have an operation. The road to recovery was taxing and time-consuming. I would make individual caramel custards and leave them in the fridge to entice him. Mashed potato would be put in a mixer with egg yolks, breast of chicken and fresh vegetables. Then I would spend ages spooning it down him. It would be a question of watching closely when he was outside because, with no warning, Carlos would suddenly feel dizzy and have to be carried indoors.

I seemed to spend all day keeping up with the different medicines and injections and making sure I didn't run out of them. We were three miles from the shops. During the year that followed, apart from check-ups every three months, Carlos missed a lot of schooling due to not feeling well enough to attend. It was a time when Carlos and I spent many days in each other's company. Often we would stroll along the sandy beach with Flicker and take long walks together.

One Sunday afternoon in a tremendous heat wave, we were all pottering about between the house and the garden. A massive explosion was heard and from our house we could see the smoke rising in the direction of the Club.

'Oh my God!' I exclaimed. 'It must be a gas cylinder that has exploded. Quick Marcos, we ought to go and help. There'll be people hurt.' The children were making a beeline for the garden gate, but I knew that what we might see would not be for their eyes to behold. 'No,' I said firmly, 'you are forbidden to leave the garden.'

Marcos and I ran, as people were all dashing towards the Club. We approached the parking area and there was a car about to transport a girl who had had half her stomach blown away. A young teenager had lost a hand and several others had been blown into the air, receiving horrific injuries. Eight or more cars were transporting youngsters to the clinic. There were pools of blood everywhere and the scene was one of total carnage.

It transpired that a group of youngsters had decided to make an explosive, choosing the parking area with cars and motorbikes all around them. They were rubbing the ingredients together and the friction, added to the heat of the day, had made the whole thing explode. We all helped hunt for the boy's hand which, eventually, was found quite a distance from the scene, and the surgeons were able to sew it back on.

Chapter 28

After moving to Vista Hermosa, Marcos and I had discussed the impracticability of having the children at schools in Jerez, so it was decided that the following year they would go locally. It was while Paloma was attending her new school that I came in contact with a lady who lived in Vista Hermosa and had her four daughters at the same school. Pizca became a wonderful friend and helped me on umpteen occasions in some truly devastating situations.

Another lady who must be mentioned was an artist named Carolina, married to a naval officer and she gave an exhibition of her paintings one evening at the Vista Hermosa golf club. She used canvas material and painted mostly with her fingers! Her pictures of flowers were quite stunning and it was while talking to her that she invited Marcos and I back to her house for a drink after the exhibition.

Father and Molli had decided to travel out together and stay for three weeks. It will always sadden me that not only was this to be their last visit, but that the atmosphere in the house was anything but pleasant. I couldn't explain to either father or Molli what Marcos was putting us through because I had no right to worry them at their age. So with a tense atmosphere, I struggled on pretending that everything was quite normal. The children and I waved goodbye to them at the end of April.

The May fair was nearly upon us and Paloma was getting so excited about wearing her gypsy dress again. One afternoon, a few days before the fair, Paloma was disobedient or unpunctual. Anyway, whatever it was, it would have been sufficient punishment to have sent her to her room for a while. However, Marcos just went berserk and ordered her to go upstairs and fetch her gypsy dress. As I walked into our bedroom, he stood there with a pair of scissors in his hand.

'Oh, no! Marcos, please, not that lovely dress,' I implored, hardly believing he would do such a thing. Paloma stood in the doorway clutching her dress with the tears rolling down her face. She hesitated, thinking her father was going to cut her hair off.

'Bring that dress here at once,' he shouted.

She clutched her dress, shaking all over. 'Please, papa, no,' she implored.

I stood motionless, not believing what I was about to see and said, 'Not her dress, Marcos.'

'You are going to obey Paloma,' he shouted. 'Watch me.'

Marcos cut through the beautiful dress, thoroughly enjoying every second of ripping the material up, until it was completely torn to bits and then threw it in Paloma's face. He then slammed the front door and drove off.

From then on, the persecutions were endless.

One Saturday I went shopping early in the morning before the heat got too intense. Having loaded the car with the week's supply from the supermarket, I then went to the butchers and several other places, so it was about 10.00 a.m. when I got back to the house. I stood aghast at seeing Paloma tied to a tree in the garden by a chain which went around her body several times.

'What on earth is going on Paloma?' I enquired.
'Papa has punished me,' she replied.
At that moment Marcos walked out of the open front door and said, 'She's staying there and don't you dare interfere.'
I unloaded the car and wondered how on earth I could get her freed. While passing through to the kitchen I said, 'Paloma wants to go to the loo and can't wait any longer.'
Thank goodness. This did make him untie her.
One evening I was given a lecture on how the business wasn't doing at all well and it was time to curb the spending. Marcos always had two refrains which were continually being aired: 'It's time to tighten our belts' and 'the cow's milk has dried up!' The real truth of the matter was that the factory was doing extremely well but Marcos had decided to give me and the children as much suffering as possible because he himself was hiding a secret.
Undiscovered as yet, there were several even greater time-bomb shocks than the previous ones waiting to hit me much later on.
I neither had a joint bank account or credit card; only the housekeeping money which I had always had to do miracles with and stretch this way and that. But believing that things were financially bad, I did without things that I needed for myself and the children. After some months of this, I opened the door one evening to find Marcos standing there with so many boxes that he couldn't see over the top of them.
'Leave the door open, I'm going back to the car,' Marcos said. He walked in with five suits, which had been made

by the most expensive tailor in Jerez. Eight expensive silk shirts, underwear, hankies, silk ties, all appeared, and a Rolex wristwatch!

I really did have something to say. 'But you told me that financially things were going badly and that we couldn't spend any more money. Here you are with suits, shirts and a Rolex watch.'

I got no further. Marcos flew into a rage. 'This is my house, my money and I have worked for everything. You haven't done anything and you are getting out because you are the foreigner here and I am arranging an air ticket for you to go back to England tomorrow.' With that he slammed the door and left the house, returning in the early hours of the morning.

Next day at lunch time, Marcos returned with an air ticket and told me, 'Don't you dare be in this house when I return this evening. Be very careful you are not here.'

I was trying not to shake as I opened the oven door and put the macaroni dish on the table. Marcos sat down and helped himself to his lunch while ordering me to get a bottle of wine. I was just getting the cork screw out of the drawer when Marcos threw his plate of food on the floor shouting, 'You know I don't like hot food.' He drank half a bottle of wine and left the house. Everywhere I looked there was macaroni with tomato sauce splattered all over the walls and a plate smashed to smithereens.

By this time, I realised that the man I had once loved just terrified me and I was a mass of nerves. Every day brought yet another nightmare.

I rang Paloma's godfather who had his mother staying

with him and asked them over for tea. I explained that I was afraid at what Marcos might do when he found me still in the house. Christopher was horrified and, while having tea, Marcos appeared. He was politeness itself, oozing charm from every pore—perhaps no one could imagine what he put me through every day. By the time Christopher and his mother left, the children had arrived home from school, so I felt a little safer when they were with me. However, later in our bedroom, I got a torrent of abuse while being hit. Marcos then picked up a treasured ornament of mine and threw it across the room, missing my head by inches, and then left the house.

I was feeling unwell due to low blood pressure and a lack of appetite. The continual worry of what Marcos would do next was taking its toll on my health. I remember getting my night-dress on, walking towards my bed and collapsing. The next thing I knew was finding myself lying on the stone floor with Marcos shaking me and calling my name. I was deathly cold for I had been lying unconscious for over three hours. Marcos helped me into bed and brought me a hot water bottle. I remember him getting more blankets because my body temperature was very low. Eventually, I must have drifted off to sleep and awoke in the morning as weak as a kitten.

I shall always remember how sweet and concerned the children were. They came in and put their arms around me as I lay there in deep depression. I didn't want to go on. I'd given all that was humanly possible and now felt quite indifferent to everything. I never wanted to get out of bed again and didn't want to eat. The morning went by and

Paloma, obviously understanding that mama was far from well, went and made an omelette all by herself. She came into the bedroom with Carlos behind her looking very worried. 'You must eat, mama,' said Paloma and proceeded to sit on the bed and fork little bits into my mouth.

Several days went by and I just lay in bed. Marcos eventually decided he ought to take me to a doctor he knew in Jerez. He helped me into some clothes and sat me in the car. The appointment with this particular doctor was a complete waste of time. I sat in a chair not uttering a single word while Marcos held forth with a long monologue about how hard he worked to give me and the children everything. How he travelled all the way back for lunch to be with me! How he had made so many sacrifices and ended by saying, 'So I really can't imagine what on earth is the matter with her.'

It was as if I hadn't been there at all, because the doctor was chatting about other things over my head and the conversation went backwards and forwards. Eventually, the doctor prescribed some injections and a tonic and told Marcos that he should take me with him for a break next time he went on one of his business trips.

In actual fact, the factory was closing for two weeks and Marcos had arranged to go to a place near Madrid for a shooting competition. I suggested that this would be ideal for me to relax at the hotel and have a rest.

'Besides,' I said, 'it will also give your parents a chance to enjoy their grandchildren.' There was no response so I left it at that and waited. Two days before he was due to leave, he flew into a rage, got out of bed, dressed, slammed his already packed suitcase shut and left the house at 11.00 p.m.

Returning from school one afternoon, the children knocked on the front door and I was horrified to see Paloma shaking all over. She clutched me and, crying hysterically, said 'Ring the clinic mama, quick, ring the clinic'. What had happened before school lunch was that Paloma's best friend, Maria, had stayed behind in one of the classrooms on the third floor. Maria suddenly decided to climb out of the classroom window and walk about on a glass roof. Suddenly, without warning, the roof gave way and Maria fell to the entrance hall below. The crash brought many of the girls out of the dining room, including Paloma. A teacher quickly covered Maria's head so that the girls couldn't see the state she was in, and an ambulance was called.

I put the receiver down slowly. Paloma was screaming, 'Tell me how Maria is'.

I put my arms around my daughter, so thankful that it hadn't been her and quietly said, 'Maria has died and gone to heaven.'

It took a few seconds to register for Paloma had thought that Maria was still alive. She screamed in agonising pain and hysterically sobbed. I held her close to me, stroking her forehead, but nothing could comfort her. She was in a highly nervous state and I gave her a sleeping pill. For a long time, Paloma sat on my lap and cried. Eventually, exhaustion took over. I helped her to bed and, with her little face red and swollen, she said, 'Mama, promise me

that you will take me to Maria's funeral.'
'Of course, Paloma, and we will take a bunch of flowers for her, darling,' I replied.
To this day, I have never understood how the school staff could have sent Paloma home on the school bus. The two little girls had been great friends and had always done everything together. I still cringe when I think that it could have been Paloma on that roof with Maria.

Chapter 29

I noticed that for some time now, Flicker would hide underneath my bed and growl if I attempted to remove her. She had become extremely nervous of late and I was puzzled by her unusual behaviour, especially as she was so devoted to me and the children. The answer came, rather unexpectedly, some time later and it was quite sickening. One morning Carlos arrived back at the house with two boys that he had met. They stayed and had some lemonade and as they were about to leave their mother appeared. Camilla was English, married to an American and it was lovely to have someone to talk to. A few days later, Camilla came to have tea with me and then invited me back to her house. It was very convenient, because I could walk along the beach up through the pine trees to Las Redes where she lived. Eventually Camilla and her husband made a date for Marcos and I to go to dinner at their house. Marcos appeared at mid-day complaining of a headache and wanted his lunch outside in the garden. Having eaten, he went into the bedroom to lie down. I followed him in and said, 'I think I'll take Flicker for a walk.'

Marcos replied that he wanted to go to sleep and on no account was he to be disturbed. It was a lovely warm afternoon, although nearing the end of October, and I took Flicker down to the beach. She loved to watch the seagulls strutting about on the shore and would stand quite motionless with a front paw suspended in the air marking them. Then, when she thought the seagulls hadn't seen her, she would move like lightning towards them. The birds would fly out and land on the water, while Flicker swam frantically out towards them. The seagulls would bob up and down cackling at her and she would have to give up her chase and return to my side.

Having walked to Las Redes, I decided to pop in and see Camilla. She was delighted to see me and, after giving me a cup of coffee, drove me back to Vista Hermosa. To our surprise we passed Marcos in his car driving at great speed in the opposite direction. On seeing us we heard the screeching of brakes and he overtook us arriving back at the house ahead of us. I said goodbye to Camilla and walked into the sitting room where Marcos was standing.

'How dare you go and see Camilla. You are meant to be looking after me,' he shouted, and disappeared out of the house.

The following day was Saturday and we had been invited to Camilla's house for dinner. Marcos got up in the morning without speaking at all and drove off. That evening I went, as arranged, for dinner and as I arrived Camilla's husband was standing in the driveway.

'Your husband is no longer welcome in this house,' said Eric. Apparently, Marcos was so annoyed that I had gone to see Camilla the day before that he had driven straight to her house. He had not only been extremely rude, but had threatened her!

Marcos came back later that same evening and went straight to bed, totally ignoring me. He hadn't spoken a word since Friday afternoon. On Sunday he stayed out all day and that evening I asked Marcos to reimburse my

housekeeping money. The gas man had repaired the water-heater and had returned three times with the bill.
'I need the money to go shopping tomorrow,' I added.
Marcos took no notice whatsoever but went over to his gun cupboard and unlocked it. He slowly removed one of his guns, opened the barrel and calmly put two cartridges inside. Swinging round, he pointed the gun at me and started to walk across the room. I froze where I stood and knew better than to provoke him.
'If you ever dare have Camilla or her children here again, I'll shoot them,' he threatened. 'You are absolutely forbidden to see Camilla again, because if you do, there will be a tragedy here,' he warned, as he prodded me in the stomach with his gun. He then put it back in the gun cupboard.
In the morning I asked Marcos again for some money for food. He took no notice, got dressed, had breakfast and on the way out of the house snatched my car keys off the table.
I rang Carolina and asked her if she would kindly drive me into town and lend me some money. That afternoon Marcos arrived with one of the factory workers in his car. The man got out and was ordered to drive my car away.
During the next few days, Marcos threatened all of us, telling our children that if Flicker barked, he would cut her stomach open with a knife. Paloma and Carlos were terrified and ran to find me, grabbing me around the waist, while I tried to calm them down. For five days, being without transport, I couldn't move from the house and it was at this point that I decided it was time to find a

solicitor.
I phoned and arranged for a hired car to be delivered, having got a friend to finance it for me. I rang the British Vice-Consul in Jerez and she gave me the name of a solicitor in Sevilla. Next morning I drove to Sevilla, saw the solicitor and at full throttle drove back again. Marcos had gone to the factory and on getting no reply to his phone call had returned back to our house. To my horror, he was standing in the main road as I was about to park some distance from our home. He glared at me and got into his car and drove off. I got on with cooking lunch and Marcos didn't appear, so I had something to eat myself. At 4.30 p.m. Marcos arrived and I asked him if he wanted any lunch.
'Yes,' he replied. The meal was left uneaten and meanwhile Marcos helped himself to some wine. 'And how are you getting down to Puerto?' asked Marcos slowly.
'I've had to hire a car,' I replied. I will never forget what I am about to relate; it stays vividly in my mind, because I was simply petrified.
I was standing in the middle of the kitchen, when Marcos appeared in the doorway. He opened a drawer and took out a carving knife. Holding it straight in front of him, he came towards me. I backed until I hit the kitchen sink and could go no further and before the knife touched me, I slid down onto the floor. There was now no escape, so I stayed there with my head bent down and my hands around my body waiting. I could see Marcos's feet a few inches from me and then they started to retreat. I looked up and saw him brandishing the knife. He had gone quite

berserk, pulling the fridge plug out of its socket and cutting it off! He did the same to the dishwasher, iron, washing machine and kitchen mixer. He tried to pull the telephone off the wall, but then decided just to unhook the receiver and leave it dangling. Turning around to face me, he bawled, 'You are the foreigner and you have to obey Spanish law. Whether you hate me or not, I am your husband and you have to obey. Don't you dare use the machines or telephone.' With that he departed in his car. On my visit to Sevilla that November morning of 1977, my solicitor had given me the name and address of a local solicitor. This, he explained, was a gentleman who would deal with the paper work and formal visits to see the Judge in Puerto. I picked up the dangling telephone and rang Sevilla. My solicitor said he would immediately ring the Puerto solicitor and get him to ring me at once. A few minutes later, the phone rang and, thinking it to be my return call, I picked the receiver up. It was Marcos testing from the Club. I heard Marcos's car roaring back and the screeching brakes and ran out through the kitchen yard to my next door neighbour. In a state of terror, I banged on their door. A young American couple with a baby had rented the house next to us and had only moved in a few weeks before. The husband opened the door and I stumbled inside. I couldn't speak a single word, only gibberish. They could see I was suffering from severe shock and helped me to the sofa. I sat and trembled uttering words, trying to explain, unable to form a sentence. The noise and banging that was coming from our home was terrifying to listen to. We could clearly hear everything, despite the fact that the houses were all detached. Marcos, on not finding me, had started to rip open all the wardrobe doors in the house. Then he started on the built-in cupboards, hurling things out of them, running from room to room. We then heard him almost taking the hinges off the long heavy wooden shutters as he pulled them sideways to see if I was hiding behind them. In the end, he gave up and we heard his car roar off at full speed. By this time, I had managed to get myself coherent and asked Mr. Deane to drive me down to Puerto. I lay on the floor in the back of the car, for fear that Marcos might be lurking about and see me. Mr. Deane left me outside the solicitor's office. Once I had been ushered into the solicitor's office, where he was sitting behind a large desk, I just went to pieces. I collapsed on the floor on my knees, unable to control the flood of tears and again totally unable to speak. Every time I attempted to form a sentence nothing came forth, except stuttering, and my whole body shook uncontrollably!

The solicitor spoke kindly and said, 'Don't worry, take your time and just sit on the floor, until you feel you can get up and explain.'

Having eventually regained control, I sat in a chair and told him what had been happening. I was given a written letter for the Judge and told to go and see him at once. I went to the local court and was sent back to my house in a taxi with one of the staff holding a writ. The Judge was giving Marcos twenty-four hours to leave the family home and, if failing to obey, would put him in prison. Although the children normally used the school bus, Marcos had gone to fetch them from their schools. I was always at home when they arrived back, so on not seeing me, they kept questioning their father. While Marcos read the contents of the writ, Paloma and Carlos shouted, 'Mama, mama,' and put their arms around me. The evening was extremely peaceful, with not another word from Marcos and the children chattering away to me in the kitchen, while I prepared their tea.

Paloma and I slept together in her single bed and Carlos had Flicker. I had taken the precaution of putting a heavy pot, strategically placed, along with two chairs by the door. If Marcos attempted to come up the stairs during the night, it would all have fallen down and given us warning. The children had heard and seen many things, so were well aware that for me to sleep upstairs, I must be very afraid. Showing great bravery, Carlos appeared in Paloma's bedroom and announced, 'Don't worry, mama. If papa comes up the stairs, I'll hit him with this' Carlos stood there with a fishing rod in one hand and a net in the other! Meanwhile, Marcos had locked himself in our bedroom and by dawn I heard him depart. He had forced my chest of drawers open and gone through all my personal things. He had taken my reading glasses, a key to The Broken House, personal correspondence, my grandmother's pearl and diamond ring, plus all the documents regarding the house and land we owned. I contacted my solicitor in Sevilla to inform him about the last twenty-four hours. He told me that he was proceeding with a legal separation through the Roman Catholic Church. He told me that I must find witnesses and that these people would have to

go to Sevilla and make a statement, independently, under oath.
By the evening, I felt completely drained, so after an early supper with the children, I went upstairs to rest on Paloma's bed. We all had our night clothes on and Paloma was busy doing homework in her room and Carlos was in the sitting room sorting out a fishing rod. Suddenly, there was a knock at the door and, before I could stop Carlos, he had opened the door to his uncle. I put on my dressing gown and stood at the top of the stairs.
'I want to speak to you,' he said threateningly.
'Look, Alberto, I don't want to talk about it now. Perhaps tomorrow,' I replied.
'You get down those stairs now or I'll come up,' he shouted angrily.
'Alright,' I said, 'I'll just get some slippers on.'
As I stood in Paloma's room, giving myself time to calm down, I heard Alberto's voice, 'Leave the door open Carlos. I'm going to the car for another packet of cigarettes.'
I ran down the stairs and locked the front door and put the security chain on. Alberto shouted, 'Open this door.'
I said, 'Alberto, it's not the right time to talk with the children here and, besides, we are all tired.'
Alberto banged and thumped the door and shouted, 'Open this door immediately or I'll bang it down.'
Paloma and Carlos were by now by my side and pleading with their uncle to go away. Alberto continued thumping the door. 'You are going to listen to me and I am coming in,' he shouted. He started putting all his weight against

the door and charging at it. I never thought that he would actually have the whole door down, but as I watched I could see that he was going to continue until the door gave way. We had to get out because God knows what he was capable of doing once inside the house!

Flicker, bless her, was standing nearby and keeping guard over us. As the door came crashing in, Alberto was about to step over it but Flicker bared her teeth, snarling, and stood her ground. I had already warned the children that the moment I ran out through the kitchen yard they were to follow.

'Get that dog out of my way, or I'll kill it,' Alberto was shouting, but we had fled. Flicker instinctively knew we were in danger and stood, hackles raised, growling viciously to give us time to escape. We fled, terrified, in our dressing gowns, and I could hear Flicker running after us. Being November, most of the houses were unoccupied and it was isolated. I saw lights in one of the houses at the end of the road and aimed for it. I banged on the door and nearly passed out. When the front door opened, I was half carried and laid on the sofa and remember thanking God that the house belonged to a doctor and his wife. Paloma and Carlos were taken off to the kitchen and given a drink.

The doctor went to call the police and meanwhile I was given a pill to calm me down. My heart was pounding and I felt sick with fear. In actual fact the doctor and his wife had some friends over from Sevilla and were just going to start having dinner when I banged on the door. They were all shocked at this horrendous attack and savage

behaviour. A police officer arrived and walked into the doctor's sitting room.
'If the Señora would like to make a statement,' he announced. My head was spinning. I felt so weak, completely drained of colour.
The doctor quickly answered, 'The Señora isn't in any condition to answer questions at the moment. She will go to the police station and make an official report in the morning.'
The police officer then said to the doctor, 'He's still standing in the house and says he's not going.'
'Well he's got to go,' said the doctor, 'or be physically taken away.'
The doctor went off with the police officer to go and sort Alberto out. He was eventually driven away. We were all helped back to our house and the front door propped up against the entrance. I was so exhausted that I was past caring whether we had a door or not and we all settled to sleep upstairs.

Chapter 30

Next morning, I went to make a full statement and had the door put in its place again with a new lock. With all these happenings, from both brothers, I was scared out of my wits as to what they would do next. Added to this was the fact that because the workers were not happy with the way things were at the factory, they had sent more than one written threat to Marcos. I was terrified that someone might decide to target our children. I decided to go and see the Head Warden and, as news travels fast, he had already been informed about the recent happenings. Something told me that there would be further incidents and that neither Marcos, nor his brother, were going to consider the children in any way. The Head Warden was wonderful and reassured me that at any time, day or night, he would come at once to the house and bring other guards as well.

'We're very vulnerable and it's isolated,' I said. 'I know we will be attacked again at night.'

'Señora, even if it's two or three in the morning, just ring my home number. I'll put a pair of trousers on top of my pyjamas and come.' I sighed with relief. At least there was someone I could rely on for help.

Because Marcos had no intention of maintaining our children, my first concern was to obtain money for food so, after getting Paloma and Carlos off to school, I put on a pair of jeans and grabbed a sponge and bucket. I walked up the driveways of the rented houses where the Americans had two or more cars parked. Having collected enough money from washing cars to feed the children, I proceeded back to the house. At the weekend, Paloma offered to lend a hand and she, too, came to help me. Meanwhile, Marcos was refusing to pay maintenance and in fact refused to pay anything. It was getting cold and I would hardly eat anything at all, keeping the little money I earned to feed the children. For many months, I would curl up in bed at night with my knees tucked almost underneath my chin, with nagging hunger pains. The hunger and fear kept me wide awake every night and the memory is so vivid that I shall never forget what real hunger feels like. I was drained of any colour; the pain, the financial worry and my desperate daily fight, trying to survive with my children, cannot be described. It was immense. I was completely alone, in a foreign country, with no family. I was not allowed to take my children to Britain and under no circumstances would I leave them. They were my life and I had brought them into this world and I adored them from the moment they were born and, for this reason alone, I had to carry on.

It was an appalling evening. The thunder was rolling, the forked lightning was illuminating the whole house. Sheets of driving rain had made a monsoon outside and visibility was almost zero. Suddenly, there was a knock at the door and Ramon and Margarita called out, 'Clare, we've come to see you.'

I opened the door and there they stood with some bottles of wine and packets of cigarettes. I couldn't imagine anyone turning out on a winter's night in the pitch dark and negotiating the diabolical weather to come and visit me, fifteen miles away. Ramon and Margarita sat and listened to all I had to say. They were the only people who really wanted to hear my side of the story, for they also knew, from experience, how badly Marcos had treated me. It must have been 3.30 a.m. when they eventually got up to leave. Ramon placed some money on the table and said, 'We want you to accept this money because we know Marcos isn't paying anything.' To this day I thank them for their great kindness and will never forget what they did that night. They were the only people who came to see if I and the children were alright.

I went to see Carolina and asked her if she would make a statement and go to Sevilla. 'I certainly will', she said, because I saw Paloma tied up the garden.' She paused a second and continued, 'I happened to be walking down a path near your house, when I heard the most ghastly yelping from a dog. That made me walk in your direction and I stood on the corner and saw Marcos kicking your dog in the stomach with such brutal force, again and again. So you see my dear, I know how cruel he is, not to mention leaving you with no transport and no money.'

Rosa, also, was only too pleased to testify and mentioned that she had seen Adela from Sevilla at her grandparents' house in Benamahoma and she had had a baby with her.

That evening, when the children were in bed, I sat for a long time thinking about what I had been told. Suddenly it dawned on me that the baby must be Marcos's and blackmail was taking place. I rang Alicia and she warned me that Adela was still ringing the factory and talking to Marcos. Alicia was convinced from what she had heard

that blackmail was taking place.
About a week later, Rosa rang to tell me that the villagers had confirmed that Adela had had a baby. She had been sent away to Tarragona to have it delivered and had not stayed in her home town of Sevilla. This was the final stab in the back!
Some English people arrived at Vista Hermosa and rented out various houses. They had come to work at a local casino. I got talking to a couple one morning and they asked me about a baby-sitter for their children and of other families. Every Saturday evening they would bring the children for me to look after. This, plus a few English lessons and washing cars, brought in money. Every day was a worry, but we scraped through.
By January, I decided that life wasn't much fun for the children with their mother looking so strained. I managed to save enough money to take Paloma and Carlos to the cinema in Cadiz and then to pop in and see Julian and Rosa. Off we set one Saturday evening and the children thoroughly enjoyed the film. Paloma and Carlos were playing happily with Julian and Rosa's children and I was having a drink in their sitting room. The front door bell rang and Rosa came back and said, 'It's Marcos and I haven't said you are here but have put him in another room.'
'Thanks,' I said. 'We'll leave,' and with that we ran down eleven flights of stairs to the car. As we drew up to our house, we saw both garden gates wide open and Flicker outside on the lawn with no collar on. I opened the front door to find that the wooden shutters had been forced

open and Marcos had used his key to unlock the veranda doors which were wide open. The only thing missing was a painting which Marcos knew I particularly liked.
The children had, in their innocence, told their father some days previously that mama was taking them to the cinema and then on to see Rosa. Marcos, having broken into our house, had then driven to Cadiz and appeared at the flat so that he had an alibi. I was terrified to think that Marcos could unlock the veranda doors and walk in at any time. So the children and I discussed what we would do and we came up with the idea of securing the outside wooden shutters with a bicycle chain and padlock. This would stop Marcos from unlocking the veranda doors.
The house all locked up with Paloma and Carlos fast asleep, I sat for many hours in the dark in the sitting room with Flicker. I felt a sense of danger and uneasiness and knew I had to keep alert.
At 2.00 a.m. Flicker gave a soft growl and I put my hand over her nose as I heard Marcos and Alberto outside the wooden shutters. Marcos was bending down and flicking a cigarette lighter on and off. 'Blast, there's a padlock and chain, so we can't get in,' I heard Marcos say. I heard their footsteps fade away and a car engine start up as they drove off. Little could I have imagined that the two brothers had earlier been tampering with my car, putting my life at risk. It wasn't until the following morning that I discovered a hole had been made through the hedge in the garden. For some time the penny didn't drop and then it dawned on me why Flicker's collar was missing. Marcos was endeavouring to make out that Flicker had run away and,

as the dog was registered in his name, to take her away from me. I reckon that Flicker had growled because she had been so brutally kicked by Marcos in the past. He had obviously planned to entice her through the hedge another day. I went and got the vet to write out a new certificate in my name as owner of the dog and got her registered in the appropriate place in the town hall. On my return from doing some shopping, the car started to heat up and, as I got a few yards from the house, smoke started to seep out from underneath the bonnet. I rang Pizca to ask her if she knew of a reliable mechanic that wouldn't cost too much and that could come out to look at the car.

That afternoon the mechanic arrived and, after inspecting the car, told me that I was lucky to be alive! It had had the electrical wires altered and had I driven a few more yards it would have caught fire and exploded! Pizca and her husband were simply horrified that I had been put in such danger. The mechanic decided that as the car had been tampered with he needed to have a good look at it. So the following morning it was towed away.

At 1.00 a.m. Flicker gave a soft growl and immediately I shot bolt upright in bed. I grabbed her and whispered to be quiet. In total darkness, I crept barefoot across the sitting room towards the kitchen. Marcos was climbing over the yard wall, immediately beside the kitchen window. I was so terrified that I couldn't stop shaking and my heart was thumping. I crawled on my tummy and lay flat on the floor just by the kitchen door and slowly put a hand up to the phone. I had memorised the Head Warden's home number and done the exercise over and

over again in the dark in case of an emergency. Thank goodness I had. I dialled and the Head Warden said, 'Yes?' I whispered, 'It's Clare, come quick!'
I crawled on my stomach away from the kitchen and through the corridor to the sitting room. I stood underneath the staircase and was horrified to see Marcos's face appear at one of the little windows at the top. He had got up on the roof and had flicked his cigarette lighter on and was holding his hand up high, illuminating his face. He was knocking on the window and calling Paloma. She appeared still half asleep and on seeing this face lit up at the window was very frightened.
'It's me, papa,' said Marcos. 'Go and open the front door Paloma.' As she stood at the top of the stairs, I appeared and put my finger to my mouth and beckoned her down. She was followed by Carlos. We stood and listened. Lights had suddenly gone on and the house was lit up outside and I could hear voices. The guards were all there and the Head Warden had turned his car lights, full-beam, on Marcos on top of the roof.
I stood motionless in front of the door with Paloma on one side, holding my hand, and Carlos on the other.
'Ah! Warden, I'm so glad to see you,' started off Marcos. 'You see, I've come to fetch my children to take them with me because their mother has abandoned them and gone off and left them alone in the house. Paloma, unlock the door and open it,' commanded Marcos. Paloma looked at me and I shook my head.
Marcos started off again. 'You see my daughter is frightened, because their mother has gone out and left the

children by themselves,' he explained to the Head Warden.
'Open the door, Paloma,' said Marcos again.
I opened the door and there the three of us stood holding hands. Marcos opened his mouth and found he couldn't utter a word. The Head Warden stood there with five guards and said, 'Leave immediately and leave this lady in peace.'
Marcos spluttered, 'But the car's not there. Where is it?'
But the guards were marching behind him as he beat an undignified retreat down the road to his car.

Chapter 31

About a week later, I decided to go and see an English lady who had her own school about a mile away. Having made an appointment I told her of my predicament and that I desperately needed a job.

'Well, I can give you temporary work because one of the English girls who was due to start this term hasn't arrived from England.' So I taught English to a class of Spanish children aged about five years and looked after a large group of two- to three-year-olds in the afternoons. I would then rush back home just as Paloma and Carlos were arriving at the front door.

One night, shortly after the incident with Marcos, the Head Warden and the guards, I did something in desperation that I would never do again. I lit a candle and placed pieces of paper with the letters of the alphabet on the dining room table. I was so upset about my grandmother's ring that I was determined to ask her for help. Amazingly enough, granny came through very quickly and I could feel her presence, for there was a distinct scratching noise from underneath the top of the table and Flicker's hackles were raised. Animals have amazing sixth sense and Flicker certainly knew that we had a spiritual visitor present.

I asked her a few questions and granny moved the glass quickly. I then said, 'Will you get your ring back from Marcos?'

'Yes,' came the answer and I knew, without a doubt, that she would. Granny had a message for me and the glass

relayed the following:
'Go to country house.'
I asked, 'When?'
She replied, 'Tomorrow.' The glass then spelt out vases and she was gone. I sat for a long time trying to make some kind of sense out of this message and decided that I was most certainly being warned about something to do with The Broken House.
Paloma went to school the next morning and Carlos was feeling rather tired so I decided we would set off for the mountains. We arrived and unlocked the heavy wooden door and I started searching through vases in the sitting room and upstairs. Nothing came to light so it was a complete mystery. However, I decided to gather together all my personal things and anything else that I could sell to give us that badly needed money. Carlos and I had been piling things together for about half an hour when there was a knock at the front door. There stood the old boy who, in the past, had taught me to skin rabbits and had brought us mountain honey. The mist had gathered and Pepe stood in the half-light of the doorway.
'Come to fetch your things, Señora?' he said.
'Yes,' I replied.
He chuckled, continuing, 'Take as much as you can because Marcos has ordered several lorries to arrive tomorrow and empty the house.'
We filled the car to bursting point and Carlos thought it was great fun sitting on top of sleeping bags and disappearing into them every time I turned a sharp corner on the mountain road.

About a week later, there was a message from Marcos. He was coming to take the children for a weekend to his new flat in Jerez. On their return on Sunday evening Paloma and Carlos dashed in saying, 'Mama, mama, we have something for you.' They rummaged through their overnight bag and produced two brass bowls which had belonged to my grandmother. They had sat alongside a beautiful clock on her mantelpiece in her Highgate flat for as long as I could remember.

'We knew these were your granny's and they don't belong to papa,' explained Paloma.

Carlos nodded. 'The bowls were in papa's flat on the hall table so we took them on our way out.'

I now knew what granny had meant! She was referring to these brass bowls and had called them vases which had been sitting slightly hidden on the mantelpiece of the chimney breast in The Broken House. In my haste, I had missed them; but the powers above have ways and means, unknown to us, of putting things right and granny hadn't finished yet!

Five days later, my solicitor rang and said, 'I have a surprise for you. In my possession I have your diamond ring and reading glasses.' I went to fetch them and asked my solicitor how on earth he had got the ring back, for I had had no way of proving that Marcos had stolen the ring in the first place. He looked me straight in the face and said, 'Don't ask me, because I'll never tell you.'

To this day it has been a mystery. The ring had obviously been given away or sold by Marcos because the cream velvet inside the leather ring box was marked with make-up. That evening I got through to granny again because she spelt out her name and I knew she was with me. I simply thanked her for returning what was rightfully mine. She stayed a few seconds, gave no messages and was gone. Meanwhile, visits to the Judge in Puerto for maintenance, both by my solicitor and myself, were not being heeded. Nor was the Judge doing anything to implement justice either. Marcos continued to make life extremely difficult and had no thoughts about the welfare of our children. In fact, he did everything possible to do the opposite. Marcos had taken to appearing at Paloma's school and sitting in the dining room while the girls were having their lunch. According to Paloma, he would make a scene, drawing attention to himself and embarrassing Paloma in front of all her school friends. On more than one occasion Marcos would wait until the school bus was full and then shout at the driver. 'If you think I'm paying for my daughter to go on the school bus, I'm not.' He would then order Paloma off the bus and shout, 'Your mother can come and fetch you.'

The next incident was none other than to actually confront the Headmistress and tell her that he refused to pay any more school fees. Marcos then drove off a couple of yards to Carlos's school and did the same thing there. It was at this point that I received official letters from both schools explaining that neither Paloma or Carlos would be allowed to attend school anymore. I was worried sick and went to talk to Pizca who had her four daughters at the same school. On hearing what I had to say she said, 'Come on Clare, get in my car and I'm going to sort it out.'

By the time we had arrived at the school entrance hall I had tears streaming down my face. How could a father stop his children's studies, their careers, their future?
Pizca was amazing. She marched in and gently told me to sit on one of the benches in the hall.
'I'm going to see the Headmistress and sort this out,' she said, and with that strode into the Headmistress's office.
Soon I was following Pizca into Carlos's school and as we entered she hailed the school priest.
'Ah, father, I'd like a word with you.' We were ushered into a room and Pizca gave an extremely good lecture on Christians helping one another and the Catholic Church teachings. By the time she had finished she had sorted both my children's education out.
Marcos was also trying to have the electricity and water cut off. He did get the phone disconnected. He also tried to stop the refuse collection and one afternoon stole the reclining chairs from the garden.
I went for an interview, along with fifteen other people, for a job as Secretary/Receptionist at the American Naval Base in their legal office. We had an examination in English and a test for typing speed and accuracy. I hadn't done much typing for over twelve years, but I was determined to get the job, because we desperately needed money to survive. To my great relief, I was accepted. I'd never used a word processor before and within five days I had mastered it. In times of sheer necessity it is unbelievable the strength, determination and survival techniques you learn.
Returning one afternoon from work, I greeted the

children and we went into the house. Flicker was nowhere to be seen and I went into my bedroom. I couldn't believe what I saw! Bedspread, top sheet and blankets were heaped in a bundle at the end of the bed draping on the floor. On investigating further, I discovered the bottom sheet in strips where Flicker had clawed into it. I rushed out and shouted to the children.

'Is Flicker upstairs?'

'No,' shouted the children.

I then saw two cushions missing from the sofa. I dashed into the spare room near the kitchen and there, crouched inside the built-in wardrobe, was Flicker. The poor dog was having a false pregnancy and had prepared a home for the litter. She had pulled a blanket inside along with two cushions and other articles of clothing. Instead of the usual waggy tail, she looked at me with beady eyes and gave a low growl. I'd read about false pregnancies in bitches and knew better than to touch her. She wasn't herself at all and best left alone. I warned the children to completely ignore her and not to attempt to even stroke her. At night she would go and eat her food, when we had all gone to bed. By morning she was inside her wardrobe again.

After a few days, Flicker came to find me in the middle of the night. Her teats were heavy with milk and she was obviously uncomfortable. From then on, every night I would have to extract some of her milk to ease her discomfort. Eventually, she returned to her usual normal self. It was at this point I vowed never to have another bitch.

Despite all the hardships, we were managing and having sent the children off for their school bus, I would drive in the opposite direction to the naval base. Soon Marcos heard that I had got a secretarial job and he went berserk! He came round one evening and drove my car away. The Judge had stated in a written 'sentence' that as there were two cars, I was to keep one, and Marcos the other. Besides, we were miles from anywhere and I couldn't get out of the residential area. Official statements were sent to the Judge by my solicitor asking for justice to be implemented. But my car never came back. Lucy's husband worked on the base and he kindly gave me a lift into work. But it was very difficult because sometimes there were days when he didn't go to work or had to stay on late. This was making everything even more tiring and a problem for me to cope with. Finally, I had to quit my job to enable me to look after my children during the summer holidays. After only three months, I gave in my notice.
During the long hot summer, I set up a blackboard in the garden and gave English lessons to Spanish children. The word soon got around and I was inundated with parents begging me to take just one more child. I divided them into groups: beginners, intermediate and advanced. Organising the house at the crack of dawn, I would have breakfast with Paloma and Carlos and then settle down in the garden to commence lessons. This would continue until the heat got too unbearable, around noon. It was then time to dedicate the afternoon to my children and after lunch we would go off to the beach. When the heat

had subsided, I would start the classes again while Paloma and Carlos would play with their friends.
Winter, once more upon us, the families disappeared leaving their summer houses and returning to Madrid, Barcelona and other parts of Spain. This meant that there were not enough children left for me to maintain a living. Added to the strain and worry was a letter which arrived from father to say that he had been taken ill. He was now in a nursing home, having sold his house. I was beside myself, ripped apart, worried sick between him and my children and without a telephone. I had no way of communicating in an emergency with my father or anybody else for that matter.
As it grew colder, Paloma and Carlos needed new clothes, books for school and above all we needed food. By this time a year had gone by since the Judge had ordered Marcos out of our house. Marcos had no intention of paying anything and was living it up, spending money as if there was no tomorrow. During the summer months, Marcos would appear carrying a shoulder bag with a young man by his side. They would sit all day by the club pool and swim in bathing trunks that went transparent when wet, covering themselves in oil and creams. Night clubs, discos, bars, parties, fairs, dancing and drinking were all on Marcos's evening agenda. During the course of an evening, he would give an open invitation to all around him to order drinks and he would pay out large sums of money.
One particular evening Marcos decided to show everyone in a bar that he had so much money he could afford to

burn it! He lit a note, worth a considerable sum of money, with his cigarette lighter and held it up for all to see. Meanwhile, I was desperately struggling through each day to buy the bare necessities for our children. Marcos's behaviour was despicable.

Eventually, the Judge tired of Marcos's scandals and total disobedience, put him in prison where he stayed over the Christmas period. Promising to make amends and maintain his family, the Judge let him free on the 31st December. In January 1979, Marcos had fled the country and gone off to the Philippines. He had got involved with a woman who was financially very well off. Between them they made a pact that if Marcos went abroad with her, he would receive an enormous amount of money on his return to Spain.

Chapter 32

Carlos had had to repeat a second year in the same class so, before the summer holidays started, the school staff asked me to go and see them. It was explained that as Carlos could not continue a further third year in the same class there was nothing more that they could do with his education. This is the way Spanish law works and it means that your child literally has his whole future jeopardised. I was completely beside myself with worry. What on earth was I going to do to save Carlos's continued studies? After getting over the initial shock, I decided to ring Cristina from a neighbour's phone. Perhaps she would know what I could do. Cristina suggested a boarding school called Campillos near Malaga. It was a school where life was tough and the boys were made to study. Campillos would take boys during the summer holidays and put them through everything they hadn't studied during the past year. 'Find out and let me know what happens if they will take him,' said Cristina.

I had a chat with one of the masters over the phone, asking the school to please take Carlos and get him through his exams to enable him to carry on with his studies. I was informed how much the initial cost would be and the date he had to attend. He was to arrive with a mattress and all his bedding as well. In a state of panic, I paced the floor for hours knowing that I couldn't raise the money, nor the transport to get him there. Carlos had to be in Campillos on Saturday and it was Monday night. On Tuesday I rang to tell Cristina the outcome and that

Carlos had to be there in four days' time. 'I don't even know how I'm going to get him there, let alone anything else,' I said.
'Don't worry anymore, my brother will give you some money and pay for a taxi to take you and Carlos to Campillos,' said Cristina. I have never been so thankful for such tremendous generosity. It was truly appreciated and will always stay in my memory as a wonderful act of kindness.
Off we set with Carlos's mattress and all the paraphernalia for Campillos. I had typed out a letter explaining my son's emotional upheaval; the situation at his school and to take this all into consideration. I also left a contact phone number in case of an emergency. The boys that studied during the week were allowed to go home on the school coach for the weekend. Those boys who failed their weekly test, through lack of studying, stayed at school. Most of them got on with their studies!
Meanwhile, I had to think of something to bring in the money to pay for Campillos and keep us all afloat. The situation was now so critical for us I had to do the only thing left for me to do. That meant selling the furniture. A few yards down from our house there was a family from Sevilla and they spent occasional weekends at Vista Hermosa. On hearing of my tremendous financial struggle, the wife offered her kind support in anything that would help me out. She arranged for a person with a van to come one evening and give me a lump sum of money for receiving things that we could live without.
People rallied round to help and someone put a notice up

on the board at the American Naval Base, advertising a sale of furniture and a baby grand piano. There was nothing I could do but put on a brave face and watch people remove pictures, mirrors, treasured ornaments and furniture. It was completely devastating, but I didn't cry, for deep down I knew that having been put in this horrific situation, my children came first above all else. Most certainly, above anything material.

A box of silver cutlery had to go and that had been a present from my parents and a whole breakfast, lunch and dinner service. An elderly American turned up who collected spinets and other musical instruments and bought the baby grand piano. The house was left a bit sparse, to say the least, but I had a fair bit of money to keep us going which was far more important. Having got Carlos settled in his studies and coming home weekends, I felt that I had to have a rest, because everything was physically and mentally wearing me down. I needed to see my father and find out how he really was. Besides, it had been three years since I had last seen him. One of the English families offered to have Paloma to stay and get her off to school in the mornings. Carlos bravely offered to stay one weekend at school and an American neighbour said she would take care of Flicker. I got myself an air ticket and went to spend five days at a bed and breakfast near father's nursing home in Brighton.

Father looked alright but was getting frail and just sat in a chair all day. His eyes filled with tears on my last day and I felt like a criminal leaving him there. It hurt me so much and here I was torn between father and my two children.

We were both so many thousands of miles apart across land and water.
On my return we had settled into some kind of routine and the English lessons were bringing in money and I had managed to save some from the furniture sale. It was the first time that the children and I had some kind of peace and tranquillity but it was to be short-lived.
At the end of June, Marcos appeared and all hell broke loose. He had been away for six months and was furious to see me coping. His father had once said, 'Leave her and she'll come dragging her feet and beg for help on her knees.' Marcos was now even more determined to do anything, that would leave me without a roof over my head and without my children. So he set forth on scheming the most horrific illegal situations he could muster. The moment Marcos set foot back in Spain my solicitor sent an official statement to the Judge asking for justice to be implemented.
The Judge totally ignored Marcos's refusal to obey his orders for maintenance of our two children and their schooling. Marcos's evil intentions knew no bounds and he set out to visit friends of his parents in Jerez to ask them to be witnesses against me for the Roman Catholic Court case. More than one couple he visited told him, in no uncertain terms, to leave their house immediately. Finding no one that was willing to accuse me of having been anything other than a devoted wife and mother, he schemed up a wicked plan.
He paid a sum of money to some men acquaintances for the act of being witnesses against me. The men in

question had never spoken to me; in fact knew nothing at all about our family life. When questioned individually, and asked by the Bishops and priests attending the court case to describe me as a person and what it was I was being accused of, none of them could answer. Instead, they described Marcos's character, his violent behaviour, the unconcerned way he treated his employees and his scandalous public life. The evidence had clearly shown that Marcos was not a good influence on his children. His bribe to procure innocence had failed. I was awarded full custody of both children by the Roman Catholic Church in a legal separation.

The Judge, however, neither put Marcos in prison again, nor did he do anything at all to see that we had some kind of financial security. Meanwhile, I was paying for Carlos's studies at Campillos. It was also extremely peculiar for a Judge to allow Marcos to have his children for half the summer holidays, when he wasn't obeying the Judge's orders. Nothing tied up at all. I went to see the Judge and my solicitor wrote asking for justice, but we were ignored. The next thing that happened was a letter stating that the family home belonged to one of the business societies and that I had to get out! This, in itself, was a mystery, both to my solicitor and myself, because when we had bought the house in Vista Hermosa, Marcos and I both signed the document with the owners present and therefore it belonged to us both. The flat which we owned by the sea was, at a later date, mysteriously sold without my signature and Marcos pocketed the money from the sale. The two plots of land bought during our marriage were sold off

too, without my signature. Meanwhile, Marcos boasted openly in Jerez to having blackmailed the Judge.
Paloma was spending the latter part of her holidays with her father, as ordered by the Judge, and Carlos would stay some weekends with Marcos, going straight from Campillos. I went to speak to the Judge and told him I had nowhere to go.
'You'll have to leave and go and rent a flat,' he said coldly.
To this day, nothing has ever been cleared and remains a total injustice of the greatest magnitude.
Pizca lent me her car to fetch Carlos from boarding school at the end of the summer course and we were both over the moon. He had really studied for the first time and had passed his exams, which meant he could now move up to the next year. I had a long discussion with his tutor and decided that whatever else happened, Carlos must stay at Campillos during the normal term time. I was not going to return him to his former school.
I'd missed him most terribly during the summer and did worry that it might be too tough at Campillos because, although he was fitter, he was very thin. At weekends, I used to send him back with things he liked to eat, or get another boy going on the coach to pass a parcel on to him. It was a frantic rush when the coach arrived late on a Friday evening, because all the dirty clothes and bed linen would appear with him and everything looked as if it had been cleaning the floors! It would all have to be washed, dried and ironed before Sunday mid-day when the coach would depart for Malaga.
When Carlos's half-term came, Marcos decided that he

wanted the children in Jerez. They were to be returned on the Monday evening. Carlos rang the front door bell as his father's car was disappearing down the road.
'Where's Paloma?' I asked.
'Papa has driven her to Campillos and put her in the girl's boarding school,' explained Carlos.
'What!' I exclaimed. 'He has no right at all and besides she's in the middle of a term.'
I stood in disbelief at the continual disruption and upheaval that Marcos inflicted on our children. 'She hasn't any clothes or anything with her,' I said.
We went straight to a neighbour's house and rang the school. I asked to speak to my daughter and was told I couldn't. I then asked to speak to the Headmaster. He was very abrupt and didn't believe I had legal custody of Paloma. He had had strict instructions from her father that under no circumstances was Paloma allowed out of the school without her father's written consent.
I put the phone down in total disbelief and, shaking all over, rang my solicitor and told him the scenario.
'What am I going to do? I'm worried sick about my daughter.'
'I want you to go down to see the Judge tomorrow morning. You will explain that Marcos has unlawfully removed your daughter to Malaga and put her into the Campillos girls' boarding school and that you want her returned,' explained my solicitor.
Next morning, Carlos and I went to see the Judge, He wrote a letter and handed it to me, saying, 'You are to go to the police headquarters of the Civil Guard in Campillos

and hand this letter to their Commanding Officer. He will escort you to the school.'

I went to see Pizca and asked her if I could borrow her car. 'Of course you can,' she replied. We set off for a four-hour drive after packing Carlos's things up to return to his school, and arrived in the evening. We were escorted to the school by the Commanding Officer. The Headmaster, on reading the Judge's letter, apologised profusely, saying that he had been totally convinced that Paloma's father had legal custody of our daughter. I was taken up to the dormitory where she was lying on her bed. 'Come on, we are going home,' I said as I gave her a big hug.

Carlos's half-term had come to an end, so we left him at his school and made our way back to Puerto. Paloma was in such a state of nerves, I gave her a pill so that she could get to sleep.

After this incident, Marcos did everything in his power to win Paloma over by letting her do and have anything she wanted.

Paloma would say, 'Papa, I'm not allowed to do this or that, mama wouldn't like it.'

'Now you're with me, you can do what I tell you to do,' Marcos would reply.

I knew that, due to her vulnerable age of thirteen, money was his most powerful weapon for bribing Paloma.

Marcos wasn't interested at all in the enormous importance of her teenage years and that she needed, above all else, her mother to prepare her for the years that lay ahead. The love and dedication I had given my little girl were to be lost forever. Paloma had radically changed

and wanted to stay with her father. There was nothing I could do. The Judge didn't want to hear anymore. Marcos went round Jerez saying that he had come to an arrangement with the Judge and it certainly became crystal clear why justice was never accomplished.
Pizca's husband was Portuguese and they had been discussing for some time the possibility of returning to live in Portugal again. It was around this time of events that they packed up and left. Pizca had been a very kind, sincere and loving friend. I was devastated by her departure.
Carlos continued at Campillos and I started to catch the ferry to Cadiz to find accommodation. Eventually, after a month and many hours hunting, I got an estate agent to show me a flat in the main avenue. I hadn't a clue how long the money I had managed to save would last, but all I could do was put my trust in God.
Having moved to Cadiz while the children were with their father, it had been legally arranged that Carlos was to return to me before he started again at Campillos. The day for his return arrived and went, without Carlos's appearance. I went down to the phone box and had Marcos shouting rudely, 'I'm not bringing Carlos back.'
Flicker was terrified of the town noises and the traffic. She would crouch in corners, make messes and wasn't adapting to a flat at all. I would take her out in the warm evenings and walk along the sand. The beach would be illuminated by all the lights along the promenade and music could be heard from the only discotheque in town. We would spend hours just walking and it was the only

time she was happy. Walking for days searching for a job, frightened, desperately worried about my children and the constant battles with Marcos made me decide that it was time to end the torture.

So, one evening I sat half-dressed on my bed and picked up a bottle of sleeping pills. I started to swallow them. All I remember was Flicker sitting beside me and, without warning or any reason, she put a paw up and hit the bottle out of my hand. It was more than twenty-four hours later when I woke up to find myself spread-eagled across the bed, still dazed, feeling sick and a broken glass on the floor with pills scattered in every direction. A few days later, a letter arrived from my solicitor to say that Carlos was to be handed over at the Tribunal.

Flicker became more unsettled, shivering and shaking every time she heard a firecracker in the street. The noise from the constant roar of traffic, hooting horns and motorbikes simply terrified her. I knew that I didn't have the right to let her go on suffering in this way. Whilst out searching for a job, Flicker would scratch doors and make messes through sheer terror. She never really recovered from Marcos's cruelty and her nerves had become chronic. She also had a bad heart condition and I knew that it wasn't fair to have her constantly frightened. I set off very early one morning before fetching Carlos and went to the vet who had always looked after Flicker. He agreed that to gently put her to sleep was by far the most humane thing to do. I hugged her, burying my face in her fur, then wrenched myself away, standing in the dust and heat with the tears streaming down my face. At least Flicker wouldn't have to suffer anymore and she would always have a very special place in my heart because she had saved my life. The vet appeared from his surgery holding her collar and lead.

'She's gone to sleep very peacefully.' I was totally distraught, arriving at the Tribunal with my face red and swollen. I hugged Carlos, knowing that I had to go on for his sake and, after all the legalities, we left for Cadiz.

Shortly after all these happenings, a job came up giving evening classes at the British Academy. This was in the centre of the old town and a good two miles away from the flat. The pay was minimal but it was better than nothing. Armed with heavy books, I walked every evening to the Academy and would stand by a blackboard in a huge classroom. There were about thirty pupils, ranging from young students to business men, but they were a nice group of people to teach. The British Academy was an enormous old building with a maze of doors and a wide marble staircase that went up three or four flights. It also had high ceilings and balconies everywhere. I would finish work at 10.30 p.m. and have to lock up, being the only teacher left in the building. I didn't like the idea at all, but was lucky enough to find that several pupils would wait for me. I would have to go through the building, checking lights, etc. and then turn the heavy key in the massive wooden outside doors. We would then all walk down to the bus stop together.

Some weeks later, the couple who ran the Academy told me about a temporary job that they had heard about. I dashed off next morning to present myself in a shipping office. The gentleman in question was Norwegian, working for Det Norske Veritas as a senior surveyor. His personal secretary had suddenly been taken ill and had been rushed into hospital for an operation. He was looking for a substitute for a month. So, until 3.00 p.m. I was doing secretarial work, and in the evenings I taught at the Academy.

In times of desperation and needing help, I have tried to put my faith in God, and always found that someone has come to my rescue. I paced up and down the flat, wondering how on earth I was to work and look after Carlos during his holidays. I didn't know a soul and had no one to turn to for help. I must have paced up and down for over an hour-and-a-half, praying hard for an answer, when the front door bell rang. I'd been living in the flat for nearly three months and had never met any of the neighbours. I opened the door to a lady who lived on the second floor and she asked me if she could have a word with me.

Once seated, she said, 'We have all lived here as residents for many years and all know each other. I must confess that not knowing who you were I did enquire through some friends of mine in Jerez about you. I was given a glowing report.' She paused and smiled. 'I was also given a detailed description of your ex-husband's goings-on and know how difficult everything is for you.' She told me that she had a son of Carlos's age and suggested that at the weekend Carlos could go up to their flat. The boys struck up a friendship and would spend hours together building model ships and planes. Jorge's mother was delighted and

after meeting Carlos she offered to have him for lunch and supper every day. She just took him under her wing and literally adopted him while I was at work.
Jorge's mother will never be forgotten because she appeared when I was at my lowest ebb and was a real neighbour. Without her help I haven't the slightest idea what I would have done. May God bless her always.
Marcos had stopped our basic medical assistance due to discharging himself from his work as unfit to continue! He didn't care about the children at all and knew that Carlos had to have a check-up every so many months with the Cadiz doctor. Not only was he not the least bit worried about his son's health but he flatly refused to pay Carlos's school fees either. It was, in short, a living nightmare, living off bread, margarine and cups of milk. I couldn't pay Carlos's schooling and the flat rent, so my solicitor kept writing statements asking the Judge in Puerto to implement Marcos's obligation to pay maintenance. Marcos told the Judge he had no money, but in actual fact he had made a pact with his brother to be paid a considerable sum of money on a monthly basis from the factory profits. Marcos not only had money to buy a luxury flat, drive an expensive car and live a lavish lifestyle, but also spend a considerable amount of money on a private detective. The detective was to observe and follow me about wherever I went. This all took place, unbeknown to me, at the time of Carlos's half-term holidays. It must have cost Marcos a fortune and the detective had nothing out of the ordinary to relate. It must have annoyed Marcos to see the written report of my

movements, stating that on various occasions, I had come out of the block of flats with my son, laughing and talking together, on our way to either the beach or the cinema.
When Carlos went back to Campillos, I would write and arrange to meet him as usual at the bus stop. The school coach would stop in Jerez and then carry on to Cadiz every Friday evening. I'd wait ages for the coach to arrive and eagerly look for him as all the boys tumbled down the steps to their waiting mothers. Unbeknown to me, Marcos would have met the coach in Jerez and ordered Carlos off it.
'I'm going on to stay with mama this weekend,' he would say. 'No, you're not, you're staying with me,' Marcos would reply.
I would stand at the bus stop until the last boy had gone and, after an outburst of abuse from Marcos over the phone, return to my lonely flat, with the tears choking me.

Chapter 33

Some months later while still working in the Academy, one of the pupils told me about a company that was about to arrive in Cadiz and would be working on a project for sixteen months. I rang the phone number that I had been given and was put through to the Resident Engineer leading the team. He was a Scotsman working for Chevron Oil Company and became my boss. I was employed through a well known Spanish construction company called Dragados y Construcciones as a bilingual secretary to Jonathan. The salary was more than I could have dreamed of but I couldn't take the job without transport to enable me to get to work. It was a good twenty-five minutes' drive to the construction site and we had to do four journeys a day. Having signed the work contract I could now go and wave it in front of the car hire purchase office. Eventually, all cut and dried, I bought the cheapest car available, a Citroën 2CV.

Carlos was due back from Campillos for the holidays and I was so pleased. He had expressly told his father that he wanted mother to fetch him, so I set out feeling that at last some of the weight was lifting off my shoulders and we were going to be alright. I arrived at Campillos and went with my son to fetch his bedding and was about to empty a bedside locker when Carlos said, 'Be careful, mama, I didn't know where to put a tortoise I found, so he's living in there!' I opened the locker door and there, resting on top of a pile of clothes which had been rammed into the locker, was an enormous tortoise.

I shall never forget our long journey home that end of term. Carlos had got through all his exams and was so pleased about the car which he named 'Chitty Chitty Bang Bang'. We chatted and laughed as we exchanged conversation and stopped several times to pour water over the tortoise, afraid it might dehydrate!

We had a few days' peace then Marcos wanted to have Carlos for the weekend. Brother and sister had been separated and obviously wanted to be together, so I didn't argue. When Carlos returned, he told me that his father had told him and his sister to sign some papers. They hadn't been allowed to read the contents of what they had been told to sign and Marcos has taken the children with him to see the Judge. On many occasions Carlos had always said, 'I'll never leave you mama. I want to stay with you forever.'

I missed Paloma very much but at least I had Carlos and things were a little easier. We would go upstairs to the flat, grab a sandwich and fruit and then take something for tea on the beach. We only had to cross the main avenue and walk a few yards. After a swim we would sit on the sand and later eat our picnic. We got a routine going and I loved Carlos's company. It reminded me of the past when we had spent so much time together at Vista Hermosa walking along the sandy beach. Our days together were to be short-lived and the bomb shell came some ten days later.

The front door bell rang and there stood Marcos with Paloma. 'Get your things together Carlos, you are coming with me,' said Marcos without even giving him a kiss.

'I don't want to go,' said Carlos.
'I have an official order from the Judge to take you for the summer holidays and you are coming with me,' Marcos replied.
'I want to stay with mama,' cried Carlos.
Marcos got hold of him round the back of his neck and started to push him out as my son and I tried to hug each other.
To this day the expression on his face haunts me as he was forcibly dragged away crying. There was nothing I could do for the Judge had given Marcos the right to have the children during the holidays. Little did I know, at this stage, that Marcos was never going to return my children. Continual statements, over many months, were written by my solicitor; visits were made to see the Judge but he did nothing, yet I had full custody for their upbringing and education. Marcos knew that what he had managed to achieve was a terrible injustice and that it would bring immensely harmful consequences for Paloma's and Carlos's welfare. Marcos wasn't interested and didn't care about our children needing their mother to love them, guide them and care for them. Meanwhile, Marcos boasted openly in Jerez to having blackmailed the Judge. Marcos had tried everything, determined to see me go under. He'd worked out his underhand scheme skilfully by lies, deceit and money. He'd left me with nothing financially, no transport, no phone, no house and no children. But there was one more thing that Marcos was determined to embark upon. It was not only to take my children away from me physically, but to destroy their love for their

mother. It was several years later before I found out what he had done to my children. It was evil at its worst and to this day I have never forgiven him.
I'd put up with twelve years, day in, day out, of physical and mental hell, because I adored my children and wouldn't leave them. The question that has never been answered is: Had dirty money passed hands to allow a corrupt father to blatantly disobey the Judge's orders, the Roman Catholic Court and all that represented justice? Everything seemed to suggest that it had.

Chapter 34

The position at the office was a responsible one with a heavy workload. There was little time to stare out of windows or go off into my miserable world. So during my hours of work I switched off from all the personal problems and concentrated entirely on performing my duties to the best of my ability.

Jonathan liked perfection but he was a kind and considerate boss with a sense of humour. On hearing that my father was in a nursing home, Jonathan gave me permission to ring now and again to speak to him. It was an extremely considerate and kind gesture and I was truly grateful.

We were allocated three prefabricated open-plan offices on site for all the staff working on the project. In one of these offices were men from Lloyd's Register of Shipping as part of the team. The mail was always put on my desk for sorting out to the different departments. On one particular morning, I picked up a large envelope and collapsed with laughter, along with my office colleagues. Some unfortunate Spanish firm had never heard of Lloyds, or someone hadn't paid attention to the correct spelling. Typed on the front of the envelope were the words—'Lloyd's Register of Shitting!'

When I rang Marcos to arrange a time to fetch the children to take them out for a meal, I would be told umpteen times that I couldn't. Invariably there would be some excuse whilst bawling down the phone at me. On one of my visits, desperate to see my children, a woman opened the front door and, on seeing me, slammed it in my face. Marcos would constantly be shouting, 'Don't open the front door. Your mother can wait at the kitchen door.'

To my horror, I discovered that Marcos had removed Carlos from Campillos and put him in a local school. My son gave up trying from then on and ended up totally disinterested in his studies. Meanwhile Paloma had been expelled from her school! It wasn't difficult to see from their behaviour and all that they related that their father didn't bother about them at all. I was sick with worry. For years the solicitors and I battled for justice and nothing, absolutely nothing, was done at all. The Judge had an awful lot to answer for because he had been put in that high position for a reason—to see that justice was implemented.

In desperation I wrote to the Ministry of Justice in Madrid. They answered my letter by referring me back to the Judge in Puerto! I was getting nowhere and by now already had a duodenal ulcer. I had been seeing the wonderful doctor who had been treating Carlos. Doctor Gissard was a sympathetic man and had also met Marcos on our first visit to his consulting rooms with Carlos. He had sat listening to me and then asked some questions. I had no one to turn to and Doctor Gissard made me promise that if ever I felt on the border of taking my life again, I was to turn up at his house. 'No matter what hour of the night it is, I shall get up,' he said. 'Get to a phone box and call me any time, promise me,' he continued. I was so relieved to know that there was someone who cared about me. I was desperately lonely and ill with worry over my children.

One morning while at the office, I got an unexpected phone call from a lady who lived in Sevilla. I had first met her whilst living at Vista Hermosa because she had a house there which she lived in during the summer holidays. Victoria had two sons who used to play with Carlos. 'I'm coming over to Cadiz this coming Saturday and wondered whether you would like to join us for a meal out?' she said. 'I've been going out with someone and he is bringing a friend to make a foursome.'

We went out to a bar and had a drink and then to a restaurant for dinner. Later we drove to Victoria's house at Vista Hermosa to have coffee. As the evening progressed we disappeared into different bedrooms. Here I was, aged thirty-eight, blaming myself for having been rejected during my married life, believing I was sexually inadequate. Nobody can start to understand how I had suffered ever since my marriage at twenty-three. For fifteen years I had tormented myself on a daily basis. I was a failure and not a normal woman. I firmly believed that this was the reason, that during our twelve-year marriage, Marcos used to order me to my bed with the words, 'Leave me alone. It's all your fault.' It seemed quite ironic that I had conceived and delivered two children into this world yet still did not know what it was to have a normal sex life or to be treated with love and respect. It was quite a ridiculous situation and I had made my mind up that I had the right to stop the constant torment and doubts about myself. There was only one way to find out!

The gentleman I was with had gone into the bathroom and when he came out I was standing with my hands against the wall, simply terrified. I just couldn't move, as my mind raced back, hearing the words that Marcos had drummed into my head. The gentleman I was with took one look at the panic on my face and sat on the bed. He patted the bed beside him and gently said, 'We don't have to do anything, just sit and tell me what has happened.' I sat like a frightened child and explained for the first time the absolute hell I had been put through. He gently held my hand as the tears poured down my face. We arranged to meet again and by the end of that particular night I knew that the long years of suffering, thinking I was inadequate, had ended at last.

But the mental torture over my children had no cure and Marcos was doing everything in his power to cut me off from them. I would phone to arrange to take them out for a meal and be told continually that it wasn't convenient. Meanwhile at the office, as the weeks progressed, the project was producing an endless mountain of paper work. Jonathan asked me one morning if I knew of someone he could employ to do photocopying etc. I had been in contact with Rosa on several occasions and visited the family at their flat. One of Rosa's daughters needed a job, so I was able to return Rosa and Julian's kindness to me. She was a nice girl and spoke very good English.

It was while working for Chevron that I got in touch with Greta. She was delighted to hear from me. 'Come and stay, it would be lovely to see you again.'

On several occasions, either for a weekend or a few days'

holiday, I would catch the train to the Atocha Station in Madrid, where Greta would meet me. Atocha connects destinations to and from the South of Spain.

On one of my visits, I went by coach to spend the day in Toledo. It is a beautiful city and well worth the visit. On another occasion Greta and I were invited to a dinner in Segovia. We stayed the night there and went sightseeing the next day. The Roman granite aquaduct is breathtaking with 118 arches and a height of ninety-five feet (twenty-nine metres).

Chapter 35

On 23rd February 1981 at 6.20 p.m. armed Civil Guards, under the command of Lt. Col. Antonio Tejero, burst into the Spanish Parliament known as Cortes. Members were in the process of registering their votes and all were taken hostage. In full view of the television cameras, Tejero mounted the podium, pointing a pistol at the President of the Chamber. He ordered the deputies to lie flat on the floor, and then fired volleys of shots into the ceiling sending shattering glass down from the chandeliers.
At the same time, General Milans del Bosch, military commander of Valencia, declared an effective state of emergency in Valencia and sent tanks to patrol the streets there.
By mid-evening, consultations were in progress opposite Cortes, in the Palace Hotel between:

> The Director-General of the Civil Guards, General José, Aramburu Topete
>
> The Chief of the National Police, General José Sáenz de Santamaria Tinturé
>
> The Civil Governor of Madrid, Sr. Don Mariano Nicolas Garcia on how to persuade Tejero to surrender without causing bloodshed.

At 1.15 a.m. on 24th February, King Juan Carlos appeared on television and addressed the country. As a consequence of the King's speech, General Milans del Bosch immediately called the tanks off the streets in Valencia. Meanwhile, those members of government who had been taken ill were allowed out of Cortes and later the women members were released. It wasn't until 12.50 p.m. that Lt. Col. Tejero formally surrendered to General Aramburu. A communiqué from Chiefs of Staff then announced that the coup d'état was over.

While all this was going on I immediately dug out my passport in case I suddenly needed to drive down to Gibraltar with Paloma and Carlos in a hurry!

One morning I answered the phone and Paloma was crying hysterically. She told me that her father had punished her and was making her sleep every night outside in the kitchen yard on the ground. He had pulled her hair out in handfuls and cut her long hair off in chunks with a pair of scissors.

'Calm yourself, darling,' I said. 'I can assure you that mama will come and do something about this when I finish work.'

Paloma didn't know her father was listening on the supplementary phone and had crept up behind her. The next thing I knew there was a scream and I heard the receiver being replaced.

How I managed to concentrate on my job I shall never know. I was shocked, worried and terrified, but never said a word in the office. After work, I drove back to my flat, had a shower, got changed and, without stopping to eat anything, drove to Puerto de Santa Maria. I went straight to the National Police and, after making a statement, asked them to please accompany me to the house. I needed them to witness my daughter sleeping on the concrete outside. They refused, saying that I should go and see the Judge in the morning. I roared off to Vista Hermosa and, on arrival, called Paloma from over the high wall. She answered me and I was just about to say something when the front door opened. There stood Marcos with a gun in his hand.

'I'm warning you to go away at once,' he shouted menacingly. 'It's nothing to do with you and Paloma is going to continue to sleep in the yard.' I was beside myself with worry about my children, but whatever I did, I was cornered.

Next morning, I didn't go to work on the pretext that I was ill, but set off very early for Puerto again. I drove up the school driveway, hiding my car behind some trees and waited. As Paloma approached, I hardly recognised her. Her face was red and swollen from crying and her hair had been chopped off in chunks. There were bald patches on her head where her father had lifted her off the ground. I gave her a hug and gently guided her towards the car. 'We are going to see the Judge,' I said. Paloma was terrified about her father finding out.

The Judge in Puerto was away on holiday and there was a Magistrate in his office. He told me to pack my daughter's clothes and take her back to Cadiz with me. This we did and in the afternoon we went to find a hairdresser. Luckily, it was Friday, so we spent a quiet weekend and went to the beach. Sunday afternoon there was a knock at the door. There stood three of Paloma's friends and she wanted to go out with them. Little could I imagine that these friends had been threatened by Marcos and been told to fetch Paloma back to him. That evening Marcos stood at my front door with Paloma and had come for her suitcase.

It became quite evident why Paloma wanted to continue with her father. He was letting her go out in the evenings, staying out late and didn't care about her welfare, her education or anything else. Paloma wanted her freedom and so, in her mind, it was worth going back with her father. She had changed so much and was so indifferent in her feelings towards me—it was breaking my heart.

* * *

The project came to its end and we had a farewell dinner at a restaurant in Puerto. Dragados promised to call me if another project came up. So the days started to drag by. The loneliness was indescribable with not even a television and my only vice was heavy smoking.

Shortly after the termination of the project I was in the Piano Club one evening when the head barman said, 'I have a message for you from a gentleman called Sr. Calve. He understands that you are looking for another job and has left his business card here.' It took me quite by surprise and the head barman was handing me a card whilst he continued to say, 'Sr. Calve didn't know how to contact you.'

'Thank you very much for the message,' I replied.

Next morning I rang Sr. Calve's office and was asked by him if I would be interested in taking a job as his PA Secretary. His company had constant dealings in the

English language and there would be travelling involved. A time was arranged for an interview and on that day I was ushered into Sr. Calve's office. 'I don't speak English and therefore need a bilingual secretary to deal with the public relations side. My company deals in various different businesses but mainly in the consignment of fish. I need someone down in Algeciras in three days' time.' Having explained further, Sr. Calve offered me the job and I accepted. I left the office thinking that this was the turning point in my life and that things could only get better.

On the morning I started my new employment, I arrived promptly at the office at 9.00 a.m. and, after being given instructions, transferred my luggage into the company car and drove off to the hotel in Algeciras. The fish depot was about seven miles away and I found two men and a young woman working in a small office. They were all very pleasant and made me welcome. Here, I was to do my paper work and also stop at random any of the incoming lorries choosing six fishes from their cargo to be weighed. I also had to drive down to the Port and see the Captain on board to find out how the unloading was getting on and any other problems that needed sorting out. The Captain spoke no Spanish at all, so anything that had to be conveyed to those loading or to the transport drivers had to be translated. I had to keep a check on board of the three vast holds of fish and at what rate the lorries were being loaded.

I soon discovered that I had to keep the same pair of shoes on every day in the fish depot and once back in my

hotel room place them outside on the balcony! Having done this ritual I would jump into the bath for a shower and then dress for dinner.
My first evening I had only got one foot over the dining room threshold before the maître d'hôtel was scurrying towards me, bowing and saying, 'Good evening Señorita, I shall show you to your table.' Sr. Calve was well known and stayed at this hotel whenever he came down to the depot. I had been told to order anything I wanted and it was to be put on the bill. In the mornings I would have breakfast sent up early to my bedroom and then I could get straight on with the day's work ahead.
On the third evening, Sr. Calve arrived and we had dinner together in the dining room. He was staying two nights and then going back to Cadiz. He had an American couple, who were business clients, arriving at the hotel the next day and the following evening we would have dinner with them. After his departure my boss wanted me to find some nice restaurants in the surrounding areas and drive them out in the evenings for dinner.
By the time we had finished dinner and had a cup of coffee in the lounge bar it was 11.00 p.m. Sr. Calve said goodnight, explaining that he was going upstairs to make some phone calls. It had been a long day and I retired to my bedroom. I'd just cleaned my teeth when the phone buzzed into action on my bedside table. It was my boss on the line asking me to go to his room, bringing a notepad and pencil with me.
I rushed along and knocked on his door. 'Come in,' he said. 'I'm making some urgent phone calls abroad and

nobody speaks Spanish.' So I spent the next hour relating in English what Sr. Calve wanted me to say and vice-versa, while jotting down notes.
The American couple were middle-aged and very charming. It was my job to see that anything they required was fulfilled. I took them to meet the Captain and we all had coffee aboard. We visited some truly delightful restaurants, one of which was in a little village, where we walked through a patio filled with a profusion of flowers and plants leading into a cosy dining room. The place was lit by lanterns and a guitarist serenaded the customers.
After the American couple left the hotel, I continued with my work, sitting in the evenings listening to the pianist whilst having coffee. Some days later, on driving back to the depot from the port, I was told that my boss had arrived to have lunch with two gentlemen at the hotel and I was to join them. The meal was taken up in between mouthfuls conversing backwards and forwards translating. However, the afternoon was spent seeing a tuna factory which was interesting. Personally, I think that if we saw how food is processed before being put into tins, we might not be so keen to eat it!
The assignment had lasted just over two weeks and it was now time to pack up and return to Cadiz.
Next morning I arrived for work along with the rest of the staff. Sr. Calve had a few words with me in his office and said how pleased he was with the work I had done. One of the girls showed me to a cramped corner in the office. There was an old table and a pre-war manual typewriter stuck on the top! I opened the table drawer looking for a

ruler and came across a piece of long wood. The chair wasn't adjustable and far too low to reach the keys on the typewriter, resulting in excruciating finger and back pain. I soon gathered that most of the staff had been there a long time and thoroughly resented me arriving on the scene. Whilst they had been sitting scribbling away doing accounts and laborious work I had been staying in an hotel.

Later that afternoon, I had a whole lot of lengthy telexes to type out and on seeing the telex machine I gasped. It must have been the first machine ever invented and I hadn't a clue what to do with it! I went over to one of the girls and asked her if she would be so kind as to explain the rudiments of the blessed thing! She was very blasé and it was more than clear that she resented my presence in the office, as did the rest of the staff.

Having been used to a large modern table with room for in-trays, telephone, diary, table calendar, etc., with stationery at hand and a separate typing stand with a massive commercial electronic typewriter, I found this situation ridiculous.

The telex machine was temperamental and definitely had a mind of its own. Having started to type out a message, it would, without warning, chew up the perforated tape and snap it off.

By the end of the fourth day, I'd had enough and not one of the office staff had spoken a word to me. I went to Sr. Calve's office and told him I was extremely sorry but I could not continue to work under these conditions and

gave in my notice.
There was nothing left now to motivate my days and when I did go and see Paloma, she always told me that Carlos didn't want to come with us. He had grown so distant and unless there was a birthday or Christmas present involved, there was no way of getting him out. Paloma felt and behaved as if it was an obligation to spend time with her mother and there was a complete lack of love for me. Being unable to cope anymore, I resigned myself to lying in bed for days with deep depression. Jorge's mother, having not seen me, rang the front door bell one afternoon, and was very concerned about how weak I had become. 'You can't stay here alone,' she said. 'Haven't you got anyone you can stay with?'
'No,' I replied. 'Well, I'll have to call someone. Surely you know a friend in Jerez?' she asked. I gave her Cristina's phone number. Cristina turned up that evening and brought another lady with her who lived right opposite Marcos's block of flats in Jerez.
'We've come to take you away from here,' said Cristina. 'Magdalena has offered to have you in her flat until you are stronger and able to find another job.'
They gathered some clothes together and we left. Some weeks later, I went back to fetch all my possessions and return the flat key to the estate agents. Magdalena was divorced and was going through a bad time herself, so we sat up into the small hours, smoking heavily and talking non-stop.

Chapter 36

As Magdalena had no transport she told me to park my car in the space provided for her use in the underground car park. Three weeks later I was invited to Sunday lunch at Cristina's mother's house. I stood in disbelief as I came out of the lift to fetch my car. The canvas roof was buckled up in the air and all four tyres had been punctured. On investigating further, I discovered the plug leads had been ripped out. The oil cap was off and silver paint had been poured into the sump. I immediately recognised the paint as being that used in Marcos's and Alberto's factory. In Spain you are obliged by law to keep car documents in your car at all times and these had been taken.

I rang Cristina to explain that I was unable to get to lunch. Cristina said, 'We will come and fetch you and after lunch we will go and make a statement at the police station.' All the family were present at lunch and were horrified on hearing what Marcos and Alberto had done to my car. The police came and took fingerprints but nothing more was ever done about it. Justice just didn't exist in Spain.

Marcos's flat was opposite Magdalena's but Paloma and Carlos didn't want to see me. There was nothing I could do but lay awake at night and cry my heart out. It was to be at least another six months later before I discovered what Marcos was doing to my children.

I'd been staying with Magdalena for about ten weeks when I received a message from Dragados to report back on site in Cadiz. The Esso team had arrived from London for the

Odin project. Once again, I took on the job of PA bilingual secretary and moved back to Cadiz to another rented apartment. My boss was American and very pleasant to work for, so I settled down and got on with the job. The project got underway and I had an assistant to do all the photocopying and filing. Some days, whilst sitting at my desk in the office, I felt I was watching a Norman Wisdom film.

The assigned assistant was one of those unfortunate men who, whatever he proposed to do in the course of his duties, would always have a mishap. The photocopier and fax machine were situated in an office adjacent to the main entrance door. It meant walking the whole length of the office and then back to his desk. You could guarantee that nine times out of ten, the assistant would either trip over a waste paper basket, trip over the leg of a chair or trip over his own feet, usually with a pile of papers in his hands. While trying to save himself from landing on the floor, he would grab at a filing cabinet, making it sway precariously or he would clutch onto a swivel chair and send that spinning around. During this performance, all the original papers would be mixed up with the photocopies scattered all over the floor. Sometimes, at this point, whilst the assistant would be retrieving papers from all directions in a most undignified posture, we would have a visitor to see the boss.

On one particularly hectic morning, I had spent a considerable amount of time sorting out papers and had placed them all in individual piles on a big table ready for filing. On my return from the WC, I found my assistant

leaping about with his arms in the air retrieving papers which were flying around the office. He had decided to do nothing better than switch on the electric fan!
All the correspondence that passed backwards and forwards with Dragados had to be in the English language. One particular letter was so hilarious that it had everyone collapsing with laughter. It read:

Dear Sir

We are enclosing to you our CCR 001 valoration and the Back-up wich justifies it. Please return the CCR 001 duly accepted, for its posterior invoice.

Very truly yours ....

Now that I was back in the flow of office work I would ring Marcos to arrange to see my children at the weekends. On numerous occasions he would give me a time on a Saturday or Sunday to visit. I would arrive at the flat to find that the children weren't there. He would isolate them from me and when I phoned it would either be Marcos or his woman friend who, after a burst of shouting and abusive language, would slam the receiver down.
Eventually, one evening, I did manage to arrange to see my children. When I arrived and rang the bell, Paloma appeared and said, 'Carlos doesn't want to come with us.'
'While we sat having a meal, I asked Paloma what was happening.'
'Carlos just doesn't want to see you anymore,' said Paloma.

'But why?' I asked.
'I don't know,' replied Paloma.
When we got back to her father's flat, I told Paloma to fetch her brother. Carlos stood in the doorway and said, 'I wish you weren't my mother. I wish you were dead.'
I ran for the lift and the shock made my knees give way, as I sat, crouched in a corner of the lift floor, hysterically crying my heart out. The children had been poisoned against me.
Blinded with tears, I stumbled out of the building and back to my car. The anguish and pain in my chest was excruciating. I drove back twenty-nine miles in the dark at top speed and couldn't see the road. It would have been a blessing to have had a fatal accident and put an end to my agonising suffering. Entering the long Cadiz avenue, I drove through every traffic light in red. I was past caring what happened.
I could not face the loneliness in my apartment, so I walked about aimlessly in the dark, not knowing in what direction I was heading. I was in such a stupor and state of shock that I wandered about for two hours. Returning to the flat I pulled drawers out searching for some sleeping pills. I sat on the bed with the top off the bottle and then remembered that there was one person who cared what happened to me. I grabbed my handbag and ran out of the flat, down in the lift and ran, without looking, straight across the wide avenue with cars coming in both directions. Inside the telephone box, I fumbled about frantically to see Dr. Gissard's phone number on a piece of paper in my bag. Shaking all over, I dialled and

hysterically said, 'I want to end my life. There's no point in going on.'
The doctor said, 'Now listen to me, you are going to get into a taxi and come to my house immediately. I shall be waiting for you at the front door.'
'Yes,' I said weakly and put the receiver down. It was 1.30 a.m. as the taxi drew up and Dr. Gissard was standing waiting for me. He put an arm around my shoulders and steered me into his sitting room where he seated me on the sofa. A large tumbler of strong whisky was handed to me and I talked endlessly. Around 3.30 a.m. the doctor and I walked along the seafront, until we reached my apartment.
'Now, are you sure you are alright?' asked Dr. Gissard.
'Yes, I'm sure.' I replied. I knew then that my life had to go on.
Shortly after this, my solicitor asked me if I would give my written consent for Paloma to spend a year at a school in Romney Marsh. I considered that it would be very beneficial for her. I rang and spoke to Marcos and asked him to let me see her before she left.
He refused to give me the date she was leaving for I wanted to see her off at the airport. I asked Marcos to let me say goodbye to Paloma and he said he would let me know. I had bought a few presents for her to take with her and waited for Marcos to ring me at the office. A week went by and then ten days, and eventually I phoned Marcos's flat. Paloma had already left for England. I went and cried uncontrollably in the office WC and, when I had regained control of myself, returned to my desk and

rattled through my typing non-stop, until it was time to go home.

The following weekend, I was wandering about in the old part of Cadiz doing some shopping. I had stopped to have a coffee and had seated myself at a small table in a corner cafe. It was quite by chance that I saw someone from Jerez who came over to talk to me. I was to understand at last the unforgivable damage that had been drummed into Paloma's and Carlos's brains. I sat in horror as I was told how people had seen and heard Marcos use his evil, wicked practice on my children whilst in his flat. Marcos would tell Paloma and Carlos to hate their mother whilst they were asleep!

The change that had taken place in my children's characters, their indifference towards me and their total lack of any kind of affection, now all made sense. The missing piece of the jigsaw had been found. This had been Marcos's ultimate goal. As a mother, it was tearing me apart—exactly what Marcos had set out to achieve.

Chapter 37

It was around this time that Eric entered my life. One evening, I had arranged to meet a friend at the new Piano Club. It was very pleasant inside with a nice bar and comfortable sofas and armchairs. On a higher floor level was a grand piano and customers could sit on stools around it.

'Have you met Eric?' the pianist asked me.

'No,' I replied.

'I'll introduce you. He comes in every evening.'

Half-an-hour later, an elderly gentleman in his seventies with snowy-white hair and moustache appeared. This apparently was Eric and he was to become a very dear friend. Eric had emigrated with his wife to Cadiz and shortly after their arrival he became a widower. His wife's untimely death had upset him so much that eventually he had a massive heart attack and the surgeons had had to fit a pace-maker. He never complained and was always immaculately dressed and had a lovely smile with a twinkle in his eyes. No matter what the situation, he was game to join in and had a tremendous sense of humour. There was never a lack of conversation and he was always genuinely interested in whatever was being said.

HMS Plymouth arrived in Cadiz port and both Eric and I received invitations to a cocktail party on board. During the course of the evening, it was mentioned by the Commander that he would very much like to take a trip around the surrounding countryside. So I offered to be his guide for the following day. I phoned Carlos and asked

him if he would like to join us. The Commander promised that on our return to the ship he would show Carlos around to see the engine rooms. I knew this would appeal to him because at heart he has always been a mechanic. So he agreed to come and we had the great honour of being piped on board the following evening.
February came round yet again and the Cadiz Carnival went into full swing, lasting its usual three days and three nights non-stop. It was during the course of Saturday evening, while dressed up as Red Riding Hood, that I was introduced to an Argentinean gentleman. It was also to be at the time of the Falklands War, not exactly the ideal situation for a relationship at such an awkward time!
We'd been going out together for three months when Guillermo announced that he wanted to go to Italy for a week's holiday.
'I have already bought the air tickets, booked the hotels, so there's nothing to pay,' said Guillermo.
It was far too good an opportunity to miss and I needed a break from the office. 'There's one condition about the Italian trip and that is that I want to go sightseeing every day,' explained Guillermo.
'That's fine,' I replied, not realising what I was letting myself in for. It was to be a gruelling itinerary.
Arriving late afternoon, we got ourselves to the hotel and, after a shower and something to eat, Guillermo got a map out and explained what we were going to see for the next three days in Rome.
Every day we were up at 6.00 a.m. and out of the hotel by 7.30 a.m. and if anyone can believe it, we kept going all

day, on our feet sightseeing, only stopping to eat a plate of pasta at mid-day, sitting outside in the street. Guillermo never seemed to be tired and at times we would literally run from one church or famous building to the next. The Vatican, Michaelangelo's ceiling in the Sistine Chapel, the Coliseum, the Forum, the Pizza Navona and the Trevi Fountain, to mention but a few. Nothing was missed out and we did see Rome in three days. It would be almost dark on returning to the hotel leaving time only to shower and collapse into bed.
It was while we were in Italy that Guillermo would buy Spanish and English newspapers every day. He frantically wanted to know how the war was progressing and would make me translate the English news whilst resting my poor feet! His remarks about the British were offensive and nasty and he didn't care about the fact that I was present at all. It was at this point that I decided our whirlwind affair would come to an abrupt end, once we returned to Spain.
On our fourth day we travelled by train to Florence and spent all day walking about visiting Duomo and its Piazza, Giotto's Campanile, Bargello and the Uffizi Gallery. It was so beautiful that I could now understand why so many generations of artists had travelled to this wonderful city to capture its enchantment on canvas.
Our fifth day was spent in Venice, being transported by Vaporetto steamboat on the Grand Canal to the famous San Marcos Square. We arrived in time for breakfast and then visited the Cathedral and Doges' palace.
Unfortunately, it was a cold, damp, foggy day and our ride

in a gondola was amongst smelly river water and floating rubbish. I found Venice very disappointing and sad because so many houses had been abandoned and it gave the impression of a ghost town.

On our sixth day we travelled by train to Pisa. Here, we visited the Cathedral, Baptistry and climbed to the top of the Leaning Tower, spending all day sightseeing. Leaving Florence early on our seventh day we travelled back to Rome for our flight to Madrid. Once inside Barajas airport I took off my shoes and walked about barefoot! My feet were swollen and they were covered in painful blisters.

I spent the next fortnight hobbling about the office and everyone kept saying how tired I looked. No wonder, I thought. Nobody would have believed me if I had told them how many hours I had walked each day. But despite the discomfort it had been an opportunity of a lifetime and well worth it.

Paloma returned from England at the end of May and it was wonderful to see her again after her year away. We would meet of an evening at the Hotel Jerez and catch up with our news.

One evening, Paloma said, 'Mama, we are moving to Vista Hermosa for the summer holidays and I am going to celebrate my birthday with a party in the garden. Would you come and help me prepare the food?'

'Yes, of course, I'd love to help you, but what about your father?' I asked.

'He has said you can come because he's in a good mood at the moment, due to not having seen me for a year,' explained Paloma, with a mischievous grin.

'Well, that's fine,' I replied. 'I shall look forward to being with you darling.'
On 19th June, I drove to Puerto de Santa Maria, through to Vista Hermosa to the house. I was really happy to be able to assist and had brought a basket of things for Paloma's party. The garden was full of youngsters and there were lots of motorbikes near the house. I parked round the corner, some yards from the house, and walked through the garden gate. Paloma came out and greeted me, saying, 'Mama, I'm so glad you have arrived. Will you help me make sandwiches?'
Before I could answer her, the front door opened and Marcos stood there with his face red with rage. In front of all the teenagers he bawled at me to get out. Paloma looked in amazement as Marcos started to advance towards me with his fist in the air ready to punch me in the face. I stepped back as Paloma screamed, 'Quick mama, run to your car.'
As I reached the garden gate, reeling from shock, four of the teenage boys blocked Marcos's exit, preventing him from following me. Paloma's friends would not have allowed Marcos to physically hurt me. Finding himself confronted with four youngsters, who would have enjoyed hitting him, he turned back to the house, which gave me time to get to the safety of my car and drive off.
In July, I decided that I must get back to England and see my parents. I hadn't taken all my holiday leave from work so, arranging a suitable time with my boss, I booked an air ticket.
Father looked well although frail and was overjoyed at

seeing me. He would sit in his room refusing to be taken downstairs to a communal lounge. This solitary confinement made me wonder how father kept so *compos mentis.* While I sat with him, making my life sound simply marvellous, I would go through all his clothes, sewing buttons on and mending. Before leaving I would buy him new pyjamas and anything else that needed replacing. The tears would roll down father's cheeks as I was leaving and I would always make sure that the Sister on duty knew that I was about to depart so that he wasn't left alone. Mother, having retired from nursing, was living in a rent-free cottage near Haslemere in Surrey. She wasn't really pleased to see me and spent her time making critical remarks about my hair, my clothes and picking arguments. Never, for one moment, did she stop to think about the money I had saved to buy an air ticket, nor was she interested in anything I had to say. At the end of five days, I felt it had all been such a waste of time, leaving me with a heavy heart and more depressed than when I had arrived. She'd never really wanted me as a daughter and, even in her old age, she hadn't mellowed.

Chapter 38

In Spain, being a Roman Catholic country, a Saint's day is celebrated even more than a birthday. As I had been unable to attend Paloma's birthday party, I decided to take her out in August for her Saint's Day. She wanted to go to the new Puerto Casino where they had a discotheque for the youngsters. Marcos agreed to her request on the condition that I drove her home by 11.30 p.m.

There was a steep descent to the casino and cars were parked on both sides of the road. I found a space and Paloma spent an enjoyable evening with her friends in the discotheque. Meanwhile, I pottered around the casino, played a few machines, had a drink and made several trips downstairs to keep a discreet eye on Paloma. She saw me on one occasion and dragged me onto the dance floor where we ended up in fits of laughter. Paloma can be great fun to be with and invariably in each other's company we have ended up giggling like a couple of school children.

At 11.00 p.m. we left arm in arm, making our way up the steep hill towards my car, while Paloma talked non-stop. Suddenly Paloma said, 'Look, there's papa's car.' Down the hill towards us came Marcos's blue Mercedes and he stopped parallel to my parked car. Marcos had got his head out of the window and said, 'Wait there, I'm taking Paloma home.' There was a parking space behind my car, so he deliberately reversed his Mercedes into my car and with his bumper scraped the whole length of my Citroën. The mudguard was badly dented and I stood in total disbelief. When, eventually, I could speak, I told him in no

uncertain terms what a real bastard etc. he was.
'Get in my car Paloma,' commanded Marcos. 'You're lucky it's not worse,' he continued and got into his Mercedes and drove off.
I struggled on with my job, the monotonous life and the constant torment over my children. The apartment was dark with no view at all and once the front door was closed it became a prison. Eventually, I came to the conclusion that perhaps I should return to Britain. My two teenage children never wanted to stay with me and the loneliness had become unbearable.
I wrote to papa to ask him if he could remember any of his past connections who might be able to put me up in London, as I was intending to return to England. He replied that his cousin Doris had a godson who lived with his family in Putney. Having sent a letter off to them, I waited for a reply and set in motion the exhausting manoeuvre of packing and planning the long journey ahead. There was one very important thing that I wanted to do before leaving and that was to drive to a little fishing village called Chipiona. Close to the beach called La Regla is a monastery and an adjoining chapel. High above the alter is the Virgin Mary carved in one solid piece of ebony wood. Her miracles are famous and people come to see her from all over Spain. Entering through a side door into the vestry, I climbed up the narrow steps. The walls are covered in a collection of crutches and irons. On reaching the top step, there is a tiny room with a massive glass cupboard which takes up one entire wall. It is filled with medals, locks of hair, small presents and letters thanking

'La Virgin de la Regla' for her miraculous power of healing those people or children who have been considered, in many cases, too ill or too disabled to be cured.
I knew a lady in her seventies from Madrid called Conchita who spent the summer months in her house in Vista Hermosa. One afternoon she told me her amazingly true story about 'La Virgin de la Regla' and the miracle that took place.
Conchita had had breast cancer in her twenties. She had three different consultations and each doctor had taken X-rays. All confirmed a large cancerous tumour. Conchita put her faith in the Virgin and travelled from Madrid to Chipiona. She prayed and asked to be cured, for she had two young sons to bring up alone. Her husband had been killed in the Spanish Civil War.
Some weeks later Conchita had to go back for more X-rays before the surgeons operated. The large tumour had disappeared completely! Medically, it was incomprehensible. Conchita returned to Chipiona to give her thanks and took with her a moulded plastic breast inside a transparent pouch. It hangs in the glass cupboard to this day.
The Virgin is adorned with a large velvet cloak which flows almost to the ground behind her. A small pew is situated there and many pray by lifting her cloak and putting it over their heads, so that they are in contact with La Virgin de la Regla. I knelt and sewed a piece of paper inside her velvet cloak. I prayed for a long time in the peace of this beautiful chapel, high above the altar. I'd come to ask the Virgin Mary to look after my children. My

message was:

I know you understand my suffering as a mother. Please guard my children from all evil. I ask that one day my children will know the real truth and the three of us will be reunited again in peace, with the love that only a mother has for her children. 31/10/82.

I knew that the hardest thing of all was meeting Paloma and Carlos at the Hotel Jerez for the last time before leaving Spain. Due to the amount of luggage, it was out of the question to travel by air, so this meant going by coach through to the North of Spain, crossing the border through France to Calais, then on to Dover and ending at Victoria Coach Station.

Marcos could not be trusted and having, myself, been at the receiving end so many times, I knew perfectly well that if he heard about my departure by coach he would have found some way of inconveniencing me further. He was quite capable of making a phone call and having all my luggage emptied and searched. So I decided I had no option but to keep quiet and say nothing at all.

I sat looking at my children and thinking that they were now individual teenagers. If only they knew of my deep hurt and torment which was just ripping me to pieces due to their indifference. I couldn't go on blaming myself and making myself ill with worry over them. I knew in my heart that I had always been there for them and could do no more than continue to love them as I had always done.

When the time came to say goodbye, I stood outside the hotel in the driveway and hugged them both tightly and told them to look after themselves. They walked off and I stood watching them, motionless, until they were out of sight. What would the future bring for the three of us? The coach was due to depart at 10.00 a.m. so I set off with a friend who was driving me down to Algeciras. I hardly spoke a word all the way and when we got there, I had to dash into an hotel. My head was thumping, my stomach was upset and the tears streamed down my face as I howled my heart out in the WC. Eventually, I got myself seated in the coach and, through a flood of tears, waved goodbye to my friend from the coach window. The journey took two days and one night to reach London.

Chapter 39

At Victoria coach station, I wondered what on earth to do. The luggage was unloaded and dumped on the ground amongst the coaches that were belching out exhaust fumes in every direction. After sitting for so many hours my back and legs were aching and very stiff. I was completely bewildered wondering, as I stood amongst my luggage, whether I had done the right thing in leaving Spain.

I eventually discovered that I had to hail a taxi outside the coach station. The taxi was piled to bursting point with everything except an obliging taxi driver. I arrived decidedly grubby and exhausted at Putney.

Neil and Ida were rather amazed at the endless assortment of suitcases, and an old school trunk trailing behind me. However, I was made welcome and for some weeks had to inconvenience them with my luggage adorning their hallway, due to the fact that most of it was too heavy to get up the stairs.

For three months I walked into every job agency in London and registered with them. Having fluent Spanish, I tried the international agency as well, but I was never chosen from the list of applicants for an interview. None of the employers wanted to give me a chance because apparently it was a crime to be forty-one years of age! I not only started to despair but got quite exhausted waiting for buses in the bitter cold and walking miles every day with blisters on my feet. The hustle and bustle of London was extremely difficult to cope with, being accustomed to

the easy-going way of life in a seaside town in Spain.
I had almost given up hope when a job came up as PA Secretary to one of the Project Managers in an office in Wimbledon. I was situated on the top floor with two other secretaries, April and Jennifer. They were very pleasant and we all got along well together and became good friends. The office building was a tall one and would get unbearably hot. My desk was in a reception area where there were no windows and this, coupled with fluorescent lighting and the heat from the photocopier, was intolerable. My skin would dehydrate and start to peel off. By the afternoon my legs and ankles had swelled up so that it became painful to move. Every day I had to walk two miles to catch my bus and then get to the office and repeat the process after work. I wasn't really settled, everything was strange, and it was just like being in a foreign country. Having lived all my life in small towns, surrounded by countryside and the sea, London was bewildering to say the least. In the end, I decided that I would have to try and get used to my surroundings and not sit in my bedroom every evening.
After making a few enquiries I joined a club where its members met at an hotel every Thursday evening for a social drink.
Since arriving back in England, I would travel by coach alternate weeks on a Sunday and go down to Brighton, spending the day with Daddy at the nursing home. He looked forward to my visits so much having nothing else to do all day but watch television.
I went and spent a weekend with mother too. She had told

me in the past that the lining was rotten on her sitting room curtains. I was able to tell her that I had brought back the lining material she wanted from Spain.
Shortly after arriving at Putney I was talking to Neil about my adoption. It turned out that he too had been adopted and had found his natural mother many years later. 'Start at St. Catherine's House,' said Neil. So I dedicated a whole day to an exhaustive search. St. Catherine's was not as I imagined it to be at all. I had the idea that it would be like a public library and that I could sit down at a table and browse through data at my leisure.
On entering the building I discovered heavy Buckram-bound volumes with vellum pages all in their respective years of date placed in large pigeon holes that almost reached the ceiling. The rooms were sectioned off and there was a complete hush, except for the turning of pages, as people were engrossed in finding the information they required. There are no chairs or seats and you have to stand whilst placing the volume on a long podium to support it.
I soon discovered how extremely exhausting and back breaking it was to pull awkward, large, heavy volumes out of shelves! I was eager to make headway and soon came across my birthdate. My natural mother's name, Eleanor Rose Emily Stapleton, had been written in but in the column where my father's name should have been, it was blank.
I started on the marriages from 1941 and more information came to light. In 1943 at the age of thirty-five my natural mother had married a Mr. Hunt. Back I rushed

to the births hoping to find a half-brother or sister. My mother had been aged thirty-three at my birth so I went through the years to forty and found that no other children had been born. I went and got a copy of her marriage certificate. By this time I had pulled down many volumes, turned pages endlessly and reached up to put them back again and was thoroughly exhausted.
Next day I went to Somerset House where the Wills are recorded. Starting again from 1941 I worked my way up through the years until I came upon my grandfather's death. This was getting exciting because I could now read his Will and also discovered that my natural mother had been the only daughter. He had died in 1963 at the Royal Hampshire County Hospital, Winchester, and a firm of solicitors in Hampshire had dealt with his Will.
One of the gentlemen from the social club, whom I had been out with several times, offered to drive me down to Whitchurch. We set off one Saturday morning to find the solicitors' office. A clerk there was able to give me my natural mother's last known address.
We wandered about this charming little village, visiting the local pub, the vicar and chatting to a few of the older inhabitants who possibly might have remembered my natural mother. No information came from all this and it was very disappointing. However, I did have an address so it was a start. I arranged to keep the solicitors informed as to my whereabouts, in case my natural mother should contact them.
Once back in London, I typed out a letter and sent a copy to each individual resident in the block of flats where my

natural mother had last lived. Some of the residents were fascinated by my research and very sympathetic, even ringing the office to say how sorry they were in not being able to help me.

My next course of action was to jump on a bus after work and go to 50 Bishop's Mansions in Fulham. Flat No. 50 had no one living in it and various residents who hadn't replied to my letter had no recollection of my natural mother. I came away feeling very down-hearted. It was as if she had never existed and I had come to a dead end.

Chapter 40

About two months into my job, I went out one lunch hour with April. We went and sat in a cafe and on our way back to the office decided to buy some sweets to help alleviate the boring afternoon ahead. Busy typing and munching away, I couldn't get a piece of humbug to dissolve. On taking it out of my mouth, I found, to my horror, a large piece of molar tooth. On further investigation, I discovered that I had half a tooth left and the filling was hanging out!

At one of the social evenings, I had met a gentleman who was associated with Mencap. We had somehow got onto the subject of dentists and he had mentioned that he went to an outstanding dentist in Golders Green. He had given me the dental surgeon's telephone number so I rang the surgery and was told to get there as soon as I could. Dashing across London on different underground trains, I managed to get to the dentist in time for him to do some emergency work. A second appointment was made for Saturday and every Saturday after that for a month. Several things needed to be put right and after X-rays had been taken Kenneth informed me that there was an impacted wisdom tooth.

'Oh, I know!' I said. 'It's been there for years.'

'Well, it must be taken out as soon as possible,' said Kenneth. 'Therefore I will have to arrange for you to go into hospital,' he continued. I stacked up with tins of rice pudding and peaches ready for the dreaded day.

I went into The Royal Free Hospital early one morning

and the nurses and doctors were marvellous. The surgeon who extracted the impacted wisdom tooth was quite brilliant and I had no stitches, just an enormous gaping hole. Anaesthetic has a peculiar effect on me and once semi-conscious, I moan for ages afterwards. It resulted in having a nurse to my bedside every ten minutes to ask what the matter was! Ida had very kindly offered to come and fetch me, so late afternoon I was wheeled outside and driven back to Putney. The wisdom tooth had been deeply imbedded in the gum and my face was very swollen for two weeks, with a lovely assortment of black and blue bruises.

Shortly after my operation, Ida received a strange phone call late one night. A voice just said, 'Please tell Clare I'm in hospital,' and then the phone went dead. In the morning I rang mother's home and got no reply so I started ringing the surrounding hospitals. After a lot of hassle, I managed to find out which hospital she was in. Apparently mother had had a stroke in the garden, lying there for over an hour. She had eventually managed to get herself into the house where she had had a heart attack. Luckily she had been able to dial 999.

I rushed off to visit her, catching a train, armed with flowers, grapes and magazines. She was sitting propped up in bed and had been in the hospital several days. 'Why on earth wasn't I called, mother?' I asked. 'I'm your only family and you know I would have come at once,' I said gently.

'I've got down my solicitor as my next of kin' she said coldly.

At this point I decided that the issue wasn't worth debating. Mother had spent my entire life dismissing me and had never had a good word for me. She wasn't going to change now. Leaving late afternoon for London again, I promised to come down at weekends and help her out when she returned home.

Mother lived a mile from the nearest bus stop, so walking with shopping loaded with heavy things was anything but easy. When she returned home, I rang to explain that I would arrive on the Friday evening after work and a friend would be staying as well. Bob was one of the gentlemen from the social club and was quite game to drive me down to mother's house and help with all the chores. He was extremely kind and not only came to fetch me, armed with strawberries for mother, but with an array of house plants as well.

Mother had mentioned that her doctor had ordered her to have a little whisky with water every evening.

'The cost is so awful,' she exclaimed over the phone. So into the car went two bottles of whisky, a large amount of food, a duvet, a pillow and new curtain linings which I had made for her sitting room along with umpteen other items.

We arrived thinking that mother would be delighted with all the trouble and money spent on her. I had spent two late nights after work sewing and machining the curtain linings. After a cup of tea, mother hissed at me, while Bob was out of the room, 'I suppose he'll be leaving now?' she enquired.

'No,' I said. 'Bob is staying to help with everything

tomorrow.'
'Oh!' said mother. 'Really Clare, you do the most peculiar things.'
'Well, mother,' I said, 'I've come to clean the place out, wash curtains and cook a whole lot of food. Meanwhile Bob will help get the curtains down and do DIY jobs. I couldn't have managed without him driving me here.'
Bob slept in the spare bedroom and I settled down on the sitting room floor in a duvet. Mother appeared and muttered something about '.......... and I didn't bring you up like this to sleep on the floor.' I could do things for her from the bottom of my heart but they were never appreciated and it hurt a lot.
Next morning I took breakfast into mother and suddenly she remembered umpteen jobs that needed doing. Bob was kept busy all morning, while I soaked curtains and did a load of washing by hand. I never understood why mother hadn't got a washing machine, but all her life she had sent the bed and table linen to the laundry. By the evening, mother had to admit that it had been a splendid idea to bring Bob. He even went out and put to rights the garden gate which was hanging off its hinges. We left on Sunday after tea, leaving plenty of cooked food.
Back in London I had come to the conclusion that I wanted to be away from the big city. So when a job as Matron came up at a school not far from mother's home, I applied for it. Day and night I thought about Paloma and Carlos so far away and it was a constant torment. I wasn't happy for the school was isolated and, having no transport, I would have to spend my day off sitting in my

bedroom.
It is extremely exhausting being a Matron and a lonely existence. In the end, I could stand no more and gave in my notice. One of the staff was going up to London so kindly gave me a lift and I went to stay with Jennifer.
'Stay as long as you want Clare,' she said. I was very grateful. Eventually, after pacing up and down Jennifer's sitting-room carpet most evenings, in a complete quandary as to what to do, it became quite clear that Spain was the answer. I decided to ring Eric and see if he could help me.
'Come and stay with me,' he said. 'I'll meet you at Sevilla airport.'
I dashed down to see father and spent the day with him, returning to Jennifer's late evening. I spent the next few days sorting out clothes that I needed and things that I could leave behind in Jennifer's spare bedroom. Then it was time to visit mother, leaving some more things with her. Jennifer came to Heathrow airport to see me off and we waved frantically as we lost sight of each other at the barrier.
The warm December air breezed over me as I stepped onto Spanish territory and Eric and his newly acquired American girlfriend were there to meet me. On arriving at Eric's flat I dialled Marcos's phone number. Paloma answered and said, 'Hello mama, how are you?'
'I'm fine,' I replied. 'Guess where I am. I'm very nearby.'
'In Spain?' enquired Paloma.
'Yes,' I said. 'In Cadiz.'
'Really?' said Paloma. 'You're joking.'
'No, I'm not,' I said laughing. 'I've just arrived this minute

at Eric's flat.'

Next day Eric lent me his car and I drove over to see Paloma and Carlos. It was wonderful to be with them again and we all ended up talking at the same time, trying to tell each other all the news.

Chapter 41

Eric's girlfriend was a member of the U.S. Armed Forces team that had been assigned to offices near the Cadiz port. There was to be a Christmas party and I was invited to join Eric and his girlfriend. The Colonel in charge of the team was introduced to me and by the end of the evening had asked if he could phone to take me out to dinner one evening.

Norman and I started to see each other quite frequently and it developed into a relationship. He had been in the Vietnam War and been shot so badly that he had had over sixteen operations! Losing most of his stomach and his voice box, he had had to learn how to speak again. I had great admiration for him and enjoyed his company very much. So horrific had been the terror and sheer hell of what he had been through that he still lived the nightmares. I would awaken to find Norman half sitting up in bed leaning on an elbow. He would be fast asleep but he was back in the war on duty, watching for the enemy with an imaginary gun in his hand. I would gently lay him back against the pillows.

We went to a dinner dance at the American Naval Base, which was held in the Officers' Club. All the gentlemen had to attend in uniform with their decorations. I have never seen so many medals worn by one soldier. Norman had been awarded the highest honour for bravery by the U.S. Armed Forces, the Purple Heart. I shall always be grateful to Norman because he was very generous in helping me get back on my feet again. He would also lend

me his car to go and take Paloma and Carlos out.
After two months, I eventually found a little apartment to rent. It was only a few yards away from Eric's flat and well situated in the main avenue.
Norman would arrive and stand in the doorway laden with big brown paper bags full of food and things for the flat. He took me off to choose material and had curtains made up for the bedroom and sitting room. Once installed in my apartment, I got in touch with Dragados again. A month later they asked me to go and do some technical translations. When B.P. arrived, I was employed for the Ula Project.
Due to problems with closures of shipyards in Spain, all the workers at the Astilleros Shipyard in Cadiz went on strike. Unfortunately, it was not a quiet walk down the main avenue, but an extremely unpleasant and violent riot. I stayed marooned in my flat all day along with other people in the same block. We all stood on our balconies and watched in horror as a group of eighty men started to smash shop windows by throwing bricks. Cars were being overturned and set alight, while others sent wheely bins crashing across the road.
The National Police, in riot gear and holding shields, followed the strikers and were forced to shoot rubber bullets at the offenders. The whole thing was frightening with quite a few men getting hurt.
By this time, six months had gone by and Norman and his team were starting to clear out their offices and pack up to leave Cadiz. He had gone to America on business for a few days and on his return I discovered that Norman was

seeing a former American lady friend again. She was also leaving the Naval Base and returning to America. I came back from work to find a letter from Norman on the day he left Cadiz. He told me how sorry he was that he hadn't seen me before leaving but that it was probably best that way. He would always remember and miss me and that perhaps one day he would get his life sorted out. Norman finished his letter by saying '.... you are a beautiful lady and were very sweet to me. Take care sweet lady and may God bless you. Love Norman.'

We had had a five month relationship and he had gone forever; as if he had never existed! The days and weeks dragged by with the daily routine and the lonely evenings. Eric's girlfriend had left too with the *entourage* and so Eric and I would console one another. He never failed to bring a smile or laughter to my face, he had such a tremendous sense of humour. Many hours were spent together and there was never a lack of conversation. It was nice to know that he was a friend and I valued his friendship tremendously. When I'd had a bad day at the office, felt down-hearted, or wondered how to get through another day, I knew I could head a couple of yards down the road to Eric's flat. He'd often open the door and say, 'Just in time for a cuppa,' or 'How about a snacker?' Eric made the most perfectly cut sandwiches I've ever tasted and was a first class chef.

Other times, Eric would appear at my front door and stop for a cup of tea or a meal. We would sometimes meet up at the Piano Club, where I had first met him, and sit listening to the pianist. Sometimes we would go and have

dinner together or he would come with me to Jerez to have a drink at an hotel with Paloma and Carlos.
At the weekends, Eric and I would walk for miles along the sand paddling in the warm water, but as much as I enjoyed Eric's company, I longed for someone around my age. I was fed up with the endless years of loneliness, always behaving in the correct manner with such self control.
On 12th October 1984 I walked into the office to hear the news about the IRA bomb which had torn apart the Grand Hotel in Brighton. Immediately, my thoughts went to my father's nursing home which was only a few blocks away from the Grand. I rang father and he told me that the noise from the explosion had been tremendous and had shook the nursing home building, but apart from that he was alright.

Chapter 42

One evening while in the Piano Club, a few of our mutual friends were discussing the forthcoming yachting Regatta in Tangier. One of the gentlemen turned round and said, 'Clare, would you like to come?' Not having a clue what I was about to embark upon, I quickly said, 'That would be lovely.'

There was a long weekend coming up, so we set off in a convoy of cars for Morocco on the Friday morning. It was extremely hot and the dust flew up from the road into the open windows. When we got to the border there was a three-mile queue of cars. We sat for nearly two hours in the searing mid-day heat waiting to have our passports checked and stamped. It was an agonising procedure and those with small children or elderly relatives in cars were concerned about dehydration and heat exhaustion.

I sat hot, thirsty and tired, consoling myself with the idea of arriving at the hotel and turning on the cold shower full blast and standing underneath it. Eventually, we were over the border and on our way again, driving over rough tracks with clouds of dust bellowing out behind the car. The convoy of cars had headed through several villages and was making its way to the hotel, but we were heading in another direction.

'Where are we going?' I asked.

Fernando replied, 'I used to live in Morocco for many years and we are going to Tetouan to visit some very close friends of mine.'

'Oh, really!' I said, far too hot to think of anything more

sensible to utter.
We arrived at a large house and the door was opened by a maid. We followed her to the sitting room door where we had to take our shoes off before entering. There were couches all round the walls and cushions everywhere. I felt and looked a mess. My hair hadn't seen a comb since early morning, my clothes were sticking to me and I was getting hotter and hotter with a thumping headache. I longed for an ice-cold lager to quench my thirst.
Fernando was whispering across the room as we lay on couches propped up on our elbows. 'We are staying for tea and it is the custom to drink China green tea with mint and sugar. Don't refuse because it would be considered unforgivable and extremely offensive.'
The couple that were Fernando's friends were very hospitable. The husband came in and after greeting us lay down on one of the couches. His wife was allowed to stay and talk to me but, had I not been there, she would not have been allowed in the room in the presence of men only!
The tray arrived with a large teapot and a dish of typical Moroccan sweetmeats dripping in sickly honey and sugar. I sat with my cup of tea and pastry, praying to God that they would disappear! I took one sip from the cup and thought I was going to be sick. The teapot had been stuffed with fresh mint leaves and the tea had been sweetened to the point of being undrinkable. After hours of conversation and completing a tour of their house, we were eventually on the road again.
On arriving at the hotel and finally closing my bedroom

door, I rushed to stand under the shower. Turning the tap on full blast, a small trickle emerged and that was all that it was going to provide. Washed and changed, we all met downstairs to make our way to the Yachting Club where we had an evening meal.
Retiring to our respective bedrooms, most of us had had a thorough mattress inspection for bed bugs before turning the lights off. All the windows were wide open and a conscious effort was made to try and sleep. I'd been lying on the bed in the unbearable heat for an hour or so, when a noisy disturbance beneath the hotel window made any intention of sleeping quite impossible. It was 1.00 a.m. and a young man was sitting on the kerbside opposite the hotel playing typical Moroccan music on a pipe. It droned on and on until after 3.00 a.m.
Saturday was packed with a full itinerary and after breakfast we made our way to the Yachting Club to await the arrival of the first yachts into port. After lunch it was time for a walkabout around the town and then back to the hotel to get ready for the evening. We assembled in extensive gardens, awaiting the arrival of the King of Morocco and other dignitaries and were then escorted to an arena. Here we sat on stone steps to watch the riders and horses perform an ancient Moroccan tradition. The riders held their rifles in one hand high above their heads and made their horses gallop at top speed. A sudden bang from the rifles brought the horses to an instant standstill. It is considered to be a great art and demands tremendous control between horse and rider. This ceremony takes place to welcome guests of honour.

Leaving the arena, we were seated on low benches in an Arabic tent. We sat in a circle with a low table in front of us. At each circle were seated ten or twelve people and our table had been positioned by the main entrance. Apart from our group from Cadiz, there was a mass of people who had been invited as guests. They had come from far and wide to celebrate this annual event. There were two tents and one of them was reserved for the King, his family, friends and dignitaries.

We started dinner with a cold soup in earthenware bowls. I looked at mine and saw a large crack and two chips round the edge of the bowl. I noticed several other people were leaving their soups as well, not relishing the idea of their lips making contact.

It is the custom to eat food with your hands and the main course consisted of a whole roasted lamb and a dish of spicy couscous with saffron. Plates were put in front of us and then we all had to tear a piece of meat off and eat it with our fingers along with the couscous which you roll into little balls and pop into your mouth!

Dessert consisted of a large serving dish decorated with fig leaves filled with fruit. Having finished our meal we were provided with bowls of water to rinse our fingers. At this point we were entertained by some musicians and a belly dancer. They then all left the tent and in came a gentleman who sat cross-legged on the ground, three feet from where I was sitting. In front of him was the Alibaba basket and out came the flute. I waited no longer and took one leap over the stool into the air in a most undignified manner and dashed to the other end of the tent, where there was another exit. As I stood pinned to it, I noticed a gentleman standing nearby and he had gone as white as a sheet.

'Are you terrified of snakes?' I whispered breathlessly.

'Yes,' he said, as he nodded frantically.

We watched as the snake charmer played his flute and this large cobra appeared, weaving its way upwards. I froze with fear having visions of it getting lost amongst a hundred of us! An Englishman volunteered to have the snake put round his neck, but the snake had other ideas and started to coil itself around him and had to be removed. Back in the garden we sat in the warm breeze, listening to a live band, returning to the hotel around 1.30 a.m.

Next morning a coach was laid on to take everybody on a tour but Fernando and another gentleman decided to travel in their own cars. This way we could stop when and where we wanted, so off we all went meeting the rest of the group for lunch. I don't recall where we stopped for lunch, but I know that it was a primitive village miles from anywhere. The men were all sitting outside in the dust and dirt, with typical Moorish sandals on their feet and dressed in the traditional long gowns. They drank sweet tea in glasses filled with fresh mint and were totally unperturbed by the swarms of bluebottles and flies that surrounded them and their drinks.

I have never been so thirsty in all my life and the temperature was soaring, but nothing was going to make me drink from such unhygienic surroundings. I doubt that our salad at lunch had ever seen a drop of water and I

began to think of it being a potential minefield for dysentery. The meat that was produced for our consumption had been hanging amongst the flies in the heat having never seen a refrigerator.
Several of us commented on the fact that we could end up in the local hospital. 'God forbid' was the general comment. I refused to eat or drink anything at lunch time, preferring to play safe. Fernando and I left well before the coach party, making our way along the dusty tracks with pot-holes everywhere. Turning a bend in the road we came across some camels for hire.
'Stop, stop, Fernando,' I exclaimed.
He slowed down and stopped his car while he listened to me saying, 'I can't leave Morocco without riding a camel!'
The animal was made to get down on its knees in order for me to be hoisted up. It was a smelly, disgruntled camel and objected loudly. Fernando by now had produced a camera and was clicking away.
If any of the readers have ever ridden on a camel, they will know what I mean when the animal stands up and leaves you perched helpless on its back. The ground seemed miles away and I prayed fervently that the bad-tempered animal wouldn't suddenly decide to take a nip out of its owner and gallop off. While perched in this precarious position, around the bed of the road appeared the coach. Everyone proceeded to get their heads out of windows calling out and waving. Riding a camel must be one of the most uncomfortable things you can do. The most terrifying part is dismounting because the animal lunges forward, nearly throwing you over its head and, with no

warning at all, collapses with a thud onto its knees.
Back at the hotel it was time to collect our luggage for the homeward bound journey. Fernando was staying on so I returned to Cadiz with some friends and their children in their boat.

Chapter 43

The self-discipline in everything I did had gone on for as long as I could remember. When it eventually snapped, I didn't even recognise myself. It came as a rebellion against my bitter childhood years, the physical and mental torture I had endured beyond human limits, the rejection from my mother and my adored children and the empty loneliness.

It all came about quite suddenly one winter's evening around Christmas time. Eric had gone to England to stay with his daughter. I'd taken Paloma and Carlos out to lunch and given them their Christmas presents. Returning to my apartment, I entered the vestibule to see a gentleman sitting on the hall bench. I'd never seen him before and I was taken aback when he spoke to me. He told me that he had been observing me for quite some time and also knew where I worked. Frankly, I was rather put out with all this and had come back to Cadiz feeling dejected and depressed, certainly not in the mood to talk to strangers!

The following afternoon, on returning from work, I again found this gentleman sitting on the hall bench. He told me his name was Antonio and that he was a plain clothes armed detective with the National Police.

On 24th December I cooked a turkey with all the trimmings and had a few people in for a meal. Paloma decided to come with her boyfriend and an English couple popped in for a drink after dinner. When everyone was leaving I went downstairs to say goodbye to them. There, near the entrance, was Antonio again. He pretended he didn't know me and when everyone had departed we got chatting in the hall again. 'Would you like to go out New Year's Eve?' he asked. Antonio's voice was deep, husky and two tones lower than average. He was of a slight build, had a captivating smile and I was finding him rather fascinating.

On 31st December I received a message to say that Patricia and her husband were on their way from Barcelona to the Costa del Sol. They planned to drive up to Cadiz the next day and would love to come and see me so that we could have lunch together. I hadn't seen Patricia for twenty years and had never met her husband. It was wonderful to see her again and she hadn't aged at all. She still looked exactly the same as when we were at the convent. We had a lovely lunch and between mouthfuls got as much conversation in as we could. Later she and her husband departed to drive back to Marbella. That evening Antonio came to fetch me and we wandered about the old town in and out of cafes and bars. On returning to the main avenue we went to a discotheque and joined in the festive mood. It must have been 4.00 a.m. when he stopped his car outside the block of flats in the square. Antonio asked me to stay a few minutes because he wanted to talk to me. 'I've been watching you for a very long time,' Antonio said. 'I work mostly by night and during the daytime sit in the bar across the road opposite your balcony window.'

I could see his face clearly from the street lighting. He gazed at me and I couldn't take my eyes away from his gaze. Very gently, he said, 'I'm married.' But I knew it was too late. Cupid had sent an arrow through my heart. I sat motionless, staring ahead out of the windscreen, like a stunned animal, hit by a thunderbolt. After what seemed an eternity of silence, Antonio gently turned my head and gave me a whisper of a kiss on my lips and softly said, 'I love you.' I knew only too well that he really meant those three words. There was no doubt in my mind at all. We sat and gazed into each other's eyes for a long time. Then I took hold of myself and made myself get out of the car. Without looking back, I went up the steps into the hallway.

Next morning the whole town seemed to be recovering from New Year's Eve and I spent a quiet day without going out at all.

We only had three days' work at the office before it was another weekend. On Saturday morning, I always went out to do my shopping and go to the bank. I was just about to leave when there was a ring at the front door. There stood a florist with the largest, most beautiful bouquet of flowers I had ever seen. The attached card had written on it—Antonio.

After that, I kept meeting Antonio in the streets, or he'd be standing gazing up at my balcony from the bar over the road. I had always vowed I would never get emotionally involved with a married man, but this was a situation beyond my control. I didn't want to control myself anymore. I'd always been known as the neatly dressed, well-behaved, English lady. It suddenly didn't matter anymore what anybody thought, or said, about me. Who

cared anyway what I did? The answer was nobody. I knew there would be a price to pay but the loneliness and agony of not being with Antonio would have been unbearable.
The following Saturday the florist arrived again and delivered a total of eight bouquets. My small sitting room was a mass of gorgeous flowers. That evening, at around 11.00 p.m. I answered a knock at the door and there stood Antonio. 'I just wanted to know if you had received all the flowers,' he said.
'Yes,' I replied. 'They are simply beautiful, but you shouldn't have done that.'
'I wanted to surround you with flowers so that every time you look at them it reminds you of me,' Antonio said. He came in and we had a cup of coffee whilst I sat in a dressing gown with no make-up on and my hair pinned on top of my head. Eventually he had to go because he was on night duty and we arranged to meet again. This was the beginning of a love affair that was so profoundly complete in every way.
For the first time in my life I knew what it was like to never tire from a man loving me. It was gentleness and passion as I had never known it before. When Antonio held me each night it was always as if we were making love for the first time. It was a desire that never failed and was totally mutual during the year that we were together.
I would come back from work and find a cigarette in the side of the door or a note underneath it. If Antonio rang the flat bell and I wasn't there he would always leave a cigarette. This was to let me know he had called.
Sometimes I would find three or four cigarettes stuffed

into the side of the door and it never failed to bring a smile to my face.

Every evening Antonio would come and fetch me and we would go off to saunter around the old part of town. We were both night owls and loved being out having a whisky in a bar at 2.00 a.m. I can only describe weekends, bank holidays and festive days as sheer hell because Antonio would have family commitments.

Shortly after I had met him we had the annual Cadiz Carnival. Paloma rang me at the office and said she was coming over with a group of friends. I was delighted and dug out my Red Riding Hood costume. Paloma arrived dressed as a witch and had been extremely clever in making her outfit. She had stuck silver stars and moons on her hat and had been busy sewing right up to the last minute. Paloma's friends were all her age but no one seemed to mind me tagging along and we had an enjoyable but exhausting evening!

Antonio and I went out the following evening. He was dressed as a lion in a costume from head to foot and made me do all the talking so nobody knew who he was. I was wearing a large bright red cape with a hood and carrying a basket of flowers. It got a bit much with people asking the continual question, 'Where's your wolf?' Little did they know, he was right beside me.

After a few months Antonio confided in a friend of his. He was so in love with me that he didn't know what to do. He was torn between me and his children. I made it clear that whatever happened I would never let him give up his family for my sake.

Our love for each other was so profoundly deep that it was a source of constant torment. The feeling of guilt about our relationship was always there but I could not end it, nor did I want to.

Chapter 44

In April I decided to visit my parents as, by this time, mother had gone into a home run by Irish nuns in Sussex. She had senile dementia. On hearing that I was going to England, a Spanish friend called Barbara asked if she could come with me. I explained that I was going to spend days sitting in nursing homes and living in Bed and Breakfast. It would be a tight schedule because I only had eight days' holiday from work. She insisted that would be fine and said she didn't mind at all. Antonio drove us to Sevilla airport.

Once at Heathrow we got a train down to Brighton and booked in at the first available Bed and Breakfast near father's nursing home. Dashing around I managed to see father just as the nurse had finished putting him to bed. He had deteriorated considerably since my last visit and looked very frail lying against the pillows. The thought of having me there for a few days brought a smile to his face. I bent over and gave him a kiss on his forehead and he closed his eyes and went to sleep.

Next morning I steered Barbara towards a well known clothes store and we did a practice walk to the nursing home. Having got her whereabouts, I left her happily browsing around while I sprinted off to see father. I spent the morning chatting away whilst on my knees sorting out a chest of drawers. Collections of underpants with elastic that had worn out appeared. Vests with buttons missing, pyjama bottoms with no cord to hold them up and tops with no bottoms! As they came back from the laundry

they had just been shoved into any available drawer. Barbara joined us for lunch in father's room and the afternoon was spent sewing and making a list of new clothes required. Next morning we arrived at the nursing home armed with pyjamas and replacement clothes for father. After lunch father suddenly appeared to be very tired and wanted to lie on his bed and have a rest. So Barbara and I decided to get on a bus and travel to Seaford. I very much wanted to see Mrs. O'Hara again. I hadn't seen her for twenty years. I wondered whether she still lived in the same house and sure enough, as I pressed the bell, there she stood, as pleased as ever to see me with the same words, as in the past, 'Come on in'. I introduced Barbara and we had tea whilst catching up with the years that had passed. As we were about to leave, Mrs. O'Hara gave me a warm hug and said, 'What a great pity you and my eldest son didn't get together.'
'Perhaps it was,' I replied.
She asked me to get in touch with him and was quite insistent about it. 'Promise me you will,' she repeated.
I promised and I did ring him but, although both divorced, we have never met again.
Shortly after our visit, Mrs. O'Hara died. She will always be remembered with great affection and for making me feel so welcome every time I appeared on her doorstep.
Next morning I popped in for half an hour to say goodbye to father. I always hated the farewells because father would have the tears welling up in his eyes and it was so painful to leave him in this way. I made sure that the Sister on duty knew I was leaving, so that one of the

staff could go and talk to him.
Our next destination was across Sussex by coach and, on arriving at Burgess Hill, we took a taxi to see mother. Due to travelling we had missed lunch so the nuns brought us tea and sandwiches. Mother had moments when she was quite lucid and then couldn't remember what we were doing in her room. I'd brought some presents and she eagerly opened them and then threw them on the bed. During tea she would keep asking who Barbara was and where had those things on her bed come from. It was all most upsetting. Of course, after my visits, she never remembered I'd been or who I was.
Our next port of call was Wimbledon. Jennifer had invited us to stay and this gave me the opportunity to keep my appointment with my dentist next morning in Golders Green.
The days had flown by and it was time to return to Spain. Antonio was at Sevilla airport and gave me a tremendous hug and drove us back to Cadiz.
During the summer Paloma came to stay for a few days with her boyfriend. It was lovely to have her company. I would dash back from the office and we would spend the afternoons on the beach. But Carlos wouldn't come and see me and it constantly tore me apart.
One evening, Eric and I decided to drive out to Puerto de Santa Maria, which is about a twenty-minute drive from Cadiz. We had heard of a new Piano Club with a dance floor which was due to open soon. On arrival we saw all the lights on inside and our curiosity got the better of us. The entrance door was wide open and we popped our

heads round the door to have a look. A gentleman came towards us and he turned out to be the owner. I muttered something about the fact that we were looking forward to the club opening.

'Come along inside and have a look, do, please.' We stepped into a beautiful lounge bar with elegant sofas and coffee tables set around a parquet dance floor. We were offered a drink and whilst in conversation the owner looked at me and said, 'You dance with great art.' I was amazed that he had seen me because I had only danced a few times in public places. Before I could say anything, the owner continued, 'Would you consider dancing here for the opening night?' I was thrilled to have been asked and told him that it would be a pleasure. 'Go and have a word with Jorge and then you can sort out what music you require.'

Jorge was giving instructions as to where he wanted the grand piano positioned. This was accompanied by the background banging of some workmen who were putting the finishing touches to the bar area. But we managed to decide on the music he would play for me to dance to. When the opening night did arrive I was well supported with Eric, some office companions and others from Dragados. I was amazed while making a gracious curtsey in recognition to the public's clapping that they had enjoyed my performance. The clapping got louder and with calls of 'encore', I danced again.

The Southerners of Spain see very little ballet—if any at all—and their traditional dances are the typical Flamenco and Sevillanas. This kind of dancing involves a lot of stamping with overhead arm waving, using the wrists and hands. Paloma has a natural flair for Sevillanas and dances them beautifully.

Chapter 45

It was around the middle of the summer when I tried to make a tremendous effort to stop my relationship with Antonio. The guilt was constantly at the back of my mind. We had a discussion about something and I asked him to give me my flat keys back.
That evening I went out with Eric and Barbara to have a drink in one of the open air cafes. I drank quite a few glasses of wine and then continued drinking at several more places. Still on my feet, but so emotionally upset and in a turmoil, I rang Antonio from a phone box to the cafe bar he frequented. 'I never want to see you again. I've had enough.' And so I went on. Then, feeling much better, I slammed the phone down. Staggering out to where Eric and Barbara were standing I announced, 'That's it. I've told him what I think.' I was now at the stage when I didn't care a damn who heard me, how loud I was speaking or what happened next. My feet wouldn't co-ordinate so Eric grabbed one arm and Barbara the other and between the two of them they decided to steer me back to my flat.
On arrival, Antonio was there and took over. Hysterically crying I implored him to leave me and never come back. He gently put me to bed and sat stroking my forehead looking at me with all the love in the world. There was no doubt that he worshipped the ground I walked on and we were both bonded together by a very true, profoundly deep love for each other.
The month of June came to an end and so did the B.P.

project which had lasted fourteen months. There had been no working team spirit or sense of humour from any of the office team. It had been so different from the last two projects and had been a real grind and thoroughly depressing to say the least. I was glad to see it terminate and be able to look back and say 'at least I did my duty efficiently to the bitter end'.

Having had two weeks' rest I was called to the employment office for an interview with Astilleros at their Cadiz shipping yard. I took on the job as PA bilingual secretary to the Resident Engineer. This foreign company had come to Spain for the conversion of a ship called FPSO VI and the duration of the project would be six months.

The out-dated building that had been assigned to us as offices was lacking in the minimum of hygiene and comfort. By mid-day the sun was pouring through dilapidated shutters which would bang in the warm wind. Around this time I was having quite horrific haemorrhages. My blood pressure would drop and make me feel as weak as a kitten. I had a course of injections to stop the haemorrhages and I suppose this helped bring my blood pressure up to a more normal level but I was drained of all energy. Time took its toll with the gruelling work and living off a few sandwiches at mid-day. The shipyard was isolated with no means of transport to get to a cafe or access to a more substantial meal.

Day in and day out for four months I kept at my job frequently sitting in the office with a hand towel because the bleeding was so bad. Eventually, struggling to keep my

job going, I developed a severe case of cystitis and no sooner got rid of one attack than another developed. My doctor sent me for an intravenous pyelogram and decided that I was no longer fit for work. Previous to this, I had been starved for over twenty-four hours and been given an enema. I felt so ill that Eric slept on the sofa in my flat all night. A nurse who was a friend of mine accompanied me to the hospital. I was so grateful because I was feeling extremely weak and in no fit state to negotiate getting home again alone. The X-rays were taken at intervals lasting up to an hour and, when finished, I removed my hospital gown in a cubicle. Suddenly my friend wrapped it around me again and before I knew what was happening we were rushing down corridors. I had come out in large raised white lumps all over my body, totally allergic to the iodine. I was immediately injected with an antidote.
One morning I caught the bus and went to the old part of the town to do some shopping. Standing by the bus stop, waiting for the return trip, who should appear but Antonio in his car. The law in Spain by this time was that seat belts had to be worn at all times except in towns. We were chatting as he drove and Antonio turned to look at me. 'I'm so in love with you,' he said. The next thing I knew was a crashing noise and the front of the car bonnet had doubled up in the air. I had been thrown forward giving my forehead an almighty bang against the windscreen. My knees and legs had hit the dashboard with such tremendous force that they had already started to swell up.
I sat very quietly bent forward with my arms round my

head. The thumping pain was excruciating. Antonio had got out and had gone to see if the family in the car in front were alright as they had two children plus grandma in the back seat. Antonio had been so busy looking at me that he had driven straight into the stationary car in front of us at the traffic lights. Antonio wanted to take me to a hospital but I just wanted to get out of the heat and get back to my flat. I lay on my bed shaken and bruised.

That evening Barbara and I had arranged to go out together so off we went to have a drink. My neck had started to give me a good deal of pain and around 11.00 p.m. we walked to the nearest hospital. X-rays were taken and I was told that they could find nothing abnormal. My knees and elbows were very swollen and puffed up going black and blue from bruising. A large lump had developed on my forehead too and I ached all over.

Having been given the all clear from the hospital, I thought it was a matter of time for nature's healing. Little could I have imagined at the time how extremely serious my injuries were. The reality was that I had severe whiplash and a fractured spine. It was to be seven years before a chiropractor took another X-ray and discovered what had really happened, and why I was in such agonizing pain.

Chapter 46

A few weeks before my birthday, Eric and a few friends gathered in the Piano Club. The evening progressed and Eric suddenly said, 'You haven't been well and you are feeling depressed, so my birthday present is a holiday.' I sat on the bar stool totally taken by surprise. 'We will rent a house near Marbella and leave in a few days' time,' continued Eric.

We set off in drizzling rain on a cold November morning and on arrival the estate agent came to see if everything was alright, but the heater in the sitting room wasn't working. It was really very cold by the evening and the estate agent had promised to return, but didn't. I had brought some ready-cooked food and after eating we decided it was pointless to go on sitting in a chilly room with the continual pouring rain outside.

Investigating upstairs, I discovered that there weren't enough blankets and got very concerned about Eric. He was very thin, not strong, with a pace maker and did feel the cold. I got worried about him getting hypothermia. Luckily, I had brought a hot water bottle and a duvet, so was able to use all the blankets from the two bedrooms and tuck Eric in! I then went to the other room and rolled myself up in the duvet.

Morning was to greet us with a miserable mist. On turning on the hot water tap to have a bath I discovered that there was a lack of water pressure so the gas heater wouldn't work. I gave up at this point and went and made a cup of tea. Sitting on Eric's bed, he said, 'If the estate agent isn't

here by 10.00 a.m. then we will go to an hotel.'
Everything that had been unpacked had to be packed up again. We drove down to the estate agent's office and then went on to Torremolinos. There was an enormous table with business men having a dinner meeting and we were ushered down the large restaurant to the other end. We were escorted to a table for two and at the next table there was a gentleman sitting alone.
Having translated the entire menu for Eric, I was busy with my head behind the menu card, working out what I wanted to eat. Meanwhile, the waiter had returned with a bottle of wine. I was hearing snippets of the conversation going on between Eric and the English gentleman on the next table.
'I'm here on business,' he said and it was obviously clear that he thought Eric was my father. The gentleman in question was finishing his dessert. Eric decided to ask him over to our table and this is how I met Andrew. If, at this point, I had known what the future held, I'd have run a mile.
All three of us had coffee in the hotel lounge and then Eric made the excuse that he was tired and took himself off to his room. From the moment I met Andrew I felt quite at peace with the world. He was heavily built and, at 6 ft 5 inches tall, was like a gentle giant with a pleasant, friendly face. Nothing seemed to worry him; life was, according to him, wonderful and everything a laugh.
Eric and I had found a bar a few yards from the hotel. Here we would sit, eating a full English breakfast letting the world go by. Andrew would join us for breakfast then

go off and come back in the afternoon, taking a stroll round the town with us.
Andrew and I went to a night club and for the next two days he spent his time with us wherever we went. On his departure we stood on the hotel steps and waved goodbye to him. Andrew had invited me over to England for Christmas and promised to phone.
Meanwhile, my thoughts were with Antonio who I had rung twice from a phone box. But the feeling of freedom with Andrew remained with me because he was divorced and I was free from the terrible guilt which engulfed me. Struggling with suitcases, yet again, we got Eric's car packed up once more for our return journey home. It had been a lovely thought and generous gesture on Eric's part to take me away from the inescapable trap I found myself in with Antonio.
Andrew, meanwhile, had rung and made a time for me to be at Eric's flat to talk to him on the phone. He told me to let him know if I wanted to spend Christmas in England. His son would be staying with him as well and it would be a good opportunity to get to know one another. I simply dreaded Christmas alone and the thought of everyone united with their families was unbearable. Andrew continued to ring and chatted over the phone as if he hadn't a care in the world.
A few days after arriving home I was out shopping one morning when an excruciating pain struck me down my back. Unable to walk, I hailed a taxi. Quite incapable of staying upright on arrival at my flat, I got myself into bed. That afternoon Eric popped in to have a chat. Shuffling

along in great pain, I opened the front door. Eric made me a cup of tea and stayed for a while, quite concerned about the state I was in. Eric couldn't speak Spanish so it was absolutely pointless asking him to ring my doctor. The next course of action was to find Antonio whom Eric found later in the bar over the road.

Antonio got my doctor in who pronounced that I wasn't to move, which I couldn't do anyway. 'In case you develop a slipped disc,' he announced, little realising that my spine was fractured and I had been walking about for a month in this condition! The male nurse arrived next and gave me an anti-inflammatory injection to try and ease the pain. These I had on a daily basis for the next three weeks. Heat treatment along with massage was prescribed so this was done every day while I lay immobilised.

Antonio and Eric got into a rota. Antonio would stay until the crack of dawn and then pop in whenever he could. Ordering my lunch from the bar he would come across with the waiter carrying lunch on a tray. Looking back, it was quite hilarious as the traffic came to a grinding halt, while the tray was ceremoniously carried across the width of the main avenue.

Around tea-time Eric would let himself in and we would have a 'cuppa' together and he'd stay and chat. Eric asked me what my plans were for Christmas. 'I can't walk, let alone carry a suitcase,' I said. 'I'll have to stay put.'

'Well,' said Eric, 'Andrew says that if you do feel better just before Christmas he will meet you at Heathrow.'

For weeks I lay in bed shuffling to the bathroom and back. Trying to read a book was virtually impossible.

Therefore, I had plenty of time to think—and think I did. What did my future hold as it was at the moment? Antonio and I could go on loving each other but it had no future. I could spend the rest of my life tied to him and still be alone. It would be impossible to terminate our relationship and for me to continue living in the flat I was occupying. We would be constantly bumping into each other and the torment would be unbearable.

One evening, now into my eighth week, I got painfully out of bed to the bathroom and back to bed as usual. I must have dozed off for some hours because, on waking, I discovered it was 10.00 p.m. I went to get up and not only was there no pain, but I could walk upright again. I tried bending and decided to get dressed and go and see Eric. When he opened the door, I announced, 'I'm fine again and I've made a decision to go to England for Christmas.' 'I'm delighted,' Eric said. 'Come on in and ring Andrew.' It was 21st December. Eric drove me to Sevilla airport on the 23rd and promised to meet me on my return.

Chapter 47

Andrew lived in a cul-de-sac in a little village a few miles from Nottingham. His fourteen-year-old son was with us for Christmas and I was impressed by this well mannered and pleasant teenager. It was a relaxing time to recuperate and strengthen my back with strolls in the countryside. During the weeks spent in each other's company I found that Andrew gave the impression that he hadn't a care in the world. His company was agreeable and he had a kind, gentle side to his nature. Andrew discussed the future and said that he was returning to live in Spain permanently. He had the house on the market and already had many boxes packed up in the attic ready for emigrating. We seemed to enjoy each other's company and, when together, both felt quite at peace.

Andrew had told me that he had been self-employed selling products to farmers and had closed down his business because of going to live abroad. At the time, everything that was explained seemed all quite logical and I never doubted him for a minute. We had got on well together and there was clearly a mutual deeper feeling. Both of us had kept in contact by phone with Eric and the arrangement was for him to meet me at Sevilla airport. Andrew asked me if I would come back in March after he had sorted out some personal things. I agreed to do this and help him with the final arrangements for packing up. On arriving at the airport, I came through with my suitcase to find Antonio standing there! I had explained to him before going to England what I was doing and that

we had come to the end of our affair. Antonio had gone to Eric's house and told him that he was going to meet me at the airport. I was trying so hard to break away and Antonio was trying so hard to hold on to me. I shall never forget when Antonio eventually stopped his car in front of my flat and very quietly asked, 'Do you love him?'
'Yes,' I replied. 'I'm going back again to England to his house in two months' time.'
Antonio carried my suitcase upstairs and looked at me with all the love in the world. His face and mine were full of torment and he was deeply hurt. He knew he had to continue with his family life and the time had come to give me my freedom from the guilt that had engulfed our deep love for each other over the past year.
Unable to bear our parting, Antonio knocked on my flat door a few evenings later. 'May I come in? I have to talk to you,' said Antonio. It took great strength of mind not to let him enter but I knew that if I did it would only prolong the agony.
'I thought you would say no,' Antonio said. We talked for a few minutes and I knew then that my firm resolution to make a new life away from Cadiz was the only thing I could do.
A week later, while shopping one morning, I suddenly saw Antonio walking towards me. I stood in the entrance of a house nearby and he cornered me. 'My God, you are so beautiful,' he whispered. He turned away to walk off down the street. It was the last time Antonio ever spoke to me. I tried to fight back my tears as I continued, almost mechanically, to put one foot in front of the other and

walk in the opposite direction. I felt torn to bits inside. The weeks dragged by and the weather was cold, damp and misty with plenty of rain and wind. I sat marooned in my flat except for visits to Eric or to wait for a call from Andrew. Eventually, I was on my way back to England once more. We had discussions about the future and decided to get engaged. Andrew wanted to move to Alicante and we would rent a flat there. Later, when monies which were owing to Andrew were sorted out we would be able to buy a house there. We had several months of very busy packing and sorting out to do. We went to visit both of Andrew's brothers and their families and give them the good news. We drove down to see father and had lunch at the nursing home. I knew that it would make him very happy to meet Andrew and know that I was no longer by myself. I had lived alone for nine years.

We went to see mother and spent the afternoon with her but she couldn't understand who Andrew was at all. Not only that, but she kept asking me who I was!

'I'm your daughter,' I'd say for about the eighth time and the same reply would be, 'I haven't got a daughter.'

Ironic really, that in her last years of life, mother's real feelings towards me expressed themselves in their true light.

One evening I told Andrew about my adoption and my search to the last known address of my natural mother. 'It may be silly of me, but I would like to go back to Fulham again,' I explained.

'Well, let's spend a day in London,' replied Andrew. We

set off a few days later and hopped on a bus arriving outside the flats at Bishop's Mansion. I rang the bell at number 50 but there was no answer. I wandered about inside and outside the building, praying for a clue, a glimmer of light to my natural mother's whereabouts. If she had died then I'd been too late but at the back of my mind was the determination that if she was still alive I had to see her.

We had wandered round to the back of the building and saw a woman come out of a side entrance. I briefly explained the situation and she pointed to a small house nearby saying, 'The caretaker lives there with his wife. They may be able to help you because they have been here many years.'

The couple were most sympathetic and said that many years ago a lady had lived at number 50 and her name had been Mrs. Worth. The caretaker vaguely remembered another woman living there with her but he couldn't remember anymore. As we were about to turn away he suddenly called us back, 'The daughter of Mrs. Worth lives in the next street with her husband but I couldn't tell you what number the house is,' he explained. There was a pause as he finished saying apologetically, 'It was a long time ago.'

Thanking the couple we walked out to find the adjoining street. My heart fell as I stood and surveyed a long street that seemed to go on for miles and miles. Front doors abounded on both sides and what I had in mind was totally stupid. An impossible task. Crazy in every way and completely pointless! But I wouldn't give up yet and

immediately put my plan into action.
'You take that side of the street and I'll take this side. We'll knock on all the doors and make our way down the street.'
We had been working our way down the street and I had almost given up hope as I stood in front of yet another lady at her door saying, 'Are you the daughter of Mrs. Worth?' Suddenly Andrew beckoned from across the road, saying 'Come here.' There stood the daughter of Mrs. Worth! My legs had turned to jelly. My heart was pounding and I suddenly lacked all physical strength.
'Could I possibly come in and sit down before I explain?' I said feebly. There was no reason in the world why this couple should let me and Andrew into their house. We were complete strangers but they did and they turned out to be extremely kind, sympathetic and hospitable.
Entering into their sitting room they stood waiting for my explanation.
'May I sit down?' I asked feeling extremely weak. 'In fact,' I continued, 'I think we had all better sit down.'
I poured out my story and, being overcome with emotion, a strong whisky was handed to me. Mrs. Worth's daughter went and made sandwiches whilst her husband went to look for a diary to see the year that my natural mother had lived as a companion to Mrs. Worth. There had been no forwarding address when she left. I'd come to another fullstop. My natural mother had vanished without trace.

Chapter 48

Previously, when I had returned to live in Putney, an English couple who had been lovely friends to me and had been returning to England, arranged to transport some things of mine back with their luggage. They had stored my goods and chattels in their house in their spare room. So Andrew and I drove to Suffolk to bring it all back to pack it up and have it put in storage ready for Spain. Having loaded the car up, we were halfway homeward bound in the dusk. Andrew had been driving along a dual carriageway when the road gradually merged into a single lane. Confused and possibly tired after our long journey, Andrew went to overtake a car and we found ourselves driving head on into a car travelling straight towards us. Andrew tried to miss it but there was an almighty crash and grating sound as the sides of both cars hit each other. The impact sent us skidding many yards further up the road until we came to a stop. By this time it was pitch dark and freezing cold. After finding that neither of us were injured, we both got out on the passenger's side of the car, covered in shattered glass. I stood shivering in shock with the bitter wind going right through me. The length of the car on the driver's side was a write-off; not only was it a miracle that we hadn't a scratch on us but the fact that the heavy boxes, sewing machine, trunk and two six-and-a-half foot long mirrors, piled in the back, hadn't moved forward on top of us with the impact. I made a quick prayer of thanks to the Virgin of Chipiona.

Peering into the dark road, we could see no sign of the car we had hit and this was cause for great concern. Suddenly blue lights were flashing and the police arrived. They had with them the elderly couple who had been driving the other car. I sat with them while Andrew went through all the formalities. Apparently this couple had come out of their driveway nearby whilst Andrew had been overtaking a car. We finished up all going back to the couple's house for hot chocolate. We waited for a van to tow Andrew's car away. At the compound, we rented another car, transferring the cumbersome mirrors and luggage. We arrived back in Nottingham at 2.00 a.m., completely exhausted.

Andrew had had several potential buyers for the house and a young couple had decided to buy it. We decided to get married before going out to live in Spain. Andrew explained briefly that financially things weren't easy but soon he would have enough money for us to buy a home in Spain. He also told me that a friend of his had a job for him with an estate agents in Benidorm. Under these circumstances I gave no thought about the fact that I had not been given an engagement ring. Our wedding took place at the West Bridgford Registry Office with Andrew's brothers and their wives present, plus his son William. After a brief ceremony we all went to a pub for a drink. The removal men had arrived the day before our wedding and taken all the furniture etc. into storage. This, at a later date, would be sent out to Spain when we had purchased a house. We returned to an empty house with not even a chair to sit on! All we had left was a cooker and one small mattress on the floor. The reason for all this was that the young couple who were buying Andrew's house had decided at the last minute to move in a week later. This of course messed up all our arrangements and the removal firm had so many bookings that they had been unable to change the date.

The day before the couple were due to move in, Andrew saw me off at the airport. He was moving into a Bed and Breakfast to sort out several things that were pending. Meanwhile, I could get on with my packing ready to move out of my rented flat. Due to the problem of excessive luggage, Andrew would travel out to Spain by coach. I would meet him and then we would spend a few days at my flat in Cadiz.

Things went wrong with Andrew from the moment we were married. He rang to tell me that the coach was arriving in Algeciras the following day at 3.00 p.m. That night Eric received another phone call from Andrew to say that he had made a mistake and it was 3.00 a.m.! In a panic because Eric's car wasn't available, a couple over the road said, 'Here, take the keys of our car and go.' Not wanting to travel the two hour journey alone by night, Eric offered to come. He curled himself up on the back seat and fell asleep. I could hear little *zzz's* emerging above the noise of the engine as I frantically drove through the darkness to meet Andrew. We eventually arrived back at Cadiz and I then made arrangements for Paloma and Carlos to come and meet Andrew. We all went and had a Chinese dinner and the following day Paloma invited us to Jerez for tea at her rented flat. I made arrangements with

her to keep all my things at her place until we had somewhere to live.
Renting a car, we arrived in Alicante hot and tired and stayed at the most appalling Bed and Breakfast. It was the only bedroom available due to the whole town being in full swing with annual festivities. The mattress was a piece of foam, the pillows were indescribable and mine promptly hit the floor and stayed there. The shower must have been the first ever invented and we spent the night unable to sleep due to the fireworks and crackerjacks in the street.
We moved into Benidorm and, after scanning the local newspaper and ringing umpteen owners about renting their flats, we eventually found a place. At this point, Andrew asked me to pay the three months' deposit but little did I realise that he had not told me the full story. We couldn't swing a cat in the tiny apartment and it became an oven by the afternoon. The balcony was enclosed by metal-framed windows and held the heat in. It became an unbearable prison during a long boiling summer. Arming myself with bleach, I disinfected the bathroom and kitchen to make the place a little cleaner.
On several occasions I asked Andrew when he was starting work with the estate agency and was told that he was going to see them. The days went by and Andrew made no attempt whatsoever to do anything. He spent his time on the beach thoroughly enjoying himself.
Eventually, I discovered that there was no job awaiting Andrew's arrival and he had no intention of looking for work either. It was at this point that realisation truly hit

me. I had no way out but to carry on.
I had left the security of my rented flat where I had lived for five years. My children were at the other end of Spain. I'd left the friends and people I knew and here I was with a husband who was draining my hard-earned savings. I was in a strange place that I hated with no one to turn to! Enjoying lazing on the beach, Andrew decided to have his son out to stay. The airport was miles away and it meant hiring a car to fetch William. The financial worry and the feeling of deception from my husband when I had put my trust in him, made me ill. Not at all worried about my health, Andrew would spend the day with his son on the beach while I lay day after day haemorrhaging. I would lie on a foam mattress in the searing heat, the bed damp with perspiration. Struggling to my feet and very weak, I would prepare supper so that when William came in there was a meal ready for us all. The whole summer we lived on salads, potato omelettes, rice, ready-cooked chickens and fresh fruit. The so-called kitchen consisted of a sliding panel door in the sitting room and behind it was an old cooker with a tiny sink and fridge. One small cupboard held some cutlery, a few glasses, one saucepan and one frying pan! With these facilities, I managed all through the summer.
It was around this time that Andrew decided to add to his untold story. There was no money from the sale of the house because he had had to pay the mortgage loan back. The car was the same story. Andrew had debts and owed money to the bank too! Apart from feeling very weak from the menopause, the worry about the future stopped

me sleeping at night. I would often sit in a chair on the balcony for hours, wondering what on earth we were going to do. Putting this same question to Andrew only brought back the answer that everything was going to be alright!

'I will soon receive money owing,' Andrew repeated, 'and then we will be able to buy a house.'

The summer months went by and Andrew did absolutely nothing and clearly had no plans for our future whatsoever. In desperation one evening, at the end of September, I knew that we had to make a move back to England. We would try and get into licensed trade which would give us a source of income and living accommodation. Meanwhile, I got hold of a magazine and wrote to various agencies dealing with the selling and renting of public houses. On receiving all the information we were able to decide what places we should look at.

We arrived back in Britain in October and it was bitterly cold. With barely enough money to cope, we had only one meal a day so that we could hire a car to start travelling about and to pay for Bed and Breakfast. Travelling all day in a car with barely enough clothes to keep me warm became unbearable. It became so bad that my feet continually hurt from the cold and in the end I had to buy myself some snow boots. My other concern was my parents and so on our travels we went to see my father. He had had a stroke and was extremely frail. Leaving Andrew in the nursing home hall I went up to see my father as he sat in his room. He was desperately thin and I knew that time was running out. I knelt in front of him and took his hands in mine, but he seemed to be so far away from me. I stayed for a long time kneeling and looking into his eyes, but there was little response. The tears poured down my cheeks in uncontrollable pain. Mother looked well enough but hadn't a clue who I was. The letters I had written and all the photos of myself, Paloma and Carlos had been torn up and thrown in the waste-paper basket. I felt depressed, unsettled with all that seemed to be enclosing my life and, most of all, very lonely and frightened of what the future held.

Chapter 49

Andrew and I travelled thousands of miles all over England viewing licensed premises. Some were out in the middle of nowhere and I wondered how on earth the landlord made a living at all. Many of the premises we visited were so appallingly filthy that I wondered how any health inspector could allow food to be prepared and given to the public under such squalid conditions. It was a real eye-opener to see dogs wandering about sniffing food and dirty laundry piled on the floor in several kitchens that we visited. We stayed at Bed and Breakfast places and sitting in a small car travelling for weeks on end became exhausting. My body and feet were constantly frozen with the cold and my back was giving me a lot of pain.

One afternoon Andrew took me to meet a couple he knew in a Lincolnshire village. Having had a meal with them, we exchanged phone numbers and went back to our Bed and Breakfast. I wrote a little thankyou letter and a few days later Susan rang and spoke to me.

'James and I want you and Andrew to come and stay. We'll expect you tomorrow for lunch.' How grateful I was because I was at my wits' end. Susan and James were very kind and made us so welcome and their help will never be forgotten.

We continued to travel all day but at least there was a hot meal in the evening and a friend to talk to. Eventually we found a hotel and licensed house in Lincolnshire. It was a tremendous undertaking and needed so many things doing to it but Andrew and I decided to make a go of it.

While we sorted out the financial aspect and negotiated this, that and the other, Christmas was almost upon us. Andrew and I made yet another visit in the bitter cold down to Sussex to see my father. He had had another stroke and I was furious with the nursing home for not getting in touch with me. I had always made a point of making sure, no matter where I was, that both nursing homes knew where to contact me in an emergency.
Twenty-four hours after our return to Susan and James's house, I was taken very ill with severe salmonella. By 2.00 a.m. I was unable to reach the bathroom and it became totally impossible to control the vomiting and diarrhoea. Never in my life had I experienced anything like it and I was dehydrating fast. Unable to cope and barely able to speak, I told Andrew, 'For God's sake, get me a doctor.' The doctor had to come from the next village and by now it was after 3.00 a.m. I had visions of being taken off in an ambulance but, thank goodness, the injection and medicine received put a stop to the flow! For a few days I was very weak and had no strength whatsoever, but soon we had to be on the road once more travelling about sorting out legal matters, loans, brewery, building society, bank and solicitors. The list was endless.
On 3rd January 1987, we went to visit my father again. I instinctively knew that it was imperative to see him. He was so ill that he was now bedridden and was unable to speak. I stayed a long while and stroked his hand in silence but it was as if he had gone already. I kissed his forehead, fighting my tears back, and left the room with Andrew. We travelled back arriving very late at night. I was totally

exhausted physically and mentally and emotionally drained. Next day was Sunday and we were all in the dining room having lunch. The phone rang and Susan said, 'Clare, there's a call for you.' My beloved father had died at 1.00 p.m. I remember someone taking the phone from my hand as I hysterically cried. I had lost a wonderful father who had adored me as his natural daughter. The only consolation was that there was no more suffering or loneliness for my father to endure.

As I write this autobiography, nine years have passed since my father's death. Not a day goes by without thinking of him and I miss him with all my heart. Endless proof that there is life after death has been given to me by my father and there is no doubt in my mind that he is beside me on many occasions.

The thick snowflakes were falling fast and furious, covering the already white ground. By morning, there was a carpet of snow and the weather was getting worse. Funeral arrangements were made over the phone and Andrew took me out for the rest of the day. I had an emptiness that suffocated me for I had lost forever a gentle, loving father and the best friend I had ever had in my life. By mid-afternoon, the weather deteriorated by the minute and we feared that the little Metro car would not make it back to the house.

Susan and James lived in a house on an estate off the beaten track and where snow ploughs were never seen! It was three miles to the village from the main road and another mile up the estate's driveway before the house appeared. The car came to a shuddering halt a few yards from the kitchen door. Andrew was up to his knees in snow but had managed to wade round to the passenger door and, after great difficulty, give me enough room to ease myself out. I fell straight into a snow drift and it was a real fight to find the stamina to reach the house.

My father's funeral was the next day and Andrew and I were meant to be setting off at the crack of dawn. By morning there was a huge snow drift outside the back door and all four of us were marooned inside the house. It lasted for four days and luckily Susan and James had a well-stocked larder of both food and wine.

I was extremely upset not to be able to assist at my father's funeral. It was arranged that the undertakers would go ahead with the service and the cremation. His ashes would be kept until I could get down to Eastbourne. When the snow eventually melted Andrew and I went to attend a Mass at Eastbourne Cemetery. Father's ashes were laid to rest in the family grave. Here, his mother, father and brother lay and it had been his last wish to be cremated because there was only room in the family grave for his ashes. I had always promised him that his wish would be carried out.

I stood while the urn was buried and laid a simple bunch of flowers. I had no money to spend, not even on a wreath of any kind, but the message attached to my flowers was all that father needed to know and worth more than money. It read: *To my beloved father, who I shall always love and miss. Your loving daughter, Clare.*

Negotiations for the hotel were dragging on and on. It was nerve-racking, worrying and a great deal of strain. No one, least of all Andrew, realised that I was in a state of deep mourning and depression. We'd been staying with Susan and James for two months and I was finding it acutely embarrassing. All Andrew kept saying was, 'It'll only be a few days now.' The weeks dragged on and we had to move into a Bed and Breakfast on the outskirts of Nottingham.

Chapter 50

Eventually, on 6th April we took over the hotel and moved in. Susan had given me two cats and I spent the journey in the car trying to drive with one hand and keep the cats in a cardboard box with the other. Susan had explained, 'One of them is wild and the other not used to being in a house but they'll keep the mice away!' The hissing, meowing and general commotion that went on in the box was incredible. Instead, I began to think that I had a couple of tigers because they spent the journey getting their heads and front paws out, nearly managing to rip their box to bits. They tried to bite and their sharp claws dug into my hand.

On arrival, I put them into the cellar leaving milk and food and left them to hopefully settle down. The previous owners had lived in the flat above the pub hotel with two small children and two Newfoundland dogs. The place was indescribably filthy and, what was more, the couple had left all their rubbish and mess all over the flat. We slept on mattresses amongst the squalor with a terrible smell from an old brown felt carpet. On investigating further next morning, I discovered all the floorboards had damp stains where the dogs had urinated. This was only the beginning of a ghastly nightmare and, as I write, I wonder where I got the strength to physically and mentally cope with all the horrors that engulfed me. I worked day and night in an endless effort to get the place into a fit state.

Two domestics and myself spent the best part of the day

in the flat scrubbing the floorboards with bleach. We ripped up the brown felt and stuffed it out of a window along with a multitude of rubbish. Regardless of the weather, we opened every window to let in the fresh air to make it habitable.

We then moved on to my first priority which was the guests' bedrooms. The building itself was a large place and very attractive inside with spacious rooms everywhere. There was a total of seven bedrooms, three en-suite, plus a bathroom and another WC down the corridor. A total of fourteen guests could be accommodated.

The task ahead was a major operation and it took three days to get the bedrooms clean and fumigated. The blankets, sheets and pillows were so unhygienic and soiled that they went out to the field and were burnt along with one of the mattresses. Eventually, all the bedrooms were a pleasure to go into. Duvets with pretty covers, snowy-white pillows, and a smell of clean air and furniture polish greeted each guest that stayed.

It was now time to tackle the lounge bar which was an enormous room. In a huge bay window were some lovely Yuccas and various other tropical plants. Sadly, through lack of watering and care, they were nearly dead. It had been used as a rubbish dump. Cigarette stubs, crisp packets, sweet wrappers etc. abounded amongst the indoor garden. Starting work early one morning, we polished every table and stool until it shone. Brass handles, ornaments and pumps gleamed and the whole place took on a look of being cared for. I spent the afternoon working in the window garden and, once the

public saw that the plants were cared for and thriving, it wasn't used as a rubbish dump anymore. It became an unusual feature admired by all.
Now it was time to tackle the Ladies' and Gents' WCs. There were a total of twelve lavatories and urinals between the main lounge bar and the pool room. Armed with thick bleach, loo brushes and cubes, we vigorously scrubbed and cleaned. There were huge commercial rolls of toilet paper and I soon learnt that this was not at all sensible to have when people had had more than the usual limit of alcohol. One evening a man was wrapped in toilet paper by his friends while several others had unrolled paper round cars and decorated the whole car park!
While I was not finding enough hours in the day—or night—Andrew had decided to have the large area of bar installed with more pumps and there was complete chaos going on. Technicians and a whole army from the brewery had invaded the place, adding to all the muddle.
Meanwhile, the cats were eating their food and milk but refused to appear from their hidden quarters behind the beer barrels. I figured out that as they were intelligent enough to know where the cellar entrance was, they would eventually seek daylight. However, this proved me wrong and the cats continued to hiss and spit, even attempting to dig their claws into one of the men installing beer lines. After nearly a week Andrew and I considered that apart from the unhygienic aspect, the cats could not live the rest of their lives in darkness. Early one morning Andrew went down to the cellar with a broomstick while I stationed myself near the entrance. After a tremendous battle,

Andrew managed to corner them near the entrance and the cats suddenly flew into the air past me at top speed. They chased across the car park and aimed for some long grass in the field. By the time I had walked over to where they were the cats had disappeared and I stood for ages calling, 'Puss, Puss,' making appropriate cat noises. For the next week I left food and milk outside every evening but it wasn't eaten and we never saw them again.

Words do fail me when trying to give you a detailed description as to what hit me when, after several weeks, I eventually got round to the kitchen. On our arrival I had popped my head round the kitchen door and said to the existing chef, 'Just carry on as usual and I'll eventually get round to seeing you.'

The kitchen was a fairly large one, with an adjoining room for the freezers. Leading off from here were two small rooms. One was a larder and the other for wine storage. It took the best part of two weeks to get the engrained dirt and grease removed. Fat fryers, griddle, oven and grill had many hours of work and a multitude of Brillo pads spent on them. The kitchen floor was meant to have red tiles but was so engrained with grease and dirt, one could hardly see its true colour! Thinking that the worst was over, the day came to pull out the freezers from the walls and investigate their contents. Stuffed behind them were piles of accumulated dust, items of clothing, dirty mop heads, broom handles and broken umbrellas etc. It made me wonder how the freezer motors had managed to work at all. Underneath all this was a thick layer of greasy gunge which literally took me two afternoons to shift, on my hands and knees, scraping off bit by bit of hardened slime with a pallet knife.

While all my time was taken up with cleaning, I also had to do all the laundry and ironing for the guest rooms. The days were exhausting and I was up at 6.00 a.m. and down in the kitchen by 7.00 a.m. preparing breakfast for the guests that were about to appear. By this time, I had decided to interview for a daily, and a pleasant, intelligent woman applied for the job. Stella would clean the lounge bar, help carry cooked breakfasts out from the kitchen and sort out the guests' bedrooms. Having finished cooking, serving and clearing away, I would sort out the guests' bills and then go upstairs to snatch some toast and a cup of tea. Meanwhile, Andrew would be wandering about aimlessly and could find no other comment but to say, 'Oh, why can't you cook me a breakfast as well?!' But by now I would be into the airing cupboard to sort out piles of clean sheets and carry them along to the guest rooms. Later Stella would leave the bed linen and towels for washing outside the flat door and I would make my way through it during the course of the morning.

Chapter 51

Having now got more established, it was time to do something about the menu. I soon discovered that although the chef was a very pleasant young lad, he hadn't a clue how to cook! Nor had he any qualifications and the moment I made the menu more varied he was completely out of his depth. His cooking was limited to sticking beefburgers etc. on the griddle and using the deep-fat fryers. Discussing this problem with Andrew, I suggested that we advertise and pay a good wage to a qualified chef who could really turn out well-cooked and presentable food, my aim being to put ourselves on the map for outstanding cuisine as this would bring in the customers. Andrew absolutely refused to pay the kind of salary you have to pay for a good chef. In the end I was landed with all the cooking.

Andrew and I had bought the hotel with a three-and-a-half acre field and every Sunday there would be a huge car-boot sale. It had been established many years and people would travel long distances to come to it. Sellers were so keen that many a Saturday night they would be sleeping in their caravans or cars to set up early the following morning. We were obviously making a good profit from both the car-boot sale and the guests' accommodation, but when I tried to sit down and discuss the financial aspect, I was always told by Andrew, 'It's nothing to do with you. This is my pub hotel and I'm the landlord.' As if this wasn't enough, considering that I had signed for all the loans we had taken out in joint

partnership with the brewery, building society and bank, Andrew continued, 'I don't discuss my personal affairs with anyone.!'
'But Andrew, I'm your wife and we have a joint business account,' I said.
'I know what I'm doing and I will not discuss it,' said Andrew.
Time and time again I tried on various occasions but he dismissed me and just would not talk. I was banging my head against a brick wall.
For quite a while now I had seen Andrew opening the post and throwing yet another bill into the in-tray. It was piling up but nothing was being done about it. I tried one last time at speaking to him.
'Why don't we get an accountant in once a week to sort out the paperwork? I'll file everything under different headings and we can then get straight. After all, I have a wealth of experience as a secretary.'
'No,' said Andrew, 'I'm not going to have anybody seeing my private affairs.'
Within a few months the bills were arriving with red lettering stamped across them—this is your final statement. The strain and worry made me sick with fear. Cooking breakfasts, lunches and dinners single-handed plus all the washing up, shopping at the cash and carry, ordering deliveries, coping with guests and all the laundry and ironing meant I was on my feet eighteen hours a day! Andrew never took me out for an evening away from it all, nor did he ever try to make time for us to have a day out together.

It was such a large building with literally hundreds of windows and entrances that I decided we really should have a dog for security reasons. We were situated on a roundabout six miles from town and it was extremely isolated. I had always wanted a Labrador retriever so when someone told me that they had seen an advert in the local newspaper, I rang the breeder. Six puppies had been born and were now eight weeks old but three had already been sold. Andrew and I drove over after lunch to see them. Yellow furry bundles with tummies that bulged played on the kitchen floor whilst I got on my hands and knees to examine them from every angle.

Having chosen a pup and got his menu sorted out we made our way back. Although I had covered my lap and the floor of the car with newspaper, the pup spent its time being sick. Back at the pub, having cleaned him up and settled him in his box, I then had to change and have a bath myself.

The open-plan kitchen was ideal for a puppy because it had a floor that could be mopped. A bit of garden trellis kept him in while not excluding him from seeing everybody passing up and down. I soon learnt that a Labrador has in its nature two things that cannot be changed—a passion for water of any kind and carrying things. They also love company and are not the kind of dog to be left for hours alone. Leaving a small dish of water, I came back just in time to see the pup tip the whole lot up with a paw. Face drenched, water everywhere, he was thoroughly enjoying himself! I tried again, refilling the dish with water but it continued to be

tipped up. Next morning, I made the firm decision to get a heavy porcelain bowl with DOG written on it!
William was coming to stay for a few days and we decided it was time to give the pup a name. Nobody seemed to be very inspired and besides there was a whole day's work to get through. Apart from feeding the pup and dashing up and down the stairs at intervals to check that we still had a trellis, the pup was left to his own devices.
He was on three meals a day and his menu consisted of scrambled egg and Weetabix. It was during the third day of having the pup that we noticed him sitting in front of his bowl. A bit of scrambled egg had fallen into his new water bowl and he was putting his head on one side gazing at it from all angles. We went into fits of laughter and wondered what the pup would do next. Suddenly, he immersed his head into the water blowing bubbles through his nostrils and he resurfaced with the bit of egg. Very pleased with himself, he then went off to find one of his toys and dropped that in the water. By this time, we were absolutely convulsed with laughter and the word snorkelling came into the conversation.
From then on the pup amused himself frequently snorkelling and so he was named 'Snorkels'. However, although pronounced as such, I changed the spelling to 'Snorkles'. Little could I have imagined that this small pup was to become such a marvellous companion. Extremely intelligent and adaptable, Snorkles learnt very quickly to be house-trained. In the afternoons, I would dedicate a playtime and this would consist of a cardboard box. Galloping up and down the corridor he would drag his

box, falling all over the place. It also served as exercise for his razor sharp milk teeth and stopped him from ever chewing anything of value.

Ten days after Snorkles' arrival I received his pedigree certificate, along with a note from his breeder. She hoped that I was pleased with the pup and he had settled in. I wrote back to say that Snorkles had immediately bonded with me. He felt quite at home with all the loving attention and had taken over our kitchen with all his puppy paraphernalia. On reading through his pedigree, I realised that he came from aristocracy.

Gt.Gt.Gt.Grandparents		=	Sandringham Sidney Sandringham Ranger
Gt.Gt.Grandparent		=	Sandringham Shot
His parents:	Sire	=	Kamasim Bracken
	Dam	=	Purdie

The pup was given the dignitary title of honour and knighted: Sir Snorkles.

One Saturday morning a postcard arrived from Spain. It was from Carlos and had been sent from Toledo. I instinctively knew that something was terribly wrong. Apparently he was travelling on business and would I ring him at his father's flat when he got back in a month's time. I put the postcard on my desk and went about the day's work.

Early evening, I came upstairs and sat down to read

Carlos's postcard again, studying the rather badly stamped postmark. I suddenly realised the postcard had taken a month to reach me. Immediately, I dialled and Carlos answered the phone.

'I want to come and see you, mama,' he said.

'Yes, of course,' I said.

'I'll get a ticket and ring you back on Tuesday,' Carlos continued.

'How long will you stay?' I asked. There was no reply so I continued quickly, 'Don't worry, you can come for as long as you want.' I knew the moment I had asked the question that Carlos would not be buying a return air ticket.

Chapter 52

I was experiencing all sorts of problems in the kitchen. It was a ridiculous situation and I could not be doing so many jobs with so very little help. A good salary would have enabled us to have a first class chef and I could then have had peace of mind in that department. But no, Andrew wasn't going to discuss the matter and just expected me to cope with everything. Desperate to find a chef, I took on a Frenchman who didn't ask for an exorbitant salary and I was surprised to find that he had qualifications. So on Thursday morning he made me some egg sandwiches and I set off to catch the train for London. Having seated myself comfortably and fumbled about in my handbag to check the flight arrival, I sat gazing out of the window. My mind was racing for it had been thirteen months since I had last seen Carlos and he was now twenty years of age.

A word of advice is strongly recommended at this point about the rather obnoxious smell that egg sandwiches give off in an enclosed area! The train was quite full and I was wedged in next to another lady and there were two gentlemen opposite. While I ate my sandwiches I had continued to watch the passing countryside and was deep in thought. Anxiously checking the time on my wristwatch, I looked up and found the lady next to me shifting herself as far away as possible. The gentlemen opposite had both lowered their newspapers and were peering over the tops with distasteful grimaces on their faces. All the passengers across the aisle were gazing in my direction and one woman was holding a handkerchief over her nose! I nearly said in a loud voice—'It's the sandwiches, not me, honestly'—but decided against further embarrassment. It was a great relief when the train arrived at Victoria.

I stood inside Heathrow airport with a group of people waiting for the passengers to appear from the Malaga flight. Tentative and emotions running high, the tears started to flow as I looked in horror at what I saw. I watched my son walk towards the railings which divided us carrying one small battered suitcase. Carlos was desperately thin with spots all over his face and great hollow bags underneath his eyes. He was exhausted, looked anaemic and far from well. I knew there and then that I had to find the strength to help him all I could.

As we hugged each other, I gave thanks that Carlos had remembered the words which I had always engraved on my children's memories— 'No matter where I am, I shall always love you as a mother. Whether I'm here or in England, the door will always be open.'—Thank God Carlos had done just that!

While travelling on the train, Carlos told me of the horrific things his father had made him endure. I sat stunned at his story, unable to believe that Marcos had taken Paloma and Carlos away from me not only to make my life hell on earth but their lives too. Marcos had been incapable of loving anyone except himself; those human beings around him would be treated with cruelty, tormented physically and mentally.

For the next week or so I was far too busy trying to spend

as much time as possible with Carlos and felt like a bit of elastic being stretched to its limit! There was little time at this point to see what the French chef was up to in the kitchen. The shock was to come later.

Carlos and I went out to buy clothes whenever I could snatch a couple of hours and get into town. He had literally left everything behind and brought only a jersey, pair of trousers and a change of underwear. One morning a few days after Carlos had arrived, I noticed blood all over his sheets. Over the next weeks Carlos had continuous nose bleeds. There was no warning at all; the blood would just pour from his nostrils.

Carlos told me how his father would come home after having been drinking or simply in a bad temper and hit him across the head or face. It was clear why he was getting anaemic and the nose bleeds had been going on for far too long. Some weeks later, Carlos had the veins in his nostrils cauterised in hospital and that, mercifully, put an end to the bleeding.

The weekend after Carlos arrived, William came to stay for a few days. The boys were chatting and listening to music and I went into their bedroom. I sat on the floor propped up against a bed and on my lap was Snorkles. It was a lovely feeling just to sit and look at Carlos and it made me realise how much I had missed him with all those precious years lost. The boys were laughing and moving about the room and Snorkles was sitting bolt upright. He watched them as if he was watching Wimbledon tennis and I hadn't realised how excited he was getting. Suddenly, a warm flow of urine went through my skirt and down my legs. It was the one and only time Snorkles ever had an accident and after that he was always quite exceptional in every way.

The weeks had gone by and Snorkles was now allowed the freedom of the flat. He had discovered the flat door open one day and had positioned himself at the top of the steep stairway. These led straight down into the lounge bar and gave a good view of everything going on. The stairs were too much of an ordeal for a small pup to negotiate so every evening he would lie on the landing with his front paws hanging over the first step. He found it very entertaining and would wait until I or Carlos carried him outside to do a wee.

I now spent an hour every afternoon in the field with his training lessons. He learnt quickly, possibly because when I could see he was getting bored we would stop and play. Then it was back to the training and sometimes a short ride in the car. This was to stop the car sickness and within a few weeks he thoroughly enjoyed being driven about.

Chapter 53

Carlos had started to look a better colour, had put on a little weight and was re-learning all the English he had forgotten. He was even helping Andrew behind the bar in the evenings.

Early one morning I was checking the larder supplies and discovered that the large container of cooking wine from the top shelf was empty and some bottles of wine had vanished. I had noticed on my visits to the kitchen or passing through it that the chef did not speak very clearly on occasions. I also noticed that the kitchen was not being kept clean and the chef had no organisation at all. Later that morning my suspicions were confirmed and I caught him swaying about with a bottle in his hand. So this meant that I had to take over in the kitchen yet again.

On Sundays, the situation with the car-boot sale was that when all the sellers had parked on the field, Andrew would go round each person and get the fee from them. Meanwhile, the lounge and pool-room bars would be getting crowded with two bar girls trying to manage the whole scenario. They would, of course, be taking food orders as well.

While Andrew spent all morning conversing with car-boot sellers and wandering about buying things we didn't need, I was slaving away in the kitchen. Every Sunday brought the same problems and as much as I complained to Andrew the more obstinate he became. He should have been serving behind the bar and changing barrels when they ran out. Instead, I would have to charge off to the field in the midst of cooking and try and find him. Not an easy task, considering there were three-and-a-half acres of field and about four hundred cars, not to mention people. After one particularly harrowing Sunday, I said to Andrew, 'Let Carlos take the entrance fee on a Sunday.'

'Nobody is taking that money except me,' he replied. His complete obstinacy would, sooner or later, be our downfall. Andrew, also, had got very stroppy with the customers and one evening we ended up with a nasty incident. Two yobbo types with a large dog marched into the bar. One of the men removed the dog and then they were told to go into the pool-room because they were wearing jeans. While Andrew was busy doing something else they got served by the barmaid in the lounge bar and stood menacingly with their pint glasses of beer. Andrew told them to move out to the pool-room but the men stood motionless. One man broke his glass on the edge of the bar and opened the flap door and threw it at Carlos. My son turned quickly and the flying jagged glass cut him on the back of the neck. While this was going on the other yobbo had spied the young barmaid crouched down behind the bar. Leaning over the side, he poured his pint of beer over her head and then both men walked out.

I had finished clearing up the kitchen and was up in the flat when Andrew appeared. There stood Carlos with blood pouring down his back and the barmaid drenched, shaking with shock and crying.

Chapter 54

One morning Andrew came into the kitchen and announced, 'I've had a phone call from a coach company. They are taking a hundred and fifty people on a day's outing and wanted to know if we could do them bar meals. They'll be here on Saturday at 12.00 a.m.,' finished Andrew and breezed out of the kitchen.

As it was I was suffering from extreme tiredness and told him that the least he could do was find out whether I could manage all this cooking single-handed. 'We need the money,' was Andrew's reply.

At this point, without consulting me, he had employed a handyman called Fred. Not only had Andrew made the mistake of paying him by the hour but had him employed nearly every day of the week. Although Fred was a pleasant man he was retired and therefore not young. He knew how to be painstakingly slow and would potter about for hours on end. Invariably, I would meet him during the course of the day two or three times and he was always on his way to fetch a tool that he'd forgotten from the boot of his car. Fred was costing us a bomb and the money that should have been paying the bills was not getting priority.

I answered the phone one morning and was asked if we could provide drinks and coffee to a coach-load of old-aged pensioners passing through our way. The coach duly arrived and while the barmaids served cold drinks I poured endless cups of coffee. Finally, the old-aged pensioners made their way back to the car park and it was

at this point that the barmaids turned to me and said, 'Most of the glasses have disappeared.' I had the embarrassing job of going out and telling the coach driver that the coach wasn't going anywhere until I had our glasses returned. Standing by the driver we watched as tumblers appeared from underneath the seating and out of handbags! It certainly was an eye-opener to say the least.
The building had an adjoining functions room which was so full of old furniture and junk that it was almost impossible to open the door. Old dirty bits of blanket and curtains hung from the bay windows and the room had obviously seen better days.
One afternoon we all had a blitz and got a bonfire going. Carlos made endless journeys with the most amazing rubbish and useless things. The room had literally had everything thrown into it and had been used as a rubbish tip. Clouds of dust and cobwebs appeared as I let in the daylight. It was going to be a mammoth task to get it up and running.
Making my way through the Yellow Pages, I managed to sell off two fruit machines, a dilapidated piano, an old potato peeler, a coffee percolator, a small griddle and a whole lot of old, heavy, ugly chairs covered in faded red material. Carlos took over the job of decorating and did a tremendous amount of work. Whenever I went to enquire whether he had had any lunch he would be painting a ceiling or wall.
'Can you bring me two beefburgers with cheese in sesame buns, mama?' he would say as he stood on a ladder. I would gaze up and see a large tin of paint precariously

balancing on the edge of a plank.
In between all of this, I had been teaching Carlos to type and giving him exercises to write in English.
In the middle of August I received a phone call from Eric. He had come over to England to stay with his daughter.
'Would love to come and see you,' said Eric.
'We'd love to have you. I'll meet you at the station,' I replied. It was wonderful to see Eric again and he was his usual cheerful self and looked very well. He stayed for four days and I would take him a breakfast tray in the mornings. There was little time to enjoy his company but I did escape one afternoon taking Eric for a drive and found a nice tea-room out in the country. While we sat and had a cream tea we caught up with our news and he could see how the worry and strain was affecting me.
In October a hundred bicyclists descended on us. They had booked a full English breakfast. Stella stood and fried eggs as if there was no tomorrow. Carlos and Andrew took plates out of the kitchen whilst I cooked the rest. The clearing up was awful and it put me off cooked breakfasts forever.
By now it was November and the functions room had been completed. I was just praying, as a last resort, that with business meetings, buffets and discos it would bring in that extra cash for the in-tray on Andrew's desk was overflowing with bills. I went to have a look one morning and was simply terrified. Andrew knew it was out of his control now and, like an ostrich, pretended the bills weren't there.
I pleaded with Andrew to let me sort out the furniture and

decorations for the functions room. I knew that with some money every week from the car-boot sale I could find some good second-hand furniture, etc. Andrew was having none of it and, to my horror, started to order brand new tables and chairs. So many filled the room that it became physically impossible to hoover the carpet without going through one hell of a manoeuvre. The cost was horrendous. 'You mind your own business, it's my hotel,' Andrew kept saying. 'I'm the landlord.'

It was around this time that I realised that I was only there to slave over the fryers and griddle in the kitchen heat up to my elbows in grease. I was expected to manage the hard and dirty jobs plus all the hotel laundry in a normal sized washing machine and dryer. Cash and carry once a week took up most of the morning and thank God I had Carlos to help me. There were food representatives and every other kind of representative to see; lists of meat and vegetables to order, staff to interview and staff problems to sort out; the cleaning out of the kitchen, changing the oil in the fat fryers every Monday morning. It never ended and the days merged into weeks and the weeks into months.

I started to feel that I hadn't enough strength to get through another day. The financial pressure and physical endurance with endless hours was making me ill. I still had the menopause and would stand in the kitchen, greasy and unbearably hot. Sometimes, I thought I was going to pass out, but knew I had to keep going; there was no escape.

On my birthday Carlos gave me a card and bought me some earrings. At the top of the card was written, 'Happy

Birthday to a Wonderful Mother'. Under this was a picture of a woman with her pinafore on standing by an ironing board trying to iron with her left hand. The right hand held a hoover, whilst her right foot was mixing a cake and her left foot was attached to a large ball and chain. Behind her was a stove with an overflowing saucepan. Inside, the card had the same lady dressed up in evening dress with a footman bowing as she entered the Ritz. The wording was, 'It's your turn to have a day off for good behaviour!' To this day I treasure that card and it never fails to bring a smile to my face.

It was a bitterly cold November as Carlos and I walked round the forest pond which was covered in a thick layer of ice. Snorkles was by now eight months old and a sturdy healthy pup. We were deep in conversation and suddenly realised that Snorkles was on the opposite side of this large pond. Waiting for the pup to catch up with us we watched in amazement as Snorkles leapt into the air and crashed down upon the ice. He had never swum before and immediately set off, rather like a steam boat, full throttle ahead. His little paws were brought down with such force breaking the ice with sheer determination to reach us. Having cut a pathway to where we were standing, he struggled up the embankment, gave himself a good shake and stood looking up at us wagging his tiny tail.

Chapter 55

By the end of November I had a young girl called Agnes as chef in the kitchen. She was a pleasant girl with qualifications but lacking experience and confidence. So when we started having buffets in the functions room I would manage these and she would keep the meals going. One evening I received a phone call from a gentleman who asked me if I would order a large bouquet of flowers. These were for his wife on their wedding anniversary. The husband booked a table for four for the following week. That particular evening, I laid a table up in the alcove by the fireplace and put a little vase of flowers on it. It was Agnes's day off so I was cooking that evening. Explaining the special event to Andrew I said that whatever he did he would have to be down by 7.00 p.m. to fetch the wine from the cellar when the customers requested it.

The two couples sat in the lounge bar and ordered some drinks. Meanwhile, the superb bouquet of flowers and other presents were handed over to the wife by the husband. Everything was ready for the evening's cooking and I personally took their order for food. They browsed through the wine list and chose a bottle. Andrew was nowhere to be seen and I had dashed back to the kitchen to prepare the starters.

I sent the waitress upstairs and she came back with the message, 'There's no answer in your flat.' We tried ringing by phone from the kitchen—no reply. The starters were sent out and I was now battling with steaks, grills and other orders that were coming in. Dashing up the stairs to our flat I found Andrew having a bath! By the time the two couples got their wine they were half way through their main course and not too pleased. There was no team work between us and I had tried with all my heart to help Andrew. Time had come to think seriously about the future.

In the middle of December I found myself with two discos in the same week. Not only did this involve a tremendous amount of extra shopping but cooking. It was a constant physical strain and a total of eighty people had to be catered for on the Tuesday and sixty on the Saturday. Six days later it was Christmas Day!

Muggins found herself in the kitchen cooking forty-five Christmas lunches. It was a nightmare and it took three hours to clear up the kitchen afterwards. I came out covered in grease, absolutely exhausted and completely congested by the heat from the ovens. I'll never forget the scenario as long as I live. Andrew was all dressed up in a suit drinking wine with the customers in the functions room and thoroughly enjoying the social scene. He hadn't even bothered to wish me a happy Christmas or even bring me a glass of wine.

I was too tired to eat and physically shattered. Eventually at 6.00 p.m. I threw myself on the bed unable to cope anymore. By now I had moved out of our bedroom and was sleeping on the sofa bed in Carlos's room. He and I would chat in the dark for ages until sleep took over from my total fatigue.

One evening in January, I felt that I had forgotten what the outside world looked like. Andrew and I had been there nine months and he had never taken me out at all. It was all consuming me and I felt that I was in a prison with no escape. The only highlight of the week was going to the Cash and Carry. This was the most tedious and boring operation imaginable. Added to this, I was in constant pain and didn't look at all well. 'Come on, mama,' said Carlos. 'I'll take you out to the Little Chef just to get away.' We walked across the road and ordered some coffee and cake. It was like heaven, just to sit there away from it all. About twenty minutes later, we walked back into the lounge bar. There were customers being served at the bar and a few others sitting at tables. At this point Andrew said in a loud voice, 'And where do you think you've been?'

'Little Chef,' I replied.

'What for?' asked Andrew.

'What do you think one goes to a Little Chef for?' replied Carlos as he made his way up the stairs. Hilarious laughter from the customers followed Carlos's remark.

The following afternoon on returning from Snorkles's daily constitutional, Andrew was standing on the entrance steps to the hotel.

'Guess what,' he announced, smiling as I got out of the car. 'We've had a bailiff here looking round and making notes.'

Carlos and I looked at each other and froze, whilst Andrew just stood and laughed!

I couldn't go on living with all these loans and debts around me, whilst the worry was destroying my health. Unbeknown to Andrew, I had already been to see a solicitor for legal advice. He came to the same conclusion and agreed that the situation I found myself in could not continue. So divorce proceedings were now underway. Not being able to cope any longer with the financial situation which was getting worse by the week, the solicitor came up with the only way out. This was to leave the hotel to Andrew, plus financial debts, sign myself out of the partnership and everything to do with the business. In February, after several X-rays, a stomach ulcer was confirmed. I was struggling to get through the days in great pain with continual migraines, but I had to keep on my feet because of the business. My doctor pointed out, 'No medicine is going to cure you while you continue with the constant strain and financial worry.' My solicitor, basically, echoed the same remarks. 'Get out before your health packs up completely through worry and exhaustion.'

On 15th March Snorkles had his first birthday. He had grown into a large friendly bouncy Labrador whom everyone adored.

Chapter 56

Perhaps the reader thinks by now I had forgotten all about my natural mother. She was constantly on my mind and not a day went by without wondering where she was. My investigations had brought me to a full stop and I'd even written to the Pensions Head Office, but they would give me no information as to her whereabouts. I wanted, above all else, to find my natural mother before she died. Time was running out for she was, by now, eighty-two years of age.

Three days after Snorkles's birthday, I received an extraordinary phone call. Someone I had met during my visit to the village where my natural mother used to live had received a letter from her. That person rang to give me her present address.

I put the phone down weak at the knees and grabbed a chair. The tears poured down my face with emotion and relief at this breakthrough. The years of misery, frustration and searching for my natural mother had come to an end. I had visions of us sitting holding hands laughing and crying as we told each other a lifetime.

After the initial shock I wrote out a telemessage, begging her to ring me and that I would drive down to Chelmsford and bring her back to stay.

There was no reply. I spent all the next day jumping every time the phone rang and by the evening was in complete despair. At 5.00 p.m. I could bear the silence no longer and got in touch with the Salvation Army. They went round to see my natural mother. The message from her

was quite clear—she did not want to see me.
Next day I contacted the local vicar who was kind enough to go and see my natural mother but to no avail.
Meanwhile, there were other important things in my life that urgently needed attention and had to take immediate priority. My solicitor had mentioned that I must sort out somewhere to live and that the moment the documents were ready for signing I would then be free to depart.
In May Carlos and I went on a caravan hunt. We were fortunate enough to find a married couple who ran a family business with their son and they were extremely kind and helpful. They managed to fix us up with a second-hand caravan at a reasonable price. At this point, what worried me most was my health. Totally exhausted and with continual stomach pain, I wondered how long I could cope. But in a crisis you cannot sit and do nothing. Life has to go on and we had to make the best of this complete nightmare. Not only had I myself to think about but Carlos as well and this made me fight for survival. Selling some jewellery which had belonged to my grandmother to raise the money, Carlos towed the caravan back to the hotel. He spent his time working underneath the chassis, painting and making sure everything was alright. Meanwhile, I sorted out the route we were to embark upon and booked a place on a camping site.
It all had to be organised like a military operation. Saucepans, cutlery, essentials, clothes to a minimum, plus one large Labrador to accommodate in a small space. Once everything was put in its place Carlos towed the caravan to a nearby site. Andrew kept stating that he was

keeping all the furniture and even had the nerve to mention constantly that he was going to keep my car to run his business with. The car was in my name and, as the solicitor pointed out, was legally mine.

But Andrew, not content with all he had, was getting stroppy. How short his memory was when I had given him my hard-earned savings to survive and stood by him through thick and thin. Having signed over the hotel and pub to Andrew and put my signature to the divorce papers, I was now legally free to leave. Due to his possessiveness and complete lack of communication I decided that the only way to leave was by doing a bunk. So Carlos and I prepared the way for leaving in what can only be described as 'in rather a hurry'!

We decided on the morning which was to be 4th June 1988. I left after breakfast with Snorkles and—of all things at a time like this—a collection of potted houseplants bouncing about in the boot of the car! Carlos stayed on to snatch Snorkles's bedding and dishes on the way out and we made our way to the site nearby where our caravan awaited us.

Chapter 57

I was in no fit state to drive anywhere and just wanted a few days to unwind. So for the next three days we took things easy. While Carlos pottered about overhauling his car engine I got down to typing letters and working out our plan of action. We also had to get into a routine in such cramped living conditions and get used to putting one thing away before getting another out. But oddly enough, there was something about the caravan that was strangely comforting. It was a roof over our heads and there were no more financial pressures or responsibilities. The feeling of relief was tremendous and the burden had been lifted.

On 7th June Carlos and I set off at 6.30 a.m. in convoy for our base in Oxford. I had chosen this county because it was fairly central for travelling from A to B for interviews. Carlos managed to tow the caravan extremely well, having had no previous experience. Map reading had never been my forte so I was more than a little surprised when I actually managed to lead the way without completely getting lost. Not that any one wants to lose their way when it means reversing a caravan. Those who have had this experience will know what I mean!

On spying a Little Chef on the outskirts of Oxford we stopped for a cooked breakfast and cups of coffee. Snorkles had been so good that you would have thought he had been travelling always. He trotted about the car park and then heard the clatter of his doggy bowl and gulped down his breakfast. On arrival we spent the day

settling in at the campsite.
Next morning we bought a magazine and Carlos saw a living in job as a barman. Ringing the pub which was forty-five minutes' drive away he went for an interview and got the job on a month's trial. The large campsite stretched out in every direction and behind us was a hedge with open fields. The reception area was right over on the other side of a river which meant crossing a bridge. It was extremely isolated and I was not happy about staying there alone.
We examined our caravan site book and found other places to see and set off to explore the surrounding villages. We discovered a beautiful place and it was run as a family business. Instantly the site gave me the feeling of being safe and secure.
Carlos left after lunch to take up his new-found job. I was still shell-shocked, feeling totally drained of any energy but the stomach pains had eased a bit. Trying to forget the horrific past, I spent my time taking long walks through the fields with Snorkles. I knew, however, that sooner rather than later I would have to find a job before the cold weather arrived and get some money coming in.
I started answering advertisements and reading through the local newspaper. The campsite phone could only be used for outgoing calls and this made life very complicated. Wandering through the village I discovered a pub where I could take incoming calls. This meant that after writing in answer to an advertisement for a job I could give the number of the public pub phone. I would then have to stand about the pub entrance in the evenings

and wait for a call. It really was most tedious but the only means of speaking to anyone. On one of my frequent visits to the pub, John, the landlord, got chatting and offered me a drink. On another occasion he introduced me to his daughter and son.

Valerie was receiving my mail and then forwarding it to me. She wrote and asked me to go and stay, so Snorkles and I went to her house in Hampshire for two nights. By sheer coincidence I had an interview with a gentleman who lived some twenty miles away from her.

Here I come to the point when I must make a few comments on what some people seem to think will do as accommodation for a living in housekeeper! On this particular occasion, I wouldn't have wished the housekeeper's accommodation on anybody. It was unfit for any human being to live in. A flight of stone steps took us down to the basement. It was cold, damp and it was June. There were no carpets or radiators. On asking the owner where one was meant to hang one's clothes, I was shown an iron rail fixed into the wall in the corridor! The windows looked out onto a concrete wall, where the sunlight never entered, making it dark and gloomy. It was quite appalling in every way.

Snorkles and I returned from Hampshire late afternoon to the caravan. Next morning whilst getting breakfast John appeared on his bicycle. 'Would you like to come for lunch on Sunday?' he asked. 'The children would love to see you,' he continued.

'Yes, that would be nice. I'll look forward to it.'

I always wondered how Snorkles adapted to whatever

situation he was put in. A large young Labrador in a small caravan was not the ideal place at all, but during the day he would be quite content if he was allowed to jump up onto one of the beds and could watch everything that was going on outside. He spent a lot of time walking with me or travelling in the car, but I did wonder on the few occasions that he was left in the caravan if he would rip it up! So, leaving him with his nose pressed up against the window, I drove off for Sunday lunch.

John's children were lovely. Elizabeth was six and Donald was four years old. After lunch the children came to see my caravan and fetch Snorkles for a walk. Later, John asked me if I would like to take Elizabeth and Donald shopping one morning. They needed new clothes and John had no transport so I was only too pleased to take the children with me.

I spent an enjoyable morning and whilst armed with all sorts of different garments Elizabeth suddenly said, 'May I call you Mummy while we are in the shop?'

I tried not to look surprised and gently said, 'Yes, of course you can.'

After trying on and buying an assortment of clothes we sat in a coffee shop and then made our way back to the pub. John had an evening off work in a few days' time and we arranged to go and have dinner in another village nearby. It was during our meal that he told me about the past. Two years previously, John's wife had walked out leaving the children with him. He was unable to drive due to having a hereditary condition which affects the eyes. Therefore, John had been obliged to take a living in job

where he could work and look after his children. John had found this small pub and rented it off the brewery.
I had worked fourteen months without a day's break!

Chapter 58

I had been on the caravan site for a month and was starting to worry about the financial side of things. The thought of winter and having to traipse across the sopping wet grass to the loo or clutching a sponge bag for a shower in the freezing cold really was an irksome thought. So in the middle of July I took a job as housekeeper with a lady who lived in a large Cotswolds stone house. We were miles from anywhere surrounded by country lanes and fields. It was very isolated but beggars can't be choosers. Once installed in a wing of the house I then discovered, when the gardener arrived, that housekeepers had come and gone on a continual non-stop basis and I soon discovered why. I had to clean the house in the mornings and then was free for the rest of the day. This was partly why I took the job because I didn't feel well enough to work full time. The other reason was that although Mrs. R. had two dogs she didn't object to mine. In the afternoons I would take Snorkles out and we would walk for miles in the surrounding countryside.

It was shortly after moving in that Mrs. R. told me one morning that I was not to have a bath at night after 8.30 p.m. 'The noise from the water tank keeps me awake,' Mrs. R. explained.

'The water's cold in the morning,' I said.

'The hot water timer is set to come on late in the mornings,' Mrs. R. said, and that was that.

More rules followed by telling me that no visitors of the opposite sex were allowed. I felt intimidated, most unwelcome and in Victorian times. I was introduced to another housekeeper called Wendy and she arranged for me to go out with her and some friends one evening to a village pub. Next morning I was told that I was not to go out in the evenings as it made her dogs bark.

One afternoon Wendy invited me round to her place for tea. It was there that my suspicions were confirmed about Mrs. R.'s behaviour. It so happened that one of the former housekeepers was passing by and popped in to see Wendy. She told me that Mrs. R. kept crates of gin in the priest's hole! No little wonder that she had to go to bed so early. In a way I felt sorry for this obviously lonely old lady drowning herself in gin. She wanted company but mine was clearly not good enough for her and I was, as far as she was concerned, only there to clean her house. Mrs. R. could be extremely rude and became quite nasty verbally, but I knew I had no choice but to put up with her. I kept the house spotless and did whatever she wanted me to do being always pleasant and diplomatic.

In the evenings I would sit alone with my beloved Snorkles for company in a badly lit, damp sitting room, whilst Mrs. R. sat on the other side of the house by a roaring fire! I was only forty-five minutes' drive from John's pub and because of the feeling of utter despair and loneliness I would drive over once a week in the afternoon and stay until the following evening.

John was happy-go-lucky, nothing appeared to bother him much and the children were always very pleased to see me and Snorkles. While all this was going on, I received a call from Carlos one morning while I was busy polishing

furniture. 'I've taken a job as bar manager at a pub a mile down the road from John,' he said.
'That's wonderful,' I said. 'I'll come over and see you.'
At the beginning of October on one of my weekly visits to see John and the children, a plan for escape became a reality. We all got on well together and enjoyed each other's company so John came up with the idea that I should move into the pub. It seemed an ideal solution and John and Carlos went into action hiring a van to move my belongings from the terrible Mrs. R.
For the first few weeks I had a spring clean upstairs as John's lack of housework was abundantly clear. The children and I spent an afternoon pulling clothes out of wardrobes and drawers to find that they had outgrown most of them. After a lot of hard work everything started to take on a more organised lifestyle. John had an old Collie dog who spent its time slumped behind the bar. The poor dog's hind legs were getting very stiff. He tried to take on a new lease of life on seeing Snorkles and actually managed to struggle up the road one afternoon, unbeknown to us. Someone in the village rang John and he had to get a wheelbarrow to bring the dog back!
On Christmas Day we laid a table downstairs in the pub and Carlos joined us for lunch. Elizabeth and Donald were so excited and by this time they had bonded with me and were very happy to have me living with them. New Year's Eve found us working hard right up to the midnight chimes behind the bar. Having worked all through the festive season, John and I firmly decided to have a day away from it all.

One evening I explained to John about my adoption and the tremendous desire to see my natural mother. Although she had told the Salvation Army and the local vicar that she didn't want to see me I still felt that seeing me in person might make her change her mind. A part of me was missing and I had a right to see the woman who had brought me into the world. Besides, time was running out because she was by now eighty-three years of age.

'Well, let's go and see her,' John said. So on 10th January 1989 we set off for Chelmsford.

Having planned out a course of action, I bought a beautiful bouquet of flowers. We found the house and whilst John walked about nearby with Snorkles, I went and rang the front door bell. A man came to the door and I asked him if Mrs. Eleanor Hunt lived there. He disappeared and after a minute or two my natural mother was standing in front of me. 'I've come from the florist to deliver these flowers for you,' I said calmly.

'Who are they from?' she asked, looking surprised.

'There's a card with them,' I said as I was about to hand it to her.

'Would you read it for me?' she said.

'It says that they are from your daughter.'

She never flinched or changed expression and then said, 'I don't want them so will you give them to a hospital?'

I looked straight into her face as I pronounced, 'You are looking at your daughter.'

There was no reaction, no catching her breath in surprise, no exclamation. She was void of all emotion as she continued, 'Please leave. It was a long, long time ago and

I'm not well.'
'Take the flowers and enjoy them,' I replied.
'No, I would rather you gave them away,' she answered.
'Will you give me your hand before I leave?' I asked. I took her outstretched hand and held it in between my hands whilst gazing into her blue eyes. Then I turned away and walked out into the street again, still clutching the flowers.
John met me and we walked back to the car. I sat for about ten minutes very quietly and just said, 'She didn't want to know me.'
My mind kept asking the same question, 'What have I done to be so rejected all my life?' I wanted to be loved so much and perhaps that is why it caught me totally unprepared when later that day, while stopping to walk Snorkles in a muddy field, John asked me to marry him. Emotions were in a turmoil and I felt very unwanted, vulnerable and totally alone in the world. There was nothing stable in my life and suddenly I felt that perhaps my role was now to care for John, Elizabeth and Donald. They all needed someone to love them and so I turned to John and said, 'Yes, I will.'

Chapter 59

John knew a couple who lived in the village and helped out running the pub when he had a day off or was on holiday. You couldn't wish to meet a nicer couple than Roger and Carol. So we took two days off and drove up to Morecambe so that John's mother could see us. The moment I saw Nancy I liked her. She was kind, pleasant, homely and made me immediately feel very welcome.
Carlos took a week's holiday at the end of January and went back to Jerez to see his sister. On his return he decided that he wanted to do some kind of training. John gave him mock interviews which were hilariously funny. Carlos would stand outside the sitting room door and then knock. John would say, 'Come in,' and then 'Good morning Mr. B......, do take a seat.'
In between breaking down with laughter, or something inappropriate that was said, the sitting room door spent a lot of time opening and shutting with repeated interviews. After numerous classes working on Carlos's English and typing out CVs, we eventually considered him fit for an interview. So I duly sent out letters to different companies and we waited in suspense.
Carlos was accepted by a well known food company to start his training as Assistant Manager. I had a mad rush to wash and iron his clothes and pack up the suitcases before his departure. No sooner had I done this than Valerie came to stay with her Labrador. The dogs behaved very well together and we were able to catch up on our news, taking long walks around the lakes and countryside.

After she left I started to go into a hundred mile an hour whirlwind. Our wedding was to be on 21st April. John, Elizabeth and Donald had to be fitted out with the appropriate clothes and then I had to go off and search for a smart outfit. In the first week of April, John could no longer ignore his Collie's deterioration and constant pain. Not being able to face the obvious, he asked me to deal with him. One afternoon when John was out, I phoned Roger and we carried the old dog out to my car. I took him to the vet to be put down and had a good cry in the car before driving back to the pub.
Luckily, Elizabeth and Donald didn't get upset by the Collie's absence for they already had a full-time nanny and playmate. Snorkles supervised bathtimes, kissed them goodnight in bed and played with them first thing in the mornings. He was a large, bouncy, crazy, friendly Labrador and very much one of the family. Participating in everything that was going on to the point of getting himself in all the photos. In fact it was impossible to leave him out, because he would always get wedged in between the children ready for the camera to click!
On the day of our wedding, I drove Nancy and the children down to the Registry Office. John had gone off to a pub with his brother for a drink so he wasn't there when we arrived. That in itself was a bad start, and later, as time went by, alcohol became a serious issue.
After a family lunch we left Roger and Carol to cope with the pub and Snorkles. Elizabeth and Donald travelled back to Morecambe with their granny. On our second day away John rang to speak to Roger to see if everything was

alright. I then enquired about Snorkles and Carol said, 'He's right beside me. I'll put the phone to his ear and you can speak to him!'
I made silly noises, told him he was a good boy and generally made a fool of myself.
'Oh yes,' said Carol, 'he's putting his head on one side, listening to you.'
On 27th we fetched Elizabeth and Donald from Morecambe and drove back to Oxfordshire. Next morning Elizabeth was taken ill with mumps. From that day onwards it became totally exhausting with one thing on top of another in a never-ending sequence of events. John and I wanted to get out of the licensed trade for it wasn't fair on the children either. So as John was unable to drive due to his impaired sight, I did all the driving. Every week from 25th June through the entire summer I would do a six-hour journey to Shrewsbury and back. It was sweltering weather and having arrived there we would house-hunt for hours seeing different places.
On 1st July there was a call from the nursing home to say that my mother had had a stroke. She had lost the power of speech and was almost completely paralysed. I immediately drove down to Sussex with John to see her. By the end of the year she had made a wonderful recovery.
I had been suffering with my feet ever since my twenties. The skin on my heels would break open in deep crevices and it was agony to walk. Since being on my feet so much, especially standing for hours on end catering, they had become quite chronic and many times the cracks would

bleed. I was constantly having to bandage them up. Eventually John decided that I ought to be seen by a specialist at the Birmingham Skin Hospital. We drove up at the crack of dawn on the 4th for an appointment at 10.45 a.m. It resulted that it was hereditary and therefore incurable but could only be alleviated by some ointment which was prescribed. This only confirmed what doctors, consultants and chiropodists had echoed in the past.
On the 16th Donald got the mumps, followed by Elizabeth with chicken pox on the 28th, followed by Donald with an extremely severe case of chicken pox on the 30th. July was a complete nightmare of illnesses.
Whilst John gave his notice into the brewery and sorted things that needed organising for the future, I set about selling my caravan. On 10th November it was Donald's sixth birthday so we had a party. He'd never had one before and I made a huge chocolate cake iced with white and blue icing decorated with elephants and candles. There were sixteen children invited and they had a whale of a time playing all the good old party games, whilst John provided the music on his keyboard.
By this time I had started buying some second-hand furniture. John would strip it down and then I would spend ages going through the process of applying various products finishing with a lot of polishing with beeswax.
We were moving in January so I decided to have a garage sale in the bottle room next to the cellar and managed to shift quite a lot of unwanted articles.
At the end of November John was suddenly taken very ill. The doctor didn't know what had struck him and said it

was some kind of virus. It seemed as if he was being emptied of all body fluid and I was worried that he might dehydrate completely. The mattress was soaked right through and I had to place bath towels underneath a continual change of sheets. It was totally impossible for me to cope with everything in the pub. Thank God for Roger and Carol who immediately stepped in to help. When John eventually got better he was extremely weak having lost a lot of weight.

December found me packing surrounded by tea-chests and boxes in the spare room. The landing and corridor was like an obstacle course with things that I kept tripping over or bumping into. In fact, without a doubt, my name should have been put in the Guinness Book of Records for obtaining an outstanding amount of bruises! It was such an exhausting month that I almost forgot to visit mother.

We set out for Sussex and John decided that he would visit Brighton while I went to the nursing home. Leaving him at the Burgess Hill station to catch his train, I drove on to mother. 'Do you think she is well enough to be taken out to lunch?' I asked the nuns.

'Oh, yes, she'll enjoy that,' they said.

'What about a glass of sherry?' I enquired.

'Oh, she can have whatever she fancies,' they assured me.

I took mother's arm and steered her towards the car. Having belted her in and about to start up the engine, she enquired as to who I was.

'I'm your daughter, Clare.'

'No,' she said, shaking her head. 'Haven't got one.'

She seemed quite happy as I drove out of the massive wrought iron gates and headed to a nearby pub. There were only a few days before the 25th and people were seated having Christmas lunches. Mother sat opposite me at the table and after we had established that she would like a sherry she sat clutching her handbag. She started to give people on the surrounding tables terrible looks and suddenly announced in a loud voice, 'They're trying to steal my handbag.'

I tried desperately to reassure her and started to talk about what she would like to have for lunch. I ordered at the bar, keeping an eye on mother all the time. While we waited for our food I was quietly telling her about her grandchildren.

'But you're not married,' she exclaimed. 'Where's their father?'

Her voice could be heard quite clearly and we had various couples staring in our direction.

'Mother please,' I implored, but she was off again.

She pointed a finger at me as she said, 'Who are you and why have you brought me here?' I was getting some very queer looks and it was becoming increasingly embarrassing.

Fortunately our food arrived and she ate some of it and then said she couldn't manage anymore. We had a sweet which she seemed to enjoy and then she wanted to go to the loo. She held onto my arm and insisted on me staying with her. We went back to the nursing home and she ripped open her presents as if she were a child again. Snorkles sat next to me and the duty nurse brought tea in before we left. The communal room was near mother's and as Snorkles padded past, all the ladies wanted to stroke him. He was very gentle and did his party piece, lifting his right paw and then his left to have them shaken, thoroughly enjoying all the fuss.

Chapter 60

The new year came in with John and I behind the bar with our departure still a secret. We raised our glasses in front of the customers and smiled smugly at each other. He had had previous trouble and was determined that we would leave in peace, without having a window smashed in or the car vandalised by those who had been banned from the pub—a common occurrence when a landlord leaves.
Upstairs chaos was reigning with boxes up to the ceiling in the spare room. Packing had to be done when the children weren't around and into the wee hours of the morning. Having to move from a pub into a house involves a nightmare of the worst kind and an experience I wouldn't want to wish on anyone. Umpteen shopping trips had to be made involving the most exhausting buying of domestic appliances. I dashed, endlessly, round the shops, down on my knees peering into cookers, then on for a set of plates, bounced up and down in armchairs and was completely bewildered by more than fifteen fat fryers, not to mention the many fridge doors I opened.
Then there was the question of what do we take, what do we leave and what do we burn? In the end we had an enormous bonfire in the field and got rid of all the old furniture from the children's playroom and all the junk from the bottle room. Elizabeth and Donald joined in watching with delight as an old bed and chairs were axed up and carted out.
Our last evening arrived and we told the children about the departure. Their little faces looked at us in disbelief

and utter amazement, because they had been under the impression that we were going to re-decorate. After the initial shock came hundreds of questions. 'Where are we going to live? Does that mean we will have a garden and never see the playroom again? Is there a big lorry coming?' And so it went on.

We could see no real hiccup the following morning when we had programmed everything to the last detail. Up at 6.00 a.m. gave us time to get ready for the removal men, the brokers, the brewery representative, plus the new landlord. At 8.00 a.m. I had the children sitting in the lounge bar with games and colouring books, with Snorkles tied to the leg of a table. John had the cellar complete, inventory ready for checking, catering equipment scrubbed down and everything ready for the take-over of a licensed house.

While John and the new landlord went down to the Magistrate's Court, the brokers were running round with their clipboards. The fruit machines and pool table were being loaded into lorries and our removal men were sweating up and down the stairs. I went to make tea for everyone.

Everything was running smoothly and it was all going to plan. It did for the first hour or so, then Bob—the incoming landlord—decided he didn't want one of the freezers and wasn't going to have all the catering equipment, so I left John to deal with him. Upstairs the men were doing a wonderful job and making good headway. It was at this point that pandemonium broke out. Downstairs John was still dealing with Bob who not

only didn't want this, that and the other, but had insisted on going to the cellar to tap a barrel. John firmly advised him not to and to allow the beer to settle for another twenty-four hours. Bob thought he knew better and the inevitable happened with beer cascading into the air drenching him. Meanwhile, Bob's wife had arrived and we met in the corridor upstairs. She suddenly informed me that she had changed her mind and no longer wanted the carpets, so wouldn't be paying for them. Two weeks earlier she had asked me not to remove two old wardrobes which John had been going to chop up and burn as they wouldn't come out of the bedrooms any other way. She now demanded that I remove them before we left!
Downstairs, Sarah, the daily, had tears streaming down her face and was blowing loudly into a hankie because we were leaving and Snorkles was pulling the table behind him because he'd had enough and wanted 'walkies'. I dashed off to find the removal men, who by now were reversing their lorry towards the back of the pub, in order to collect some furniture from the bottle room. When I explained my dilemma, they went into action, lifting all the carpets, rolling them up onto the van. Bob's wife appeared and confronted me as I checked rooms. 'I thought you were going to leave the carpets down.' By this time I had had enough, so my reply was, 'You didn't want them, they're not staying,' and with that I charged off downstairs to put the children and dog into the car.
John told his broker that if Bob wasn't going to have the catering equipment etc. he wasn't leaving and would be quite happy to sleep on the floor in his pub if need be.

Bob knew that he had gone too far, and that he had better keep to the original agreement made with the brokers two weeks earlier. He went on about wanting a freezer removed but John came to find me and said, 'Get into the car, quick. We're off!'

After an hour's drive, we stopped for lunch and then on to Morecambe. We had had to abolish the idea of living in Shrewsbury, due to the buyers of John's house backing out at the last minute. While we thought about what we were going to do, we decided to start working on the house. John had been having terrible cluster headaches and, worse still, pains across his chest and heart. Needless to say, the months prior to leaving had been extremely worrying.

As the weeks passed, John slowly started to look a better colour with the headaches and chest pains slowly easing. He enjoyed the challenge of DIY and became amazingly good at it.

Elizabeth and Donald had never had their own bedrooms before, so there was a continual to-ing and fro-ing of little feet and knocking on doors. Whilst chaos reigned, we managed to sell off quite a few items including the rolled up carpets. It was a three-storey house with an open-plan staircase. The view from the kitchen window on the first floor was just ghastly. Imagine eighty-eight flag stones with weeds growing round them like a jungle, plus a hideous grey wall at the rear. The two surrounding fences were made of wood which had once been white but were now green with lichen. The rest was tarmac, which went round the side of the house, with no gate and an old brick

barbecue. It was a complete eye-sore.
For a week or so, I made scribbles, designs and notes as to various ideas but I was determined that, whatever happened, a garden it would be. John started negotiating and eventually everything was decided on. A lorry arrived with three men and they took all the flagstones up, put down the soil and turf and knocked down the barbecue. Some weeks later, John was drilling to enable him to put up wire supports for the Russian vines to cover the back wall and had taken Snorkles out with him. Now, Snorkles had never seen a lawn before; he was used to fields. My mother-in-law came round in the afternoon. We stood chatting at the kitchen window admiring the newly laid turf and then we looked again quickly. Snorkles had his bottom in the air and his front paws buried in a massive hole with bits of turf flying in all directions. I got down the stairs two at a time, grabbed his collar, seriously reprimanding him, and sent him inside.
A week later John took Snorkles onto the lawn again thinking that he had learnt his lesson, but after a while he was rushing up and down with a whole carpet of turf. He was having a marvellous time, shaking it from side to side and was just on his way back to help himself to another piece when John got hold of him. It was obviously time to take action, so we went to a builder's yard and obtained some old floorboards and John set to work, making a fence and a wicket gate. Having installed a five-bar gate on the side of the house, he then covered everything he could find in white paint, including himself.
There were so many changes going on in the children's

lives, but they settled into their new school quite happily and were delighted to have left the playroom and the pub and live a life of normal citizens. Two months after we had moved, I was sorting and filing personal papers. I came across the information that I had jotted down about my birth. This had been scribbled on my visit to Somerset House. Reading through it, I suddenly realised that I was registered as having been born in the district of Bakewell. My natural mother's address had been in London, so why had I been born in the County of Derbyshire? Could she possibly have had relations there?

All that I had ever been given by my parents was an Adopted Birth Certificate. On it had been the Christian names that they had given me and the surname PRYOR. My parents had been registered as adopting me with no mention of my natural mother's name or address. I had always been under the impression that this was the only Birth Certificate that existed.

'Let's drive down for the day to Bakewell,' I exclaimed to John. 'My true Birth Certificate must be kept there.'

'I'd like to do that,' he replied. 'It's a very pretty town. Haven't been there for years,' he added.

So at the end of March we set off at the crack of dawn. It was market day in Bakewell and we had lunch at a pub, surrounded by farmers. Having found the local registry, I asked for a copy of my Birth Certificate. As indicated in Somerset House, there was a line crossed through 'surname of father'. My natural mother had named me Marion Eileen Stapleton and I had been born at Willersley Castle in Matlock.

It was getting late and there was a long drive back home so the mystery of why I had been delivered in a castle remained unknown. It wasn't until 1994, quite by chance, that I found out why.

Chapter 61

We had no sooner got the house sorted out when in April we got a call from Carlos. 'Can I come and leave some things with you?' That meant he was visiting, departing and coming back to live with us. I moved Donald into Elizabeth's bedroom and ploughed my way through mountains of clothing which Carlos had left, washing and ironing ready for his return. He came back in May and it was at this point that I discovered he had been living with a girlfriend. In July he decided to go back to her and off he went to Kent.

John decided that we should set up a Relief Management Agency involving courses for those wishing to enter into the licensed trade. In a joint venture we became Company Directors and I did all the administration and typing. John found a pub where there was a large adjoining functions room for his lectures. The students would also spend an afternoon in a brewery nearby where they could learn and experience cellar management.

I went off to look for an old blackboard and easel at one of the colleges. A projector, slides and television screen were all rented which had to be put in the car every time there was a course, along with boxes, books and stationery. I would drop the children off at school then drive to the next town to the functions room. In the evening the children and I would go and fetch John. Having been on the working side of the bar, I couldn't imagine anyone wanting to spend their lives on the wrong side of the bar! It prompted me to write the following:

HAVE YOU GOT THE BOTTLE TO BE A PUBLICAN?

So many people want to become licensees, but not because they have really analysed or fully understood what it involves or the commitments. They are fed up with commuting, sitting in offices and are under the impression that being a licensee is a social event every evening. May I take this illusion away right now? If you think along these lines, then you are completely mistaken. Being in the licensed trade is a way of life and a total dedication. You can't take Saturdays and Sundays off, you can't take a long Bank Holiday weekend and you can't put your comfortable slippers on and sink into an armchair after 5.30 p.m.

The grass always looks greener on the other side. So often people are not only envious of their boss, but consider his job far easier than their own. So sailing into the position of licensee may seem an extremely comfortable way of earning a living. Wrong, because you are summing it all up from the customer's side of the bar. Remarks such as 'Wouldn't mind being on the other side of the bar', 'He must be making a fortune', 'I'd like late mornings, with free afternoons, free drinks, and a social life every evening'. At some time or another, most landlords/landladies have had a similar remark made to them.

A publican's job is a surprisingly complex one of great dedication and judgement, made even more difficult by the fact that a licensed house is no longer just a drinking place but also a restaurant. The increasingly growing demand for better quality food, more varied menus and the catering for vegetarians. If you keep a good pint of bitter, but fail to have appetising food, you could find your customers going elsewhere. The same applies if it is vice-versa. Food delicious but you haven't done your homework in the cellar. One of the biggest mistakes a licensee can make is not bothering to clean out his beer lines frequently. The pints are pulled cloudy with an unpleasant taste and a customer who pays for that kind of pint will move on to another pub. An easy way to lose trade.

Your cellar will be the most vital factor in your business and should be looked after with pride, rather like a baby. No matter how busy you are, time has to be dedicated to a strict maintenance routine, to prevent contamination. All important is a high standard of cleanliness, monitoring casks, tapping barrels and learning how to keep the right temperature in summer and winter, to ensure the best quality beer at all times. The cellar can be a dangerous place in the hands of an untrained person and could lose you a considerable amount of livelihood in a surprisingly short space of time. So it is vital not to let Tom, Dick or Harry into it.

The customer relationship is of great significance. A licensee should be friendly and host to all who enter his establishment. He has to be a listener, discreet at all times, a confidant, with a good knowledge of psychology—in fact everything rolled into one. Through that pub door will enter people from all walks of life; from the customer who is no trouble, to the one who comes to make trouble

The drinker who is a regular customer and makes a bee-line for the bar stool and can't wait to tell you all his domestic problems.

The drinker who complains about the beer, the crisps and anything else, just to seek attention.

The drinker who comes with his mates, slapping each other's backs and roaring with laughter.

The drinker who has a repertoire of jokes and thinks he is so terribly amusing but is boring you witless.

The drinker who slumps over the bar and spends the entire evening staring at you while you serve.

The drinker who arrives with a pal and has come to cause trouble—in capital letters.

The drinkers who come in determined to get served and are underage.

It isn't until you become a landlord/landlady that you suddenly realise how complicated the human race is. Having to deal with customers, as if that wasn't enough, you are also expected to interview staff, sort out wages and, no matter what is thrown at you, keep your business running smoothly. But staff can let you down and are not always reliable, nor do they want to understand your position, with all its responsibilities and financial problems. They don't always take kindly to a new licensee changing their routines. You are expected to listen to the family ailments and be told why so and so can't come into work tomorrow or that little Johnny hasn't got a baby-sitter to look after him. There's a wedding, there's a funeral, my mother's been taken ill, my transport has broken down, the Cock & Bull down the road has offered me more salary and here's my written resignation.

Through all this, and much more, you have to cope because it's your livelihood and you, as boss, have to keep it going. A pub is a constant hive of activity, not a shop you can close and forget. There may be bedlam going on in the kitchen, draymen delivering the wrong order, bar staff missing and a waitress not turned up for work, but you have to appear unruffled with a calm and collected appearance smiling at your customers with a 'Good morning' here, and a 'Good morning' there. You inwardly curse all mankind and rush from behind the bar to balance a tray of food from the kitchen door to the customer. It also goes without saying that more and more pressure is being put on the licensee to maintain hygiene where food and drink are served. Gone are the days when the licensee smoked behind the bar and looked as if he had just fallen out of

bed to serve. His appearance and that of his staff are all important factors to the public as are so many other aspects of running licensed premises.
Situations can arise which are like nightmares but unfortunately for the licensee they are reality and have to be dealt with. Dealing with the general public is anything but easy, and as a landlord/landlady you have to be prepared for any event, and know how to handle difficult situations. One of my most embarrassing moments was during a very hectic Bank Holiday Monday. The chef was ploughing his way through his orders, the kitchen looked like a battlefield, and the waitress and I were dashing backwards and forwards. Having just served a couple with a ploughman's and a salad, I was busy clearing a table when a shrill voice, for all the customers to hear, shouted, 'I've got a caterpillar in my salad!' You only need one person to complain and then you have the whole lot looking at their food too. The whole room was in a hush as I picked up her plate. There was a small strip of lasagne verde which, in the chef's haste had managed to land on her salad. The lady in question had left her glasses at home!

Chapter 62

It soon became abundantly clear that the days that John had no work to do he was just going to lounge about the sitting room. He'd walk Snorkles round the block whilst I would be careering about in a mad rush to get the children to school. I would come back to find the clutter still on the breakfast table with John having no intention of lending me a hand whatsoever. His evenings were spent walking down to the pub leaving me to baby sit.

As time went by I soon realised that he was under the impression that I could now be taken for granted. John was forty-one years old and I was eight years older than him. He'd acquired a wife, a step-mother for his children, housekeeper, cook, nurse maid, baby sitter, gardener, chauffeur, secretary and car washer.

It wasn't until after we were married and had left the pub that the verbal abuse started. On wearing my glasses for driving, typing, reading or viewing the TV, I would continually be referred to as *hatchet features*. Whilst in the car he would make remarks about my glasses, telling me that they made me look *school marmish*.

One morning I went to give John a kiss and was told, 'Ugh! Don't kiss me with those glasses on.' It was upsetting, hurtful and humiliating but, worst of all, it was giving me an inferiority complex.

When Nancy offered to baby sit I would go and fetch her and then drive her back on our return. We always had to go to a pub. John would not consider going anywhere else. On one occasion he wanted to meet up with his cousins for a pub crawl. I offered to chauffeur them all around for the evening. While seated at a table and conversing with one of John's cousins, he suddenly announced in a loud voice, 'Clare speaks the Queen's English, but hasn't the intellect to go with it.' John despised anyone who hadn't been to University and continually aired the fact that he had obtained a degree.

When John was out of the house I would spend my time galloping upstairs from the laundry room to answer the phone. The dining room table had been taken over as an office and I would have to pretend that that was what it was! There would be enquiries about the courses and when the next one was commencing, plus all the questions people wanted answers to. Frequently I would have just got up to the third floor to sort out the bedrooms when the phone would start ringing. Down I would go at break-neck speed to answer yet another call.

The evening routine for John would be to eat his meal and then immediately get up from the table and settle down in front of the TV. I would be left with bathing the children, washing and drying hair, and getting them to bed. Coming down to the kitchen I would be faced with a sink full of washing up. By the time I had cleared the kitchen, John would be ready to go off to the pub in the knowledge that I was there to baby sit. Many evenings, for lack of hours in the day, I would catch up with all the typing that needed doing. There were many occasions when I would have to drop whatever I was doing to drive John to the next town or to the station to catch a bus or train. I spent my time continually ferrying the family around from one place to another. Elizabeth started Karate in the evenings and I would have to drive her to the next town, fetching her after her lesson.

I would often have Nancy round for a meal and occasionally during the summer weekends she would join us for a picnic out in the glorious surrounding countryside. While I prepared food for five, organised the children, packed up all the necessities, plus doggy bowls etc., John would be off downstairs to play his keyboard or guitar. Then there would be all the driving to do which John was under the impression was simply the act of sitting comfortably and pressing a foot pedal. He would decide on some place for us to go for a picnic, and when we got home I had, often, driven over one hundred miles! Having arrived at a suitable place for a picnic, no sooner had we got settled than John would disappear to find a pub. On a really hot summer day, we would wait until it was cooler before setting out homeward bound. The children would be hot, sticky, grubby, tired and wanting to get home and get into a bath. On every occasion it was imperative to stop on our way home at a pub. Once home, John never lent a hand. Instead he would switch on the TV while I coped with everything.

On more occasions than I wish to remember I would try to explain to John that if he would only co-operate and share some duties then I wouldn't feel so exhausted. I'd already brought up my own children and had been through all this once already. To start again with bringing small children up at forty-nine years of age with no help from their father was very selfish of him. I would stand bending over the bath with a sponge in my hand whilst supervising bathtime and my blouse would be drenched with perspiration. I was feeling very drained with an extremely bad menopause. There was nothing the doctors could do since I was allergic to all forms of HRT. But John didn't want to know and had no sympathy for anyone who wasn't feeling well.

At the very least I thought he could help with the shopping because the lifting of heavy bags would give me a lot of back pain. But no sooner had we arrived at the supermarket than John would leave me with the children to wander off to fetch tins of beer from the drinks department. On one occasion I asked him if he could come and, at least, look after the children. He turned round and said, 'I'm not coming anymore. You can do the shopping alone.' And that was that.

I was being slowly taxed physically and mentally and there was no consideration, no appreciation, no willingness and no sharing of the daily responsibilities.

Chapter 63

In September, Roger and Carol came to stay for a few days. It was lovely to see them again and hear all their news. On Sunday 21st October, I was just about to take the roast potatoes out of the oven to serve dinner when there was an almighty scream from Donald. He had run headlong into the side of a door. I took one look at the one-inch gash, grabbed a face flannel and towel and we were on our way to the hospital. In Spain, in an emergency, you hang a white hankie out of the car window and hoot. Everyone gets out of your way. Here, in England, you sit in a one-mile queue trying to get a bleeding child to hospital in the next town. It wasn't until we were in the Casualty Department that I realised I was covered in blood and still wearing my apron. Poor Donald had to have two clips and was a very brave little boy.

In November I made a sickly chocolate birthday cake—Donald's express wish—with lots of chocolate spread in the middle. We had a family tea-party with granny present. He was given a blue budgie named Gypsy. Snorkles was not impressed, being beside himself with jealousy, so Gypsy had to be placed out of his reach on a shelf. He would stare with beady eyes at the cage in sheer indignation while his whiskers quivered!

December found me icing a large cake in the evening before Elizabeth's birthday and a week later was Christmas. I really enjoyed shopping for the children's presents and wrapping them all up. Since looking after Elizabeth and Donald, I had always made up large stockings for them, creeping in to place them at the foot of their beds on Christmas Eve.

Chapter 64

The events of 1990 were full of surprises with three unexpected happy visits but it was also a year of deep emotional upheaval and despair.
On 13th January the phone rang in the morning and Ursula was on the line.
'I'm with mother travelling back home and thought we might pop in and see you.'
'How lovely. What a surprise. Do come and I'll rustle up some lunch.'
It was wonderful to see Molli and Ursula again after all the years that had passed but they had to leave fairly soon after lunch, due to getting on with their long journey.
Paloma and Carlos have always had the tendency to tell me something, usually over the phone, at the last minute! So it was with only four days' notice that Paloma rang to tell me she would be arriving on the 16th! We met at Manchester airport and, talking nineteen to the dozen, made our way to the multi-storey car park. Snorkles went berserk, barking and growling as if he was a baby tiger. However, once Paloma was seated in the car, he decided she warranted a session of licking.
She stayed a few days and then jumped on a train to see her brother and his girlfriend. Then she spent a few more days with me and John and I saw her off at the airport. As she waved goodbye from a distance I broke down in floods of tears. It had been three long years since our last encounter and I missed her more than words can express.
Two days after Paloma's departure, his Majesty returned

from his daily constitutional with a nasty gash in one of his hind legs. He finished up at the vets having to have an anaesthetic and stitches.

In April, Carlos paid a fleeting visit staying only overnight and away again. One afternoon in July the front door bell rang and who should be standing there but Heidi with her husband. I hadn't seen them since I was at boarding school. It left me quite speechless as we hugged each other. 'We are travelling round England and thought we would do a surprise visit.' They ended up staying the night and we sat over a long pleasant dinner catching up with all the past events.

At the beginning of August things came to such a point that I told John I just needed to get away. As much as I dearly loved Elizabeth and Donald, I had had no rest from them at all in nearly three years. There had been no holiday either and I had lost track of my last holiday, some six years past. I had never understood people who said, 'I need to go away' or 'I need space'. But I did now.

I had obviously come to the end of my tether and John couldn't have cared less.

'I'll be away for a week,' I said, 'staying at a bed and breakfast wherever I stop on my travels.'

'Okay,' replied John, totally devoid of any emotion as he continued to watch the TV.

Setting out with some clothes in a small suitcase and Snorkles, I drove off quietly towards Worcester and booked into a bed and breakfast in the countryside. Next day Snorkles and I ambled about along the River Severn occasionally stopping to sit on a bench just letting the world go by. In the afternoon we drove on to Tewkesbury and stayed there the night. The third day I took a leisurely drive to Oxfordshire and went to visit Roger and Carol. They immediately made me very welcome and insisted on me staying for two nights. On the fifth day I drove back to Morecambe in the hopes that John would have missed me and perhaps had had time to realise what was happening to our marriage. The moment I entered the house I knew that he had no intentions of making amends. The household had ground to a halt with congealed washing-up piled up in the sink, newspapers dropped wherever they had fallen and a collection of dirty mugs in the sitting room. Upstairs it was the usual story. John's dirty clothes strewn on the bedroom floor. He was incapable of putting them into the dirty-linen basket. Elizabeth and Donald had been told that I had gone to visit Carlos. They greeted me with big hugs and I gave them a present each before preparing supper and baths. Once the children were in bed I went down to the sitting room. 'I have to talk to you John,' I said.

'Well, go on then,' he said as he continued to lie on the floor in front of the TV.

'Would you mind turning the television off and perhaps sit on the settee a minute?'

John sat down and said, 'Well, go on.'

I gave a deep sigh and said sadly, 'I can't go on like this. I'm going to have to leave.'

Totally devoid of any emotion, he replied, 'Okay. I'm a survivor.'

I looked at him and there was no love for me at all and my

reply was, 'So am I.'
He got up, walked over to the TV and switched it on again.
For some time now I had had my suspicions about John and, at a later date, these were confirmed. All the verbal abuse and emotional turmoil during the years had given me the beginning of another peptic ulcer.
In September I was lucky enough to contact a member of St. John Ambulance who was able to teach me first-aid from home. This meant that I could answer business enquiries at the same time. An examiner arrived in October bringing a lifelike dummy with her and, after I had resuscitated it, thankfully passed my exam.
At the beginning of November, I accepted a job as House Matron at a college. Nancy was spending Christmas at John's brother's house and John, Elizabeth and Donald were leaving to join them on the 24th. On the 20th I went to say goodbye to Nancy. She had been a sweet mother-in-law and I was very fond of her. As I was about to leave, she gave me a present and I have treasured the mantelpiece clock ever since.
John had told Elizabeth and Donald that I was going to spend Christmas with Carlos. He also told me that I was not to say goodbye to them, so when they all stood at the front door to get into the taxi, John just said, 'Goodbye,' and I hugged the children and they were gone.
I sat at the dining room table for a long while playing with a bit of paper. Then I remembered that I needed some receipts to do with servicing the car. Whilst hunting amongst the in-tray papers I came across day-return

tickets which had been purchased for two people on quite a few occasions. It all became clear, that my suspicions had been right all along, and what had been written by John in the business diary didn't correspond with the rail ticket destinations.

I packed up all my things and took a single bed, two chairs, armchair, bathroom cabinet and curtains that I had made with me. The Matron's flat was empty so I needed some furniture and I arrived at the college with a van in tow on 27th December.

Chapter 65

The flat was freezing and I had driven 264 miles and felt exhausted and cold. The housemaster and his wife invited me to dinner in their part of the house. It was beautifully warm with the heating on full blast. I enquired about some heating for the flat and was told that there wasn't any until the term started. I discovered, at a later date, that the other housemasters had had separate heating installed for their Matron's living quarters but here it was going to be different.

The weather was bitter and I just couldn't get warm but struggled on trying to unpack and get myself a little organised before the new term started. Not surprisingly, I got a chill which upset the digestive system because I was run down. I developed a temperature and had the doctor in but kept on my feet living off hot Bovril drinks.

On 31st December—four days after my arrival—there was a phone call at 8.00 a.m. from the nursing home. Mother had passed away during the night, after failing to recover from Asian flu. I got dressed and went down to tell the housemaster's wife who gave me a cup of coffee. I went off with Snorkles and walked about trying to come to terms with the shock of everything.

Returning to the flat I stayed there the rest of the day and cried bitter tears sitting with my arms around Snorkles. It was that evening that I realised that there was a complete lack of kindness in this house. There was a supplementary phone connected to the housemaster's living quarters and it wouldn't have taken much effort to ring to ask if I was

alright.
On the 3rd the housemaster's wife wanted to speak to me before the arrival of the boys. At my interview I had been told that I was to have nothing at all to do with the domestic side of things. It was all dealt with by her. That was fine by me for it gave me time to get dressed at 6.30 a.m., give Snorkles a short walk before appearing at 8.00 a.m. in the dining room to be on duty whilst the boys had their breakfast.
Due to the term starting on 6th January I felt that as I was new to the job I really should be present when the boys arrived. Mother's funeral was therefore delayed another four days. The evening before the boys' arrival I was informed by the housemaster's wife that there had been a change of plan. I was, as of tomorrow morning, to be down in the kitchen by 7.15 a.m. to prepare trolleys with milk, bread, butter, marmalade and make tea for all the individual tables, then put everything out in the dining room. I was also expected to wash out all the milk bottles. This now meant that I had to get up at 5.45 a.m. and walk Snorkles in the pitch dark.
The nuns at mother's nursing home never gave a thought to my long drive to get to mother's funeral. The service was to be in the nursing home chapel at Burgess Hill. I set off at the crack of dawn unable to even contemplate any breakfast. Having never driven the route from the college to Burgess Hill I discovered all sorts of new road layouts and in my panic to get there, got onto a different route. The nuns hadn't bothered to wait for me and on arrival I gave Snorkles some water in the car and followed the

coffin into the chapel.
I was so very grateful for the support of my mother's firm of solicitors who had sent one of them to attend. This gentleman was not only extremely professional but kind, sympathetic and helpful. He beckoned me to his pew and I stood beside him as the uncontrollable flow of tears engulfed me. All the childhood memories came flooding back, everything that had happened with mother and I wished with all my heart that it had been so very different. She had gone, still rejecting me and having never appreciated the slightest thing I had done for her. It hurt even more to think that I had never caused her anguish or pain, and despite all her criticism I had always tried to be a loving daughter.
The service had by now finished and we were following the coffin to the cemetery. I stood next to the solicitor a few yards from the hearse while the bitter north wind blew right through us. The priest had gone round to the back of the hearse and was spraying holy water over the coffin before the bearers removed it for burial. There was a long wait as we stood in the cold and the ceremony didn't progress. Meanwhile the bearers had all gone *walkies* round the cemetery. After another interminable wait, the funeral director came over to mother's solicitor and muttered something in his ear. He in turn looked at me and said, 'There's a problem. They can't bury her.'
'Why?' I exclaimed, absolutely amazed.
'Well, apparently there has been a misunderstanding with the gravedigger and he hasn't dug a hole.' I was totally speechless. The solicitor then smiled and muttered, 'I

hope your mother had a sense of humour.'
'No, she didn't,' I replied with a faint smile.
There was to be a delay until 4.30 p.m. and it would be pitch dark by then. I had a long journey back and was feeling totally drained and very weak. We went back into the nursing home and were asked to remove all my mother's clothes and personal things from her room. Apart from the nuns, there had only been one family present who had known mother. In her Will she had left them her 18th century Hepplewhite chair and an inlaid cabinet with drawers which mother had always used as a bedside table. These were the only things left of my childhood home and I was devastated to think that what I cherished was to be given away to people who were not even family. It distressed me so much and my eyes filled with tears. My mind went back to the dreadful day when our furniture was removed and sold and the family home auctioned. The solicitor could see my anguish and said he would have a word with them and was sure that the family concerned would let me have them. A few moments later, they stood at the door of my mother's room waiting to grab the chair and cabinet and load them into their car. Human beings can be so cruel and senseless. I'd grown up with that furniture as a child and they were all that was left of our family home. Despite everything that I have endured in my life, I'm thankful that I have never been intentionally unkind, money-grabbing or mean. There is a side to me which has great compassion and kindness. Had it been the other way around, I can truthfully say that I would have been incapable of taking anything. The

sentimental value of any object to an individual cannot be priced!

The solicitor packed up things whilst I went through the unpleasant task of emptying drawers, handbags and all that death involves for those still living to sort out. On the way back to drop the solicitor off at the railway station he suggested that we ought to eat something. I sat in a pub with a sandwich and a drink, devoid of energy, completely drained emotionally and physically. Then I wearily drove back to the college with a dog that had more compassion and understanding than many human beings. Snorkles sensed my distress and insisted on laying on the passenger seat with his head resting on my lap.

Chapter 66

It soon became apparent that the gossip that went on in the kitchen quarters was true. I came down one morning to fetch some food for a sick boy and found cook swaying all over the kitchen. The housemaster's wife was doing her level best to pretend nothing unusual was going on and she and the rest of the staff were endeavouring to cook lunch!

A few weeks later I came down to prepare the tables for breakfast and had to open all the windows in the dining room, despite the cold weather. Cook had turned all the gas taps on in the kitchen but forgotten to light them.

Every day I noticed that all the food left on the boys' plates was chucked into a large bin. I asked the housemaster's wife if I could occasionally have the scrapings for Snorkles.

'Yes, ask cook,' she replied. Little did I know at this point how pally the cook and housemaster's wife were. On the day that the boys had stew I asked cook, after the tables had been cleared, whether I could have the scrapings for Snorkles. I was given the bits of meat and gravy that had been left on the boys' plates. I thanked her and went upstairs to get on with my duties. Next morning, after having done surgery, I was busy in the laundry room when the housemaster's wife appeared.

'I want a word with you in your flat,' she said. 'My husband went to the kitchen yesterday evening and wanted some stew. He was told by cook that you had taken it all for your dog.'

'But I wouldn't do such a thing,' I replied. 'All I had were the bits that the boys had left on their plates.'
'Well,' she continued, 'my husband was not at all pleased about it.'
'Honestly, I can truthfully say that I didn't take anything that wasn't going into the bin,' I replied.
'That's what you say but cook has told me differently,' she continued. I realised then that cook could do no wrong and between them they were out to make my life a misery. Things went from bad to worse and I had continual interference in all I did on the medical side. It so happened that out of all the resident house matrons at the college, there were only two of us that had first-aid qualifications. There were nights when I would have a knock on my door and one of the boys was either feeling sick, had been sick or had a temperature. So I would naturally have to attend to him and that of course was part of my undertaking as Matron. But what was not acceptable was the fact that there was no member of staff supervising the boys in their dormitories.
The oldest boys would come to bed late and start fooling about until I thought my bedroom ceiling was going to crash in. Thump, bang, bang, crash, wallop. On more than one occasion, in desperation to get some sleep, I would don my dressing gown and slippers and march upstairs. There would be boys out of bed, pillows on the floor and a real rumpus going on. I no sooner went downstairs, got settled in bed and it would start all over again. Many, many a night I would lie there until 2.00 a.m. unable to get any sleep.

There were too many unpleasant incidents to relate here but I did get a tremendous amount of support and sympathy from the other matrons, sanatorium sister, and members of staff. Life was made so difficult that in the end I gave in my notice and was so touched by the cards and presents I received from staff in other houses and from the boys themselves. Many of them didn't want me to go because they knew that I had genuinely cared about them and their health.

I wrote and explained the situation to Valerie and she immediately offered me a place in her house until I could find another job. I was very thankful for her kindness because I honestly didn't know where I was going to go. The two dogs settled down quite happily in the kitchen and Valerie would cook with one foot in each basket! On several occasions Valerie would accompany me to an interview and we would agree on our return journey that it had been totally unsuitable.

One day in May, Carlos and I arranged to meet in Guildford. He was coming by car and would meet me at the railway station. He now had a Labrador pup of five months and she was lovely. We drove out of the town and found an ideal place where the pub had a large garden. We took the pup for a walk in the afternoon and spent a very pleasant day together.

Chapter 67

In June I took a job as housekeeper with a young couple near Salisbury. They lived surrounded by fields and woods and it was extremely isolated, but I desperately needed a job and there was a little bungalow in the grounds. After the van had dumped all my furniture, I set to in getting everything as straight as possible before starting work.
On the first day, I was left all day from early morning until late evening with a little boy of three years and his baby brother. I soon experienced that once you have taken a living in job, your employer seems to think they have the right to own you. Time off is very seldom yours to relax; you have no rights at all. They seem to be under the impression that they can treat you as their mood takes them. I can see anyone who has been a live-in nanny or housekeeper frantically nodding their heads in full agreement as they read these truths.
If I'm going to take a job or commitment, I get on with it and do it properly. I haven't time for idle gossip, stretching my work out or pretending to clean something when I'm not. So very soon my new employer's wife was saying, 'Goodness, have you finished that already?' and 'I've never seen the house so clean and tidy.'
The mornings were taken up with applying wax with a mop to parquet and tiled floors and polishing with a machine. Endless trips were made with loads of washing to the garden line. Invariably there were visitors and never ending changing, washing and ironing of sheets and duvet covers. At mid-day I would dash back to the bungalow,

snatch a sandwich and give Snorkles a quick walk in one of the fields. The afternoons were spent solidly ironing until 5.30 p.m. Some evenings I would be back at the house to baby-sit until midnight.

It was a large five-bedroomed house and there were windows wherever you looked. I had been cleaning the insides as I went along, but one morning discovered, to my horror, that I was expected to wash the outsides as well! Within three weeks I started to get back pain and made a visit to the surgery. That proved a waste of time so I continued on.

One morning, having done my normal round of collecting up dirty clothes off the bedroom floors, tucking sheets into heavy kingsized mattresses, hoovering, polishing etc., I went to have my usual sandwich and see Snorkles. I was about to get down to the ironing that afternoon when I was told that the boys had made the playroom carpet so dirty that it needed shampooing.

'I can't stand the orange juice stains and the dirty marks any longer,' I was told. She continued, 'I'm going out to a birthday party this afternoon with the boys.'

'If you would kindly show me how to use the machine for shampooing, I'll get on with it,' I replied.

'Oh no,' she exclaimed. 'I want it cleaned by hand,' and with that she handed me some carpet shampoo and drove off.

I set to on my hands and knees the whole afternoon. It was left spotless! But my back had been giving me a lot of discomfort and this exertion had caused excruciating pain. I don't know how I continued on, but it was fear that drove me on; like so many other times in my life it was a matter of survival. If I stopped work, I had nowhere to go and no roof over my head. I was worried sick thinking what might happen to me and terrified of being parted from Snorkles. Above all else, I would not and could not live without him nor was I going to!

I made an appointment to see a chiropractor at the Salisbury clinic. It was after two X-rays were taken on 11th August 1992 that the chiropractor discovered that I had a compression fracture at the fifth thoracic vertebra. It came as a complete shock. This had been caused in 1985 during the car crash with Antonio, when the radiologist at one of the Cadiz hospitals had taken X-rays and confirmed that there was nothing abnormal!

I was by now having trouble breathing, because of muscle spasms secondary to a lumbo-sacral sprain. The altered mid-thoracic mechanics were making me short of breath due to its constrictive nature.

The thoracic pains began on starting the housekeeping job because of the constant lifting of heavy mattresses, carrying very heavy washing, carrying a heavy hoover up and down stairs, lifting a heavy baby in and out of his cot and carrying him about. I was told by the chiropractor to stop my work before further damage was done. That, I explained, was impossible. I had nowhere to go. I had no option but to carry on if I was to survive. My employer's wife knew that I was suffering from back pain and it was on the Friday afternoon, while finishing off the ironing, that she asked me if I would come in to work on the Saturday. She was having some friends to stay and needed

beds making etc.
I told her I was very sorry but, apart from needing a rest, I had already arranged to visit a friend for the weekend. It was all quite amicable and she said, 'That's alright. I'll see you after the weekend.'
Next day it was pouring with rain and not ideal for driving so I cancelled my weekend to Valerie's house. Besides, I was tired and needed to rest my back so I took Snorkles out on Sunday for a short walk in the morning. Opening the front door on my return I found an envelope. I was being dismissed from my job and had been given a month's notice to leave. This bombshell left me stunned because several weeks earlier I had given my employer's wife some house plants for her sitting room. She had thanked me and said she was so pleased with everything I did.
On Monday morning, drained of all colour, I went in to work and, while in the kitchen, was called into their sitting room. Her husband was standing in the middle of the room and she stood by one of the armchairs with her head bent down, studying her feet. She wasn't going to give me eye contact because she knew that the dismissal was totally unfair and that I had nowhere to go.
'We just want you to know that we are not asking you to leave for anything that you have done. We feel that it's getting too much for you,' he said. Looking him straight in the eyes, I replied, 'I'm in your hands and it's up to you whatever you want to do with me.' I ran out of the sitting room with the tears pouring down my face and disappeared into the laundry room to recover.

Chapter 68

I went to see the local council and stood in a queue of people. A woman was seated behind a desk in an office and, having explained my situation, she abruptly said, 'We can't help you because you're not pregnant, haven't got a child, not disabled and not an OAP.' Dismissing me, she called out, 'Next one.'

The weeks started to go quickly and I still didn't know what to do. In desperation, I made a final decision that the most important factor was Snorkles and myself; not material things. I had lost everything four times in my life, so I would have to do it again.

I drove to the nearest little market town and went into a shop that sold second-hand furniture, clothes and other nice things. When the shop was empty of customers I told a lady named Penelope about my predicament. She was so kind and quite horrified to think that people with money could be so heartless. 'I'll come up and see the furniture this evening, if that's alright,' she said.

'Oh, thank you,' I replied, 'because it's all got to go and I need the money.'

Having seen everything that I had to part with, she promised to return on Saturday afternoon. Penelope and her husband arrived with a van and loaded all my worldly possessions into it. Meanwhile the couple that had dismissed me stood at the window watching the whole procedure. I'd collected boxes from supermarkets so after work set to in the evenings packing up what was left. A week before leaving I was hanging a load of washing on the line in the back yard. The gardener appeared and asked me where I was going. 'I really don't know, probably have to sleep in the car.' He said nothing and I continued to peg out the washing, while he went off to do the garden. Next morning, the gardener appeared round the back yard again. 'I've spoken to my wife and we both agree that you are coming to stay with us,' he announced. 'Come round after work and have a cup of tea.' There, again, was living proof that someone had been put in my way to help me in a desperate bid for survival.

The gardener and his wife had ten cats and my immediate question was how will the situation be with Snorkles? As always he sensed my distress and understood at once that if we were to survive together it was imperative for him to behave. Within seconds of arriving he was summing the situation up as the cats appeared round doors and on the draining board. I knew exactly what Snorkles was thinking as he watched them all. Can't cope with ten cats ganging up against me—one dog—so I'll ignore them. That is exactly what he did!

They tried during our stay to provoke him, arching their backs, waiting for him down the corridor and even went into my bedroom to sleep on his bed. Snorkles's most treasured possession without exception is his bed and he has always been quite possessive about it. I would leave my bedroom door open so that when he felt like it he could pad down the corridor away from the daily commotion and rest. The first time he entered and found a white cat in his bed he had the intelligence to come and find me. He put his head round the sitting room door and

stared at me until we had eye contact. Usually that stare was saying, 'Get up, it's time to feed me,' but on this occasion he definitely wanted me to sort the problem out. If it hadn't have been for the gardener and his wife, without a doubt, I wouldn't have managed to keep Snorkles and in desperation would have more than likely ended both our lives. So when I was given three soiled mattresses on the stone tiled floor to sleep on, I was just grateful to have a roof over my head and able to keep my beloved dog. I covered the top mattress with blankets before putting some sheets on. The walls were damp, running with condensation. It was cold, bleak and depressing. I started to lose weight rapidly and went from a size twelve to a size eight. I binged on biscuits which I bought at the village shop because I was so hungry. I didn't dare say anything despite paying my way for fear of being asked to leave.
One Sunday, I came to the end of my tether trying desperately to find another job without success. I drove into Salisbury and, going into the Samaritans, broke down hysterically crying. Just to talk to someone in my solitary misery over a cup of tea was amazingly comforting. On leaving and stepping out into the street, it somehow gave me the strength from somewhere to renew my search for a living-in job.
Two interviews came up near Oxford so I stayed with Carol and Roger. They insisted on me staying a second night as we scanned newspapers and put cards in shop windows.
The night before leaving for Oxford, an elderly gentleman

in Nottingham rang in reply to my advertisement in a magazine. I told him I was going for two interviews and wouldn't be back for several days. On my return he rang again asking me to accept the position of housekeeper. He liked the sound of my voice and didn't need to interview me.

'What about a Labrador?' I enquired. 'He's very well behaved.'

'Yes, that's fine. We like dogs and have a large house and garden,' he replied. We had a chat about the job and salary. There was a pause, as he anxiously asked, 'Will you come to us?'

'Yes, I will,' I replied.

I had been getting very worried about money and also knew that the gardener and his wife expected me to leave soon, as I had already been living with them for five weeks.

Chapter 69

Having received a letter of confirmation, I set out in the first week of November. On arrival, I noticed Snorkles's back legs were shivering and he seemed to be in pain. So, after a cup of tea, instructions were given to me on how to get to the nearest vet. Unfortunately, the problem was diagnosed incorrectly and considered to be cystitis. An anti-inflammatory injection and prescribed antibiotics seemed to put Snorkles back to his usual happy self.

It was a beautiful four-bedroomed house with oak panelling in the spacious hallway. A wide staircase led up to a bay-window and then continued on to the landing. The rooms all had the original tall leaded windows but the carpets had seen better days. The bathroom was hilarious, having one of the first showers ever to be installed in Britain. Judging from the pipes and antiquated taps it would have looked more appropriate in a museum. The first evening after having a bath I went to pull out the plug to let the water flow away and it swept away roaring like a lion!

Time had stood still and the couple I was to care for had done nothing to the house for many, many years. Neither furniture, decorating or renewing anything to modern standards had taken place. My bedroom had a parchment lampshade over the bed with a pull cord and the mattress was made of horse hair, full of lumps and bumps. After several nights I decided this had to be changed, due to my bad back, and bought myself a new one. The curtains were stained, faded from the years of sunlight, and with the lining ripped. There was one chair covered in satin material and after sitting in it several times it just started to disintegrate. The bedrooms that were unused had a musty, stale smell to them and so one morning I threw open all the windows.

My employer was eighty-eight years old and shuffled about with a walking stick, having arthritis, but his mind was still very active. Sometimes over a meal we could have a stimulating conversation and Arthur would congratulate me on my cooking. Other days for no apparent reason whatsoever, he could be obnoxious, rude and stubborn. On more than one occasion I would go to my room after finishing my duties and cry my heart out. He refused to let me have a weekend off and gave me one day a week, until I got so exhausted that after nearly a year of putting up with this, I managed to get my weekends free.

His wife, Lilian, having arrived home—previous to my arrival—from a third hip operation, had fallen outside and broken her leg and was convalescing in a nursing home. She was due back in a few days. This gave me time to sort out some kind of routine, get my bearings, stock up with food, do the laundry and clear out the kitchen.

I stood in utter amazement as I looked around for an electric kettle and saw an old battered whistling billy can on the gas hob. Many months later, I eventually got a new one, but the old boy wouldn't spend the money on an electric kettle!

The cupboards were old wooden ones and what I discovered in them made me wonder how this couple hadn't died of food poisoning! There were so many food

products, not just a few months out of date, but years out of date. Products that were so old that they hadn't even got a sell-by date on them.
Cooking utensils from pre-World War II appeared; many dangerously rusty and a potential health hazard. It was late afternoon when I eventually got the kitchen into a fit state to cook in and the freezer cleaned out and stocked up with food.
Lilian was due out of hospital the following day and I decided that it was time to get some washing done. The automatic wasn't in the bathroom and it wasn't in the kitchen—so where was it? 'Go out through the kitchen door and you'll find the machine in the boiler room,' explained Arthur.
Words fail to describe my shock and surprise, for there stood a massive old fashioned washing machine with enormous blades inside. Beside it was a free-standing mangle. I took the dirty linen and drove off to the launderette. After a few weeks of this I found it all too time consuming and managed to persuade Arthur that we must have an automatic.
Lilian was far too thin, having been put through so many operations at her advanced years of eighty-five. She had a lovely face with delicate skin and a sweet nature. Never once did she complain about the pain she was obviously suffering, but would smile through it all. As the weeks went by, I soon realised that the continual surgery had taken its toll and she, sadly, had Alzheimer's disease.
I was still having extreme pain in my back which was not surprising after what I had been put through previously.

So on my day off I would go and see a chiropractor, recommended to me by the gentleman I had seen for treatment in Salisbury. Not only did I have pain but was still very underweight with continual tiredness. I made an appointment to see my new doctor, who in turn arranged for me to see a gynaecologist.

In December I was able to spend the day with James and Susan. We drove out to a country pub and sat by a roaring fire having lunch whilst snowflakes started to fall thick and fast outside. Susan was coping with James single-handed since his stroke and he was far from well.

At Christmas I filled the vase in the hall with holly and made some floral decorations for Arthur and Lilian in the sitting room. The three of us sat in the dining room and went through a full Christmas lunch spending the day together.

On 11th January I walked out of the hospital appointment in a stupor of bewilderment. The gynaecologist wanted me back on 5th February for an operation. I would have to stay overnight and then need a week's recuperation.

I explained the situation to Arthur.

'I'll arrange meals on wheels while I'm convalescing.'

'You can't stay here,' he said abruptly.

'But I have nowhere to go,' I explained.

'Well, you can't stay here, you'll have to go into a nursing home.'

I rushed up to the surgery to see my doctor and burst into tears. He was quite horrified at this totally unreasonable behaviour. He promised he would ring and speak to Arthur and reassure him that I wouldn't need nursing being quite capable of moving about. I didn't want to put Snorkles into kennels unless I really had to because the weather was extremely cold and damp. So I decided to put a card into the local pet shop window.

As I got out of my car with Snorkles sitting in the back, a gentleman was making his way back to his car. I immediately recognised him as we had met previously while out walking and he had told me about two Labradors that he had owned in the past.

'I need someone to look after Snorkles while I'm in hospital. Just going to put a card in the window.'

He turned and said, 'We'd love to have him. Come and meet my wife. She's sitting in the car.'

Having exchanged phone numbers we decided that it would be a good idea for Snorkles to make a visit to their bungalow. This we did one evening and I could see that he would be thoroughly spoilt and well looked after.

Chapter 70

I hadn't been out much so didn't really know many people but I had met our next door neighbours. She offered to drive me to the hospital and I was very grateful.
Having had nothing to eat and sitting by my bed in a ward since 8.00 a.m., terrified of the forthcoming operation, I suddenly felt I was going to pass out. Empty stomach, nerves and low blood pressure took over, and tottering over to one of the cleaners, she put me in a chair just as I was about to black out. One of the nurses was called and I was wheeled back and put to bed. I don't remember the journey to the operating theatre because I had been sedated, so came round back in the ward, drinking cups of tea and drifting in and out of sleep for the rest of the day. In the evening, I was able to eat some mince and vegetables. Having slept all day I was no longer tired and by 2.00 a.m. was wide awake. There was a lady next to me sitting up in bed who was in under observation and couldn't sleep either. We scoffed our way through a whole box of chocolates whilst all around us the other patients were snoring, grunting or moaning.
Feeling still a bit wobbly on my legs, we decided to go walkies to the end of the ward in search of the night nurse. After some persuasion she put the kettle on and made us a cup of tea.
Next morning, arriving back at the house in a taxi, I used Arthur's and Lilian's electric chairlift which whizzed me up and down the stairs. The first three days I slept most of the time feeling absolutely exhausted. Eight days later I

fetched Snorkles and he'd made himself so at home that when I appeared at the front door it took him a few minutes to realise who I was. The rest of the day was spent cooking and getting loads of washing done.

The D&C had been a success and the removed polypi from the womb turned out to be non-malignant but I continued to be thin and desperately tired. The surgeon who had operated thought I should be put through the scanner for possible osteoporosis. It proved negative, thank God.

One morning in April I received a letter from Carlos. It read '..... and hope you will give us your blessing as we got married last week at the Registry Office.' I must admit I sat down with a thud, as I came to grips with this sudden news which took me totally by surprise. I knew precious little about this lady who had become my son's wife. There was little chance of driving the many miles to meet her with all that was happening my end. Besides, I hadn't been feeling at all well—although two months had passed since my operation—to embark on such a journey.

Here I shall give the reader a brief summary of what plagued me for seven months. Neither doctor nor consultants could find an answer, which I found incredible!

April	Feeling so ill that blood tests were taken for suspected anaemia. Negative.
May	No improvement. Doctor suggests I take a holiday.

June	Pain, nausea and feeling very ill.
July	Severe stomach pains, nausea, frequent migraines. Doctor prescribes medication for suspected peptic ulcer.
August	Symptoms continue, but now agonising pain in chest, stomach and back. Nausea so bad that it's getting worse by the day. Doctor changes medication.
26th	Seen by hospital consultant.
September	Endoscopy performed in hospital—camera down stomach—no trace of ulcer.
October	Extreme pain across chest and back, visit surgery in floods of tears.
4th	Sent to another hospital and was told by the consultant 'I have terminally ill patients to see and you are wasting my time. There is nothing wrong with you.'

It wasn't until nearing the end of October that a friend mentioned that her husband had had two months off work and eventually the doctors discovered an allergy to dairy products. Laying in bed that night it suddenly dawned on me that mother had once mentioned that as a

baby I had been allergic to cow's milk and orange juice. I came off all medication and gave up all dairy produce, plus anything with oranges. It took three weeks for the digestive system to cleanse itself of all the toxins. The pain and nausea disappeared.
Through all this I had worked every day and kept everything going. Fear drove me on relentlessly. The fear of losing a roof over my head and having nowhere to go. The fear of having no job and the fear of losing Snorkles. We had come through so much together and I was determined that we would not be parted by anything or anybody.

Chapter 71

One afternoon in May I popped my head round the sitting room door to speak to Arthur. He was trying to read his newspaper and said he couldn't focus properly on the words. He was having difficulty with his speech and he was totally incoherent. I realised immediately that he had had a slight stroke. Making the excuse that I had left something on the stove I dashed upstairs to phone a doctor. Apparently it had been a momentary lack of oxygen to the brain and not the first he had had. But he recovered within a few hours and was quite alright. Later that evening I rang his daughter who turned up two days later to stay the night.

The days were long and tiring as they always are when looking after elderly, disabled people. I'd be down in the kitchen by 8.30 a.m. and after breakfast would take Snorkles out for a ten minute walk. Arthur insisted on all food being home cooked and really enjoyed eating, so I always made a dessert as well. He wouldn't have a light meal in the evening but insisted on a full dinner served at 7.30 p.m. This meant that by the time I had finished washing up and left the kitchen tidy it was 8.30 p.m. or later. It was virtually impossible to have a social life of any kind.

On Sundays a full roast lunch had to be produced and no weekends off were allowed. He also refused to buy me a television for my room. If I went to sit in their sitting room with them and was in the middle of watching an interesting programme or film, and Arthur didn't want to watch it, he would switch off the television.

It was now over three years since setting eyes on my daughter and I had been with Arthur and Lilian for seven months. Time for a break considering that I had worked through Christmas, Easter, and all bank holidays. So it was arranged that I could have two weeks off to travel to Spain. I found wonderful kennels for Snorkles. They were run by a lady who was devoted to the dogs in her care and it was a small family concern. Having seen several other kennels, I decided that this would be the place to leave him.

My idea was to have a week in Madrid to completely rest and then travel down south to spend my second week with Paloma. Greta met me at the airport and we just picked up our conversation from where we had left off last time. My goodness, what a lot to talk about after so many years without seeing each other.

I rang to speak to Paloma, but she was out and when she received my message, she rang two days later.

'I can't wait to see you. I'll be on the train next Friday,' I said excitedly. 'You will meet me at Sevilla, won't you, as arranged?'

'Yes, mama,' Paloma replied. We chatted a bit and then rung off.

Unfortunately, there was so much work at the Embassy that Greta was unable to take time off but we did manage to meet one evening after she finished work and go to the theatre. It was lovely just to unwind, catch a bus into the city and saunter along the streets, stroll into a bar ordering a drink with a tapa and sit outside on the pavement watching the traffic roar past.

Approaching the end of the week, there was a phone call from Paloma.

'Don't come on Friday because I have to fetch my fiancé from Sevilla airport on the Monday. Like that I can fetch both of you,' explained Paloma. I put the phone down and looked completely stunned.

Greta said, 'What's happened?'

'I can't believe what I have just heard. I've spent all this money to travel all this way to be with my daughter and we will have three days together instead of a week.'

Luckily the connections between Madrid and Andalucia are very good and what used to be an eight-hour journey is now done in three thanks to an extremely high-speed, modern Ave train. We had a good drive back to Jerez and that evening we all had dinner sitting under the orange trees in the street.

Next morning, I went to visit Marcos's uncle and his wife. They had always been very kind to me but they were not at home. On my return to the hotel there was a message from Ramon and Margarita inviting Paloma and I to lunch at their home. It brought back many old memories and we caught up with the family news. Margarita had really gone to a lot of time and effort in cooking a delicious lunch and I was very grateful that she still valued my friendship.

That evening Marcos's uncle and wife turned up at the hotel while I was waiting for Paloma.

'Why didn't you take up our offer? We are most hurt,' they said.

At that moment Paloma appeared as I looked in surprise and replied, 'I don't understand. What are you talking about?'
They turned to Paloma. 'Didn't you tell your mother she was invited to stay with us?'
'No,' said Paloma. 'I thought it better to put mama in a hotel.'
Marcos's uncle was not at all pleased with her behaviour and didn't mince his words. He then said, 'We have come to take your mother and you out to dinner'.
We had a delicious assortment of fried fish, olives and a bottle of sherry. I was very touched by their kindness in coming to take me out for a meal.
Paloma and I managed to go and visit La Virgin de la Regla in Chipiona where we prayed a while in the chapel. Then we had lunch and sat on the beach having a long conversation. We went to visit a friend of hers who does Tarot readings. She fetched me later from the hotel to go to a night club where we danced, meeting a group of her friends. We got back at some unearthly hour of the morning!
As I had to catch the Ave back to Madrid next morning, I particularly wanted to have another chat with my daughter before arriving at Sevilla. It was arranged that we would stop on the way and have lunch, taking a leisurely drive. At the arranged time I stood with my luggage waiting in the hotel lobby. Several friends of mine came to say farewell. Paloma arrived late and was in a bad mood. She was extremely rude, lacking all respect and it upset me a great deal. We didn't have time for lunch and it was a mad

rush to catch my train with only minutes before its departure. Hot, flustered, terribly upset, I gave Paloma some money, hugged her and boarded the train as it was about to leave. Once the Ave was moving I broke down and cried relentlessly, unable to stop my tears.
The past came flooding back and the fact that it had been three years since last setting eyes on my daughter. How could she have put me in an hotel when I had been invited to stay at her aunt's and uncle's house? She knew that I had saved up to come and see her and that I was short of money.
I had been in such high spirits to see my adored daughter and had come away so disillusioned. It was made far worse by discovering that she had delayed our reunion on the Friday because she wanted to go away to a party for the weekend, leaving us with only three days together. It hurt to be treated like that by my daughter, and I didn't deserve it.
Being churned up emotionally and the lack of food must have lowered my blood pressure. An hour later, I crashed on to the floor unconscious. The next thing I remember were two ladies, one with a fan in her hand and the other with a glass of water, as I regained consciousness.
My hair was all over the place, my dress crumpled, my face red with swollen eyes and mascara all down my cheeks. I stumbled out onto the platform feeling decidedly faint having had nothing to eat since early morning. Greta was at the barrier, took one look at me and, putting her arm around my shoulders, she gave me a big hug.
'What on earth has happened?' she asked in total

amazement.
At the crack of dawn we were up and Greta was driving me to the airport. We gave each other a warm hug and kiss, for she had always been a truly lovely friend.
On arriving back I drove straight to the kennels. Snorkles was overjoyed to see me and scratched me all over at being reunited. He sat on the back seat with his head resting on my shoulder and we travelled back to the house. The holiday had done me no good at all. I had come back exhausted, emotionally distraught and generally not feeling at all well.

Chapter 72

I have always been interested in the tarot cards and all that goes with clairvoyance. On many occasions during the years I have visited many tarot readers. Every time they have given me a reading, they have always said, 'You would do well reading the tarot cards.'
The years went by with so much happening that there certainly wasn't time to learn the tarot. Having broached the subject of a television for my room to Arthur, the question had been totally ignored. So it was shortly after my return from Spain that I decided to buy a pack of tarot cards and teach myself to read them in the evenings.
On one of my days off a friend and I decided to drive out to several caravan sites. I needed to have a bolt-hole and an old mobile home seemed the only answer. We found nothing at the price that I could even consider and, as it was, I would have to get a bank loan anyway.
On my next day off I drove out into the countryside about twenty miles from Nottingham. Taking a walk with Snorkles through the corn fields, I discovered a little village and near it a mobile home complex. The site manager offered to show me around and we went to see a simply filthy mobile home which was for sale. The place smelt awful and the soles of my shoes stuck to the carpet. We wandered round the site and saw two other homes which were way out of my price bracket. We were passing by a field and there stood an eighteen-year-old mobile home.
'What about that?' I exclaimed.

'That one has got to be moved, bricked in, new cladding, new radiators and new roof. It's dry and sound as a bell.'

'How much?' I asked.

The site manager gave me a quote and I jumped at it. 'May I have a look inside?'

We struggled across knee-deep grass to get to it and scrambled up to the door. There were two good sized bedrooms, bathroom, open plan kitchen and sitting room. It had a wide corridor down one side of it and had plenty of light. Despite its age, it was dry, clean and had been kept in good condition. This was my answer and it was like finding a palace. The field had nothing in it but one small spindly growth of wild rose fighting desperately amongst the weeds and grass to survive.

The next week Snorkles and I returned to sit down in the site manager's office and discuss the final settlement.

'We will need two months to complete all the work,' explained the site manager.

'That's fine,' I replied and then added, 'You are going to have the roof renewed as well as the cladding?'

'Oh yes,' he said, nodding. 'It will all be done as agreed.'

Meanwhile I would make visits wandering about taking measurements for curtains and furniture. The mobile home was moved out of the field, the brick skirting was laid and the radiators changed. It was therefore with total disbelief that whilst practising readings with the tarot cards I asked the specific question, 'Should I buy the mobile home?' and the cards gave me a definite warning that something was amiss and not to go ahead.

At the time I didn't believe in my own ability to foresee

the future through the cards; I thought it must have been my inexperience with the tarot.

On my next visit I spoke to the site manager and asked him why the work on the mobile hadn't continued. 'Had a lot of work to do lately,' he said. 'Cladding will be done next week.'

I'd got a bank loan, made some curtains and sorted out furniture in a second-hand bric-a-brac. There were three weeks to go before the mobile home would be mine.

Sitting up in bed one evening, I spread my tarot cards out and did another reading on the mobile home. It gave me the same warning. This time I did take notice and decided to drive out the next evening after work to the site.

Knocking on the site manager's front door, his wife appeared and I asked her if I could have a word with her husband. He didn't appear and she guided me across to the site office. She sat on one side of the desk and enquired, 'Well what can I help you with?'

'There's two weeks left for work to be completed and neither the cladding nor the roof have been replaced.'

'Oh! I can assure you the cladding will be done this week,' she said.

'And the roof?' I enquired.

'The roof doesn't need replacing. It's not being done.'

'But your husband and I had a lengthy discussion when I signed the contract about the new roof replacing the old one.'

'But it doesn't need a new roof,' she continued.

'I'd like the name and address of the director,' I asked.

'Can't give you that,' she said.

'I'll find out myself, thank you,' I replied and, with that, departed.

My next step was to phone and ask to speak to the director. I was told that I couldn't speak to him but that I was speaking to the general site manager. The conversation was making me doubt all of them. He ended saying, 'Quite impossible for our site manager to have said anything about a new roof.'

'But you don't think for a minute that I would have contemplated buying an old mobile home with a bow roof that has been on it for eighteen years if it wasn't being replaced.' I wrote a letter demanding my deposit back and a few days later a cheque arrived in the post.

In the middle of September, Snorkles was in pain again so the vet put him on another course of antibiotics for cystitis. Unbeknown to me it was not what he had at all—it was far more serious.

Chapter 73

One of the best ways of meeting people is doggy walking and during my time in Nottingham I made friends with what was known as the 'doggy brigade'. It consisted of about ten of us who would invariably meet on a football ground early in the mornings. We would walk the length of three football pitches with an assortment of dogs. This was how I met Myra and we became great friends. She had an old dog and on many occasions I would drive round to her house to spend an evening chatting over a cup of coffee. It was early in November when on one particular morning a lady was walking next to me and suddenly mentioned Willersley Castle.

'I've been there with my late husband. It's now a Methodist Guild Holiday Centre. You can go and have lunch there and walk around the grounds,' she explained.

'Really? How interesting,' I exclaimed in surprise.

'Yes' she continued. 'I've got a book all about the castle's history. I'll lend it to you.' I was even more determined now to visit the place I had been born in, but the next two months were full of activity. So the visit would just have to wait.

Nearing the end of November, I managed to escape for what was meant to be a long weekend in Kent. I was going down to meet Carlos's wife and stay at a bed and breakfast nearby. Snorkles and I set off very early on a bitterly cold morning. After driving 172 miles, I arrived armed with presents for all the family and was looking forward to meeting my newly-acquired daughter-in-law. It had been a long journey and I was tired and hungry. At 3.00 p.m. I felt so faint I had to ask Carlos for a sandwich. There was a definite feeling that I was resented and intruding in their lives so at 4.00 p.m. amidst thick fog I drove back onto the motorway. The feeling of total rejection overwhelmed me.

A week later, Snorkles was in pain again and was having difficulty urinating. By now I had come to the conclusion that this was something serious and decided to take him to another vet. He immediately emptied Snorkles's bladder and an X-ray showed that he had developed bladder stones. During the next twelve days he was put on a special diet to try and dissolve them but three times he had to have a catheter inserted to empty the bladder. On the third occasion it was decided to operate next morning, 14th December.

It was snowing when I went to fetch him at 2.30 p.m. after his major operation. I had tremendous trouble on arriving back to the house because he was lying in a heap on the back seat unable to get himself out. Gently putting his front paws in the position of the car floor I spent ten minutes coaxing him to get out. Just as I was about to go and ask my next door neighbour to help me, Snorkles got himself out and struggled to his bed collapsing into it. Covering him with a blanket, making him as comfortable as possible, I kept a watchful eye on him in the corner of the breakfast room adjoining the kitchen.

The vet had assured me that he would be his usual self within a week, although I was warned that his undercarriage would turn black and blue from the

bruising.
Snorkles had been left extremely weak and so I bought a rabbit from the butchers and had it chopped up, simmering it in the pressure cooker. Having strained all the bones out of the soup I let it cool and spooned thick gelatine down his throat every two hours. His favourite food has always been chicken but he refused to even try a little from my hand.
I bought the best beef possible and had it finely minced. This he lapped up as he lay in his bed and like this I fed him at intervals during the day. For the first three days I would settle him at night, very gently placing more dry towels on top of the wet areas, unable to do anything else until he felt well enough to get out of his bed. During the course of the night I would creep downstairs at intervals to make sure he was alright.
He made a remarkable recovery and was able to go for a short walk four days after his operation. That same afternoon there was a phone call to say that James had passed away. Leaving a cooked meal ready for Arthur and Lilian I was able to attend the funeral and be with Susan. It was held on 20th December and James was laid to rest in the village churchyard in Swinstead.
I managed to get four days away at Christmas as Arthur and Lilian were having family to stay. So on the 23rd, having taken Snorkles to have his stitches removed, we set off for a hotel near Birmingham. It turned out to be ideal as I had a room on the ground floor with easy access to the outside. There was a park not far away and so after taking Snorkles for a walk I went and had a swim in the

hotel's pool. Taking a leisurely shower, trying to unwind, I dressed for dinner and appeared in the queue waiting to be allocated a table.
'I hope you don't mind Madam,' the Spanish maître d'hôtel said, 'but I have put you at a table with two other people who are also by themselves for Christmas. If after dinner you do not wish to continue sharing a table, please let me know.'
Having ordered a glass of wine I was admiring the decor, observing—as one so often does when alone—people walking across the dance floor being shown to their places and looking at the assortment of clothing. Totally relaxed and at peace with the world, I was looking forward to the forthcoming dinner. I suddenly spied Billy Bunter himself being ushered along to my table. His tweed jacket was rumpled due to his train journey and the buttons trying to hold in his stomach were bursting to be released. The wire-rimmed glasses were pinching into the chubby cheeks and all that was missing was the school cap.
The conversation was enthralling and went a bit like this:
'Have you travelled far?'
'London.'
'Did you come by car?'
'Train, don't drive.'
After a few minutes of complete silence, I tried again.
'I look after an elderly couple in Nottingham, come away for a few days' rest. What do you do?'
'Civil Servant. Live with my parents.'
At this point I could see an elderly lady walking with the aid of a stick towards our table. She turned out to be a

'grumbler' and nothing—absolutely nothing—pleased her. 'Oh,' she exclaimed when seated, 'You're all dressed up and I feel awful sitting next to you.' She pulled the material of her trousers as she continued, 'Didn't know what to wear so I didn't bother.'

I'd just beckoned a waiter over and asked for another glass of wine. He asked the other two if they would like a drink.

'No,' said Billy Bunter, 'Only drink water.'

'Yes, I would,' started off Grumbler, 'but I don't know what to have and I certainly don't want wine,' she finished off pointing to my empty glass. Eventually she chose a soft drink.

Burying my nose behind a menu card I tried to switch off from the immediate company and was busy sorting out what I wanted to order. 'There's too many things on the menu,' Grumbler moaned. 'Don't want that and I certainly don't want turkey.' She carried on whining while Billy Bunter made grunting noises across the table.

The dinner was beautifully served, quite delicious and couldn't be faulted in any way. During the meal we didn't say much because Billy Bunter was busy stuffing himself with food and gave an occasional 'yes' or 'no'. Grumbler got her starter and then decided that she didn't want it. She complained loudly about her main course being far too much food to eat and then decided that she didn't like the vegetables she had chosen on her plate.

By now the band had started playing background music and a waitress came round with a coffee cona. 'Coffee, Madam?' she asked Grumbler.

'Oh no!' she exclaimed making a grimace as if she had

been offered poison. 'I don't know how you can drink that,' she continued whilst staring at my coffee cup and finished her statement by saying, 'It's got such a nasty taste.'
Suddenly she changed tack and enquired, 'Have you come far?'
'Nottingham,' I replied. 'Takes about an hour in the car but I did stop on the way to let my dog out.'
'A dog, ugh,' Grumbler said as she made a face of disgust. 'Can't stand dogs, horrible things.'
That was enough conversation for me. I have no time or sympathy for those who don't love God's creatures and even less for someone who refers to dogs as horrible!
While the dancing was taking place I went to find the maitre d'hôtel. 'Would you please see that I have a table by myself, as of tomorrow morning?'
'Si, Señora,' he replied. 'I understand.'
'Thank you very much."
Next morning I was seated at a table for one and had just fetched some fruit salad for breakfast. I was about to put the spoon in my mouth when I saw Grumbler being escorted over to the other side of the dining room. Halfway across the floor she suddenly grabbed the waitress's arm and pointed towards my table with her stick.
'My friend is over there,' she said in a loud voice. She headed towards me and there was no escape from her continual complaints throughout the entire breakfast. I eventually got away with the pretext of having to walk my dog!

The maître d'hôtel was in the reception area as I was leaving the hotel's main entrance. 'What can be done?' I asked. 'I've come away to rest and enjoy my stay.'
'I have the answer, Señora, leave it with me.'
At lunch I sat and thoroughly enjoyed my meal while Billy Bunter and Grumbler were seated at the far end of the dining room. The maitre d'hôtel came over while I was having coffee. 'I told her that you were being joined by a gentleman for lunch,' he explained with a smile.
On Christmas day we had a treasure hunt all over the hotel which had a huge adjoining conference area. Snorkles was allowed to join in and trotted up and down corridors thoroughly enjoying all the attention he was getting from everyone. He was also allowed in the lounge in the afternoons where tea was served and loved the fuss that people were making over him. He has always had a sociable disposition and is accustomed to being taken everywhere with me. In fact he would rather sit in the car and wait for my return than be left alone at home. We've had so many moves, so much travelling together that I call him the 'New Age Traveller'!

Chapter 74

On 3rd January 1994 it was a bank holiday Monday and, amazingly, Arthur had allowed me to have the day off. Myra and I set out for Derbyshire with the dogs. We stopped on the way for coffee and then made our way to Cromford in Matlock.
A long steep driveway led us up to Willersley Castle which commands a wonderful view, surrounded by woodland walks and hills as far as the eye can see. Below winds the River Derwent with the old cotton mills once owned by Sir Richard Arkwright. The Castle was built for him around 1788 and his descendants lived there until 1927. As we entered the main entrance we stopped in the porchway to read the two plaques on the wall. They read:

1. This building was used as an auxiliary hospital during the great war 1914-1918.

2. Between 1940 and 1946 the work of the Salvation Army's Mother's Hospital and Training School was evacuated in part from Clapton, London, to Willersley Castle, during which time over 4,000 babies were born here.

It is a magnificent building with its original heavy mahogany doors all beautifully preserved. The white cornices against a sea of pale blue and the Adam fireplaces look superb. It has all been lovingly protected along with modern facilities without losing its majestic appearance.

We entered into a large hallway and on to the dining room for lunch. It was a plain meal but nicely cooked and we sat at a large round table with other people who were staying overnight. We sauntered back to the reception desk in the hall and told the lady behind the desk that I had been born in the castle.
'You can't imagine the amount of people who have visited us to see where they were born.'
'Really?' I questioned.
'Oh, yes,' she smiled. 'Would you like to be shown round the castle and see the room where you were born?'
'Oh, yes, please, I'd love to.'
We were led up the stairway and we went into one of the guest's rooms. 'This was the delivery room where all the babies were born.'
I walked in and went towards the tall windows trying to imagine what it must have been like in the month of November with no heating. It wasn't difficult to conjure up the idea because as I gazed out of the windows the mist was swirling down engulfing the tops of the limestone tors and there was a fine drizzle of rain.
After being shown round we donned raincoats and, despite the pouring rain, walked the dogs all through the grounds. By the time we got back to the car the heavens had opened and it was teeming down. The dogs were drenched and so were we and there was no hope of going on to Bakewell, as we had planned, so we drove back to Nottingham.

Chapter 75

A week later after our visit to the castle, I got a frozen shoulder due to carrying some heavy shopping back to Myra's house. I tried to ignore it but it proved very painful and lasted for over a year. It affected my arm socket and collar bone giving acute physical discomfort to my back due to my spinal injury.

Five months later after treatment with my chiropractor, there was no improvement. Eventually, I gave in to the idea of having two cortisone injections in my shoulder which turned out to be a total waste of time.

At the beginning of March I had to take Snorkles to see the vet again. He had been curled up, shivering, whining and wouldn't eat at all. I immediately thought there was a bladder problem again. It had been ten weeks since his major operation.

'I'm almost certain it's the hips that are hurting him,' the vet announced.

'It can't be,' I replied, 'He walks the golf course every afternoon and runs about very happily.'

A blood test and X-ray had to be done and the verdict was severe hip dysplasia. Snorkles's seventh birthday was coming up in two weeks' time. I looked at the X-ray as the vet explained how chronic the hips were.

'But he's never given any indication of pain. He's got such a happy disposition and loves walking. When do you think the hip dysplasia started?' I asked.

'At the age of three years,' replied the vet.

Snorkles had a course of gold injections and soon we were

off with the rambling club again. As the years have gone by, I am convinced that due to never letting Snorkles get fat and keeping him exactly the right weight has helped him no end. His regular exercise and long walks have built up a lot of muscle which has helped cushion the pain. He has learnt to cope with it very well and to watch him walk no one would know how severe the hip dysplasia is.

On one of my days off I drove over to Susan's house for lunch and in June was able to spend a weekend with her.

On 24th June I had an extraordinary experience. Not only was I interested in the tarot cards but also had read a book on crystals and their amazing powers of healing.

Wandering about doing some shopping I decided to buy myself a rose quartz. While in the shop one of the girls and I got chatting and she informed me that there was a Psychic Awareness meeting starting up the very next evening.

I managed to get to the meeting because it started late. A married couple who were both mediums were helping others develop their psychic abilities. It was most interesting and so I went along again for the second meeting on the 24th.

The evening ended and people were saying goodnight and leaving. I had just picked up my handbag from under the chair and was chatting to a lady next to me. From across the room I saw the medium's wife point in our direction and say, 'I have a message for you.' She came over and stood in front of me. Having had messages from my father in the past, I immediately imagined it was him. But it wasn't. The message conveyed was a very accurate description of Eric. The snowy-white hair and moustache, the eyes that twinkled, thin build, sense of humour, impeccably dressed and, as always, wearing a cravat. 'He tells me that he wants you to know that he has passed over to the spirit world.'

I thanked the medium and, extremely upset, made my way back to my car where I tried to stop my tears. That night I lay in bed unable to sleep because I didn't like to think that I had lost a good friend whom I would never see again.

Thinking about it while working the next day, I knew I wanted the information I had been given confirmed. Not being able to bear the suspense and uncertainty any longer, I rang a friend who lives in Cadiz on the evening of the 26th. Before I could say anything down the phone, my friend said, 'Hello Clare, I have to tell you the sad news that Antonio was buried last week.'

'What are you saying?' I replied, totally stunned.

'He had cancer in the throat and recovered from the operation and was walking about again. Two weeks later he died,' explained my friend.

Too shocked to take in the horrific news, I failed to ask much more, still believing that there must be some terrible mistake. Antonio had only been forty-eight years old.

'Is Eric alright?' I asked.

'Oh, he's fine. We saw him the other day walking down the avenue.'

After saying goodbye, I put the phone down trying to come to terms with it all. After a while, I realised that Antonio had conveyed his message by describing Eric. He knew that I would ring a friend in Cadiz and would be instantly told about his own death.

Chapter 76

One August morning, I was walking Snorkles on the playing fields as usual when a man appeared with a large mongrel dog. It made a bee-line for Snorkles and I watched in horror as this dog ferociously attacked him. Hysterically shouting at the dog's owner and imploring him to remove his dog, the man just stood and watched. Snorkles was howling in agony as the dog viciously sunk his teeth into his hips and stomach. I had visions of Snorkles being ripped to pieces and it was only seven-and-a-half months since his major operation. The owner had no intention of even calling his dog off and by this time I was screaming as Snorkles yelped in pain. Two ladies who lived by the field and were from the 'doggy brigade' came out of their houses and ran across towards me. By this time Snorkles was lying very still on the ground and I was kneeling beside him totally distraught. The dog and man had ambled off down the field.

One of the ladies put Snorkles and me in her car. I was shaking from shock as she drove off down the road towards the dog owner and gave him a verbal attack which he truly deserved.

Snorkles was very bruised but thank goodness hadn't sustained any wounds. It has left us both extremely wary of owners who do not know how to control their dogs. They should never be allowed to have a dog in the first place and as for thinking they have the right to maim someone else's dog is quite beyond belief. If they were true animal lovers—which they are not—these dog

owners wouldn't want other dogs to get hurt in the first place. Neither do they consider the shock and total helplessness to the owner seeing their beloved dog being attacked and in many cases severely hurt.
It was by now sixteen months since my visit to Spain and time to have a holiday so I made arrangements to travel down to Sussex. Arthur and Lilian were going to stay in an hotel near their daughter's house while I was away.
About eighty people from an association were all going to Goodwood races in September so I booked in to join them. Snorkles and I set off to stay in a lovely log cabin in the heart of the glorious Sussex countryside. The couple who managed bed and breakfast turned out to be charming and would come across their lawn each morning with a full English breakfast on a tray.
We were surrounded by fields so it was very convenient for letting Snorkles out. He would bound off chasing the rabbits. There were literally hundreds of bobbing white powder puffs and Snorkles would stand mystified as they disappeared into their warrens.
After a brisk walk in the crisp cold air of the autumn morning, we set off for lunch to Kenneth's house. His wife had cooked a lovely meal and we spent a pleasant day, leaving after tea to drive back to our haven.
I had booked Snorkles into kennels not far from where we were staying and, as it had been recommended to me, thought it would be alright. So, all dressed up for Goodwood, I arrived at the kennels with his bed. I took an instant dislike to the sullen-faced man who appeared in the driveway and felt uneasy about leaving Snorkles. I

insisted on putting his bed in his kennel, much to the owner's obvious annoyance. I soon discovered why, because on entering into the kennels, the smell of urine was overpowering. There wasn't time to look for anywhere else so, already late, I drove off for the sherry reception.

After an excellent lunch a few of us went off between races to view the horses in the enclosure but the bitter wind was blowing across the South Downs and it was very chilly. I felt a sense of unease about Snorkles so, after a cup of tea, I left.

Arriving back at the kennels, I went straight in with the owner to fetch him. I'd left his food prepared but the owner hadn't bothered to feed him and once out of his kennel Snorkles headed at top speed for the car. I'd never seen him behave in this manner before and had to let go of his lead before I went crashing to the ground. He couldn't get into the car fast enough and away from that terrible place.

I spent the next three days just taking life easy, driving out to country pubs and walking with Snorkles. I was feeling physically and mentally exhausted and thought that it would pass as the days went by but it didn't. Looking back, I realise now that this was a warning that the human body and mind can only take so much strain before it becomes ill. But there was to be no rest because of my circumstances and there was no alternative but to carry on.

I'd arranged to meet Carlos in Tunbridge Wells in the second week of my holiday so we set off to find somewhere to stay a few miles out of town. I stopped at several places but they were fully booked and eventually, late in the afternoon, found a bed and breakfast. From the outside it looked very attractive and had a small restaurant serving light meals and teas to the public.

We had to walk through the restaurant to get upstairs which was inconvenient with Snorkles and several trips backwards and forwards to unload the car. The room was plain with barely any furniture and inside the wardrobe were filthy stained pillows with an equally dirty blanket stuffed into it. I decided that we would move on to somewhere cleaner the next day. Placed on the spare bed were two towels and on picking them up I found that they were dirty too, having been used by the last occupants! Investigating the bed, I discovered another quite revolting pillow full of stains and decided that action had to be taken.

Going downstairs to find a member of staff in the kitchen I asked to see the owner and with no apologies of any kind a clean pillow and towels were produced.

I took Snorkles down to the garden and had tea outside and then thought that later on I would go and have a meal at the local pub. It wasn't until I got back to my room that I felt totally incapable of even walking Snorkles. I'd been feeling terribly tired, but now I was unable to stand. Feeling sick and extremely ill, I decided to go to bed early and tomorrow would be another day. Snorkles has always been an exceptional dog and understood at once that I was far from well. So instead of going for walkies, he settled down quietly by the side of my bed.

I didn't rest but tossed and turned, trying to get some sleep. A thumping headache with nausea raged all night and I lay there with a cold face flannel on my forehead. I seemed to be getting worse and felt far too weak to do much at all. The idea of getting marooned in this awful place with a large Labrador in the bedroom and no one to help either of us eventually got me to my feet at 6.00 a.m. I struggled with some things to the car and let Snorkles potter outside. At 7.00 a.m. one of the staff was in the kitchen and I told her that I had decided to leave due to feeling unwell. She helped me with my luggage and cooked breakfast while I sat in the restaurant. When the food did appear I was totally incapable of eating anything with waves of nausea engulfing me. There was nothing for it but to get onto the motorway and head straight back to Nottingham. Snorkles as usual was wonderful and lay quietly stretched out on the back seat while I drove non-stop in torrential rain until we arrived back.
The house was empty and it was freezing cold so my next door neighbour's husband kindly sorted out the burglar alarm and put the heating on for me. For three days I lay in bed and hardly ate any food while one of the 'doggy brigade' who lived opposite took Snorkles out to the field in the morning with her Labrador. I had rung Arthur to explain that due to having been taken ill I had returned to the house.
One of the lady doctors from the surgery came to see me and immediately realised that I was suffering from total nervous exhaustion. She told me to rest and take another two weeks off. Meanwhile, Arthur and Lilian had decided

to terminate their stay near their daughter and come home.
By now I was on my feet again but feeling decidedly weak. The phone rang and Arthur's voice said, 'We'll be home tomorrow, so I want you to go shopping and stock up with food.' There was no consideration as usual and I staggered off wandering about the supermarket, endeavouring to concentrate on filling a trolley with the appropriate necessities.
There was no need for this procedure because Arthur knew perfectly well that I kept the freezer filled to bursting point with cooked food in case of an emergency. The larder was equally well stocked with tins of every conceivable food imaginable, not to mention toilet rolls, household cleaners, light bulbs etc.
The daily came in two mornings a week and would help out if necessary.

Chapter 77

Having spoken to Susan she immediately suggested that I stay with her.
'Why don't we stay at an hotel for four days because it would give you a rest as well,' I said. So that is what we did and then I spent the next week recuperating out in the countryside at Susan's bungalow.
She wanted a tarot reading so then I suggested that she rang her friends to see if they would like to come too. I wanted to put into practice my clairvoyant abilities with the cards. Those that came all said, after their readings, that I had been very accurate in what I had told them about their personal lives. By the time I left I felt better and able to face my tiring work once again.
Lilian had become a source of constant worry as her health deteriorated. That alone was exhausting apart from everything else. On several occasions complete strangers asking for money or selling articles would be ushered into the sitting room! She let Snorkles out one morning while I was doing the weekly shopping. Thank goodness Arthur called him back before he managed to reach the road.
While preparing a meal or cooking several dishes, I might pop out to the washing machine or the garden for parsley. By the time I had got back to the kitchen the cooking utensils had disappeared, food had been put away and what was cooking on the gas hob would have been turned off!
On one occasion she put peas into a chocolate blancmange that I had made. She didn't want to wash or

change her clothes and I would have to coax her with infinite patience. If I was in my bedroom on my day off, she would invariably appear and as I had no lock on my door would just come in. Not understanding that I was meant to be having a rest from work, she would ask me to come and help her find something she was looking for. I hadn't the heart to ever say no but I did need my time off, which I wasn't getting.

On two occasions Lilian choked on her food during lunch. I managed to get a bowl just in time but the second time there's no doubt I saved her life. She had just put some food in her mouth and after a minute or two started to choke. Getting up, I gave her some sharp slaps between the shoulder blades but she was by now fighting for her breath, unable to speak and making frightening gasping noises. Immediately I pulled her chair away from the table, got her false teeth out and gave her an abdominal thrust. Mercifully this brought up the offending obstruction.

At the beginning of October on a beautiful warm sunny autumn day Myra and I took a day's outing to Calke Abbey in Derbyshire. We decided to stop for lunch wherever a nice pub appeared en route and found one at Breedon-on-the-Hill. On arriving at the Abbey we sauntered round the gardens with Snorkles and then went inside to look at the building. Tea was being served in one of the out-houses so we sat and enjoyed the pleasant surroundings. Making our way back to Myra's house she rustled up a light snack that evening.

Two weeks later, Snorkles was urinating blood and I immediately drove him to the vet. There were crystals in the bladder again—ten months after the operation—and these would eventually form stones once more. He was put on a special diet to dissolve the crystals.

At the beginning of November I drove down to Essex for an interview. A lady in her eighties had advertised for a driver. She lived with two dogs and a cat and didn't mind Snorkles, so it was decided that I would come to live with her. After receiving written confirmation I went to give in my notice to Arthur.

The next few weeks I spent frantically packing in the evening and finding a man with a van to follow me down south. On the 22nd I was invited over to a friend's house for a farewell party. She had walked Snorkles for me on several occasions in the past. I was quite overwhelmed by her kindness for she had gathered together the entire 'doggy brigade'. I was given several presents and cards and it was all totally unexpected.

On the 26th while the man was loading the van I went to say goodbye to Arthur and Lilian. He stood on the landing. 'I suppose you're going now?' he stated in a gruff voice.

'Yes, Arthur,' I replied. 'Nearly ready.' I wanted to go and say goodbye to Lilian but Arthur was shutting the bedroom door as he retreated. There were no thanks at all. I had already been dismissed as something from the past. It hurt to think that I had looked after them with loyal devotion, giving them the best possible care during two years of my life.

Chapter 78

I stopped at a Little Chef on our journey and ordered a cooked breakfast for the driver and myself. Once on the road again we were travelling along the motorway when I saw the van's lights flashing. I pulled over to the hard shoulder and saw the driver getting underneath his van.
'What's happened?' I enquired anxiously.
'The water seems to be at boiling point,' he announced. 'Have to go slower. She can't do much over thirty miles an hour,' he explained as he reached for a grubby rag to wipe his hands.
The journey was never-ending as we crawled along the motorway towards Essex. I had visions of us getting marooned with this clapped out van with all my worldly possessions in it or perhaps worse still it might catch fire! By the time we arrived I was exhausted from the packing, the painfully slow journey and the worry of getting my goods and chattels safely to their destination.
Winifred greeted me and was a little overwhelmed by the boxes and baggage that was being carried up to my newly acquired bedroom. The cottage was bitterly cold and unless you sat by the fireplace there was no other way of keeping warm. Winifred had been asthmatic all her life and because she insisted on keeping her bedroom and the kitchen quarters like a freezer I soon discovered why she was continually have asthma attacks. These would develop into a chesty cough leaving her unable to speak. The bouts would put her in bed for a week at a time.
My first evening Snorkles, not used to the layout in the

house, slipped on the polished floor at the top of the stairs. He was in pain and unable to walk properly. I knew that he would have to see a vet and he turned up after surgery late at night to meet Snorkles and I was very grateful.

After my first week I had a day off and went out to find my way around town. I brought back something to eat in my room and settled down to write a letter. Around 6.45 p.m. Winifred called from downstairs and I opened my bedroom door.

'Don't you think it's about time you got my supper?' she enquired. I was completely taken aback.

'But it's my day off Winifred,' I replied.

'Well, I think you could bring a tray for me,' she continued.

At this point I totally gave up and, rather than argue, went into the kitchen, cooked her supper and mine. Bringing the tray as we did every evening to the sitting room, I sat and talked to her until she went to bed at 9.30 p.m.

Next day, Winifred was taken ill and spent the next week in bed. The doctor visited and said it was a virus, but her bedroom was perishing cold with draughts coming from every angle. I was under the impression that we would be spending Christmas together but she had made arrangements to go to a daughter-in-law in the west country.

Not used to such a cold house I developed a sore throat after her departure which developed into tonsillitis. It became extremely painful to swallow and I felt anything but well. I didn't know a soul. Everything was strange and

I had barely had time to find anything in the house. The dailies took an instant dislike to me from the moment they saw me. I actually overheard one of them saying that she didn't think I would be able to cope with the shopping and was totally unsuitable!

They took great delight in telling me about all the previous people who had worked for Mrs. X and managed to make me feel uncomfortable by constantly telling me to leave as soon as possible and find somewhere else.

It wasn't long before they grumbled about the floor getting dirty due to Snorkles. This was all totally out of order because he had been taught as a pup never to enter the house with dirty paws until they had been cleaned. He would always stand outside and wait for the bucket and sponge routine.

There was constant tittle-tattle, making my life a misery. However, Winifred and I got on well together having great conversations over the tea and supper trays. She wanted me to walk one of the dogs—the other being too old—and I would take the little dog out with Snorkles.

Christmas Day I went down to have lunch with Carlos and his wife. Snorkles wasn't feeling very well and by the time I arrived back to the empty house he was violently sick outside. Since the second formation of bladder crystals he had been put on dried food for life. He simply hated it and his stomach couldn't tolerate it. He tried so hard to eat because he was hungry but eventually he gave up, taking one look at it and walking away. Snorkles started to look emaciated, his coat became dull and he was miserable. I wrote a note explaining all his past history to

the vet and on my day off went to see him at his surgery. Urine and blood tests were taken and it was decided to put him on chicken and green beans. Small portions were fed three times a day and Snorkles started to pick up and was once more a happy dog.
Winifred had had an exhausting Christmas and I had guessed right from the beginning that the long journey and a house full of people would prove far too much for her. She came back looking flushed and not at all well. I suggested a few days' rest but she wouldn't. It resulted in her being taken ill a few days after her return spending another week in bed. Feeling recovered but not looking well, she insisted on having ten for lunch! So the morning was spent cooking as it was every Sunday when a full roast lunch was produced for visiting family.
Five days later Winifred was back in bed ill again. She spent another week recovering. Meanwhile, I had a continual bout of swollen glands and was generally run down. It was bitterly cold, even in the sitting room, due to the stone floors and a draughty gale coming from the front door. I had no television in my room and by 9.30 p.m. would be expected to go to my bedroom. Winifred's dogs were put in the kitchen at night so I was unable to go and make a hot drink. Neither could I sleep at night because my bedroom was above the kitchen. The dogs would start about 11.00 p.m. when there would be growling, snapping and barking going on. They would start fighting without fail every night. The walls were paper thin and it was as if the dogs were in my bedroom. It was totally impossible to sleep. I mentioned it to

Winifred but unfortunately her dogs could do no wrong. There had been con-fabs going on behind my back non-stop so after seven weeks Winifred suddenly announced over a cup of tea, 'I'm sorry, but you'll have to leave.'
It stunned me because for seven weeks I had spent most of my time running up and down the stairs with trays, walking dogs, shopping, cooking, taking prescriptions to the chemist, feeding animals and generally keeping the house going. I had been employed as a driver!
'May I ask why?' I replied.
She paused and there was a long wait, 'I think you go out too much in the evenings.'
'But Winifred, I've only been out four evenings since I've been here and have never gone out when you've been ill.'
'You can stay until you find somewhere to go,' replied Winifred.
It was never established why I had been asked to leave, although I broached the subject again some weeks later, but I knew that the tittle-tattle going on around me on a constant basis had influenced her decision.
A week before all this, on my day off, I had passed through the kitchen to fetch Snorkles's lead from the corridor. Winifred turned round and said, 'You are taking my dog for a walk as well?'
'I'm on my way to fetch my car from the garage to go to Chelmsford.'
'But aren't you walking Snorkles?'
'No, I'll give him a run later.'
'Well, I do think you could walk mine.'
'I'm sorry Winifred, but it's my day off.'

'Oh, don't worry, Mrs. X, we'll take the dog for a walk,' chorused the dailies.

It is outrageous, selfish and totally unfair for people who employ someone to live in their house to think they own them. There is no respect for their time off and they are not expected to have a social life at all. They are no longer a human being with feelings but a piece of furniture—insignificant—to be pushed about wherever it takes their fancy. When they decide you don't fit anymore or they get tired of seeing you, they just get rid of you.

It is all summed up rather neatly by those who advertise for living-in staff in which they so often announce: .... and mustn't have any ties! In other words you must no longer be a person once employed by me because I shall command you to do this, that and the other and you will do it.

Who are these people who think you are not entitled to have weekends off? You're at their beck and call all day and then they want an evening meal cooked and all the kitchen cleared up at some unearthly hour.

Chapter 79

I had decided to spend my day off in Chelmsford and go back to where my natural mother had been living. I really can't describe why I felt the need but perhaps I was longing for just a little bit of comfort from someone and still wondered whether she was alive.

I rang the bell but there was no answer and the house looked as if no one lived there any longer. I went and rang another bell nearby and a couple came to the door. They hadn't seen anyone there for quite a while and hadn't had any contact with my natural mother.

Eventually, I drove about wondering what to do, when it occurred to me that a nearby post office might know her whereabouts. No light could be thrown on the matter so I decided to try a row of shops. In a fruit and vegetable shop I was directed to a lady who lived a few doors away from where my natural mother had lived. I knocked on the door and after explaining why I was there she ushered me into her sitting room. This lady turned out to have been a friend of my natural mother but had no idea that she had had a daughter. She sat down in utter amazement as I related my search for my mother and how I had found her in the past.

My natural mother had died in 1991 and had been buried in Chelmsford. This lady gave me the name of the cemetery and, after thanking her, I started to drive in that direction. Whether I was exhausted physically or emotionally or both, I don't know, but suddenly I just couldn't face it and turned my car round heading back to

Winifred's house.
I'd like to try and put into words a message to parents who have adopted children. In many, many cases they bitterly resent an adopted child wanting to find its natural mother or father. So frequently they are deeply hurt by this fact, when they feel that there should be no need for the child they have adopted to search for their natural parents. I have heard it said so often '...... and we have loved them as our own. We've given him/her everything and made many sacrifices, so I don't understand why he/she should want to look for a parent who gave them away.'
Well, unless you are the adopted person, it is extremely difficult to understand. The fact remains that no matter how much love and attention has been bestowed upon you it wasn't and never will be your natural mother who brought you into the world.
The feeling of rejection is tremendous. The agony of not knowing who or what your parents looked like and why they got rid of you is a mental torment. There is a very great need in many people's lives to find out why and to set eyes on their natural mother or father. Many times it leaves a deep scar to the adopted person and a feeling of sorrow, anger and resentment. My sound advice to all parents who adopt children is put aside your feelings. Think what it would be like yourself, never to have known your own parents, not to have known what they looked like. The hurt is so profound in being adopted because your real parents didn't want you as a baby girl or boy. Parents will gain a much better relationship with their

adopted child if they support that wish to find out who their natural parents were.

I shall always be so grateful to my father for understanding my need to know the truth. He didn't stand in my way but helped me by going to a lot of time and trouble in finding out my natural mother's name. Without his deep love and ability to unselfishly comprehend what was tormenting me I would never have found her.

I learnt through my own search that my mother had been single at the time of my birth. She had been thirty-three years old and had obviously been left to cope with it all by herself. Not only was it a disgrace to have an illegitimate baby in 1941 but it was also the time of the Second World War. She never had another baby despite marrying two years later almost to the date of my birth.

It hurt that my natural mother had not wanted to know me and that she asked me to leave when I found her, but I did set eyes on her and saw the woman who had brought me into this world. Since that day there has been a peaceful acceptance which ended the long years of wondering who she was, what she looked like and her whereabouts.

Chapter 80

Two weeks later in February, Winifred was looking decidedly ill again but when I wanted to ring the doctor she wouldn't hear of it. The house was extremely cold and there were draughts everywhere. By the end of the week she was so ill that she had to stay in bed. At the same time I had totally lost my voice with laryngitis, feeling far from well and battling to keep on my feet.

Next morning, I struggled into a dressing gown suffering from a high temperature, sore throat, earache and inflamed tonsils, to take a breakfast tray to Winifred. She looked very ill and I picked up the phone pleading with her to call the doctor. She absolutely refused. I returned to my room and collapsed back into bed shivering and shaking. The perspiration was pouring down me and my night-dress was drenched. The dailies arrived and eventually convinced Winifred to call a doctor in to see her. She had pneumonia and was taken off in an ambulance.

I was left alone in the house with a raging temperature. By this time I was worried sick wondering what to do, where to go and getting thinner by the day.

Winifred spent six days in hospital and I had by then recovered sufficiently to fetch her home. It wasn't surprising that I was ill because I spent my time off out in the car in the perishing cold, damp weather with Snorkles, driving about in an exhaustive attempt to find somewhere to live. One day I went to various towns and did a total of thirty estate agencies. Finding a one-bedroomed flat was like looking for gold. The worry was consuming my health as the physical and mental exhaustion took over. It was like being an animal which was down on its knees and being goaded on and on with no mercy. I'd been run into the ground and the continual years of homelessness, fear and terror had all been far too much to cope with. I was at my wits' end.

A priest, the Citizens Advice Bureau, the Council and various organisations for the homeless were contacted but no one could help me. I travelled many miles away from Essex to see if there was a chance of a flat elsewhere. I began to think in desperation that I would have to end Snorkles's life and mine—it seemed the only answer.

One afternoon in March a housing officer came to see me at Winifred's house. She could obviously see that I was anything but well, very weak and at the end of my tether. I can honestly say that had I not been housed, I would have collapsed and finished up in hospital.

It wasn't until some weeks later, after moving into a little maisonette, that I realised how terribly ill and tired I was and then it hit me full force.

Winifred knew in her heart of hearts that it was a totally unfair dismissal and gave me a cheque towards some furniture. It meant that I was able to buy a new cooker and fridge.

I shall never forget the first day in the flat. The sitting room floor had boxes, suitcases etc. strewn about. Snorkles and I sat next to each other at the top of the stairs. We had no electricity, no gas and no furniture but we had a flat! I put my arms round him and he lent against

me in a comforting sort of way. I was just wondering if I had made the right arrangements about a bed being delivered when there was a knock at the front door. There stood an elderly lady with a lovely smile on her face.
'I live downstairs below your flat and thought you might like a cup of tea?'
'That would be wonderful because I can't get anything connected until tomorrow.'
As I was about to close my front door, she added, 'Bring doggy as well.'
Gladys turned out to be a true Christian neighbour, a real friend who I could pop in and see at any time. She's lent me a shoulder to cry on when I've felt ill or upset. Gladys knows that I am here to help in any way and she can knock on my door day or night. How much richer people's lives would be if all neighbours helped each other instead of living their own selfish lives.
A month later, Carlos came to lunch and it was lovely to see him. There is only an hour's drive from his place to mine.
I was very fortunate in registering with a lady doctor. I say fortunate, because she is a lovely person and dedicated to her patients. I was suffering from deep depression and had been on the borderline of a nervous breakdown. The body and mind had taken so many continual batterings that it was incapable of going on without a complete rest. It was time to let nature restore me in its own time. I literally switched off from the outside world. By that I mean that I slept when I was tired and ate when I was hungry, regardless of time. Snorkles was my main

motivation in getting well again and where he was concerned he never failed to get his walkies twice a day. Many times I would struggle out with Snorkles, feed him in the afternoon and go to sleep, incapable of getting through a whole day. I would wake up in the evening and despair on many occasions thinking that I would never get better.

To all those people out there who are suffering from depression, don't give up. You will pull through and come out of it and believe me there is a light at the end of the tunnel. As difficult as it is, when you feel so unwell try to have positive thinking. There will be good and bad days—the bad days can be diabolical—but each day brings hope to will yourself back to health again.

Chapter 81

Paloma and I have kept in contact by letter or phone; Carlos comes to visit and have lunch with me whenever he is able to find time.
In September Susan invited me to stay but, unfortunately, I was by now suffering from severe migraine attacks, resulting in having to rest whilst at her home. I came back to my flat feeling anything but well. I'd suffered from migraine for many years but as time went on it was becoming more and more frequent. They were also getting worse and lasting up to three days. This slowly began to have a cycle of five days to a week clear and then another attack was imminent. It wasn't until I got severe toothache in two molar teeth in the upper jaw that I decided to go and see my dentist in Golder's Green. I always associate him all those years ago with the offending humbug that left me with half a molar whilst sitting in my office!
By November 1995 the constant toothache and migraines were making life unbearable. I wanted the molar teeth out but my dentist didn't think that was the answer. He sent me to a dental hospital for a second opinion. Fortunately, my dentist had read about teeth causing migraines. It was definitely a bite problem and although I had ground my front teeth most of my life, I was now grinding the back ones as well. This was sending the pain up into my head, causing horrific migraine. A light dental plate was made to wear at night. Without a doubt it did reduce the migraine attacks for two months and then they started again. Anybody suffering from migraine attacks has my full

sympathy. It is a dreadful thing to live with, never knowing when the next attack will strike. Work becomes a tremendous worry and social life difficult because of having to cancel at the last minute.

I have cried many a time in despair because of the extreme pain which can only be described as a knife being driven through the head. Everything comes to an unexpected full-stop and you are left completely helpless. The attacks leave you totally debilitated for several days afterwards due to the severity of the pain and strong medication. Whilst recuperating there has been a lot of solitude and time for meditation. There is without a doubt a spiritual feeling of peace in my flat and yet there is the constant roar of traffic outside. All that have entered have felt this lovely atmosphere and have immediately remarked upon it.

Last year I started going to a Spiritualist Church and eventually became a member. Some weeks later a guest medium gave me a message whilst sitting in a pew.

'I have your father here,' she said and described him exactly. 'He tells me that he has been watching over you and has made his presence known to you.'

'Yes, that's true,' I replied smiling.

I've had proof that father has been surrounding me with his love and giving me strength. On two occasions I have walked into the sitting room and there has been a strong smell of father's pipe tobacco. No one has ever smoked in the maisonette and when I opened the windows it was to no avail. After forty-eight hours the smell disappeared.

A friend who is a healer and medium came round to tea one afternoon. She sat in an armchair and I sat opposite

her.
'What are you staring at?' she enquired. Behind her on the wall was an old heavy picture frame with a portrait of me as a child.
'I didn't see it move but the picture frame has gone completely crooked.'
'Really?' she replied not batting an eyelid. By the time she was ready to get up and leave I glanced back at my portrait. The picture frame had returned to its original position and was completely straight again!
My quiet reflection without a television to clutter up the brain has helped to develop my clairvoyance. I have been able to help people along with their problems through my predictions with the tarot cards and give advice. Added to this the experience of all that I have had to endure in my own life has enabled me to help others who seek assistance.

Chapter 82

In January, Carlos announced that he was to become a father. I immediately spoke to Paloma and her grandmother to give them the exciting news.

In July it was discovered that Snorkles had developed a heart murmur. He is now nine-and-a-half years of age but doing alright considering his saga of medical history. He still seems to cope with his hips and is considered by the veterinary surgeons to be a walking miracle. I am well aware that time is of a premium and when his time is up it will totally devastate me. Snorkles is a joy to have because he is so exceptional in every way. He gives so much love and companionship and there is, without a doubt, a very special bond between us.

One evening, Susan rang and said, 'Just pack a bag and come. Don't forget your tarot cards,' she added. So Snorkles and I travelled up to Lincolnshire and stayed at Susan's house for ten days.

The countryside was glorious with clumps of red poppies dotted amongst the golden corn and wheat fields. Snorkles loved ambling down the country lanes while I gathered wild flowers. It revitalised me and I returned home feeling I had been given a new lease of life.

This autobiography is a true and accurate story of all that I have had to cope with. It has served as being tremendously therapeutic and has helped me come to terms with the past.

On Sunday 18th August 1996, my daughter-in-law gave birth to James Christopher.

This is the start of a new life and my joy at having my first grandson. May he be blessed always.

THE END

AFTERTHOUGHTS

In Chapter 79 I write about adoption and my feeling of rejection, sorrow, anger and resentment. At a later date, I tried to put all that to rest by eventually visiting Chelmsford Cemetery. Arriving there, I made my way through the churchyard, thinking that I would just stand in front of my natural mother's grave and say a prayer. Nothing prepared me for the overwhelming and uncontrollable emotions. The tears poured down my face in agony and I was down on my knees in front of my mother's unmarked grave. My hands dug into the surrounding earth, breaking my fingernails unable to stop the uncontrollable noise of the deepest pain that came out of my mouth. It was the final goodbye.

My mother had rejected me, not once but twice, and it left me with a desire – stronger than anything else in my entire life – to be truly loved and wanted by someone.

My search for that someone took me into two marriages that turned out to be legally null and void! All I desired was to be loved and wanted for the human being that I am.

One final word about my beloved Labrador. We moved to Bourne, Lincolnshire in 2001 to a bungalow. Snorkles was put to sleep and buried in the garden at the age of 15 years old.

He was the most extraordinary animal I have ever had the honour to live with and was the inspiration for me to become a Registered Speaker for Canine Partners. A charity based in Sussex, who train Labradors/other breeds to look after and care for disabled people in wheelchairs.